ADMINISTRATION OF POLICE TRAINING IN INDIA

ADMINISTRATION OF POLICE TRAINING IN INDIA

By

Dr. Krishna Mohan Mathur

Foreword By

J.F. Ribeiro

GYAN

Administration Of Police Training In India

ISBN : 978-81-212-0100-1

First Published 1987, reprint 2018 in India by
Gyan Publishing House
5, Main Ansari Road, Daryaganj,
New Delhi - 110002
Phones : 011-47034999, 9811692060
E-mail: books@gyanbooks.com
website: gyanbooks.com

FOREWORD

I AM happy to introduce the book on "Administration of Police Training in India" written by Dr. Krishna Mohan Mathur. The changing socio-economic and political environments (including legal, technological and scientific advances) necessitate reciprocal changes in the training of the police personnel all over the world and particularly in a country like India. The present study is the first pioneering research effort in the field of police training in India. This training has been surveyed by the author with the help of various research techniques like interviews, random samplings, field observations, use of questionnaires and visits to a large number of police training institutions in various states. The study is based on the authentic data collected by the author from primary and secondary sources.

The author says, "In the context of democratic society and the nation's commitment for social, economic and political justice, the new breed of the policemen is to be moulded and trained to fulfil their role expectations and this calls for an indepth study of the police training in India". The author has scientifically analysed here the relevance of training to police work. He has identified training needs of the police officers at three distinct levels i.e. policy level, supervisory level and operational level. The training has been viewed as an "integrated process in which development of job standards, identification of training needs, determination of training objectives, development of course curriculum, selection of training methods, obtaining of instructional staff, actual conduct of training activity, evaluation of feed-back of training are considered as basic steps". Various training concepts have been analysed from the systems approach. The author has brought out the history of police training with distinct landmarks in a very scholarly and scientific manner.

The author has analysed the basic and in-service training programmes and has presented the environs of police training with their both tangible and intangible constituents in a very simple and straightforward manner. The socio-emotional and inter-personnel relationship between the police trainees and the trainers is one of the most important determinants of training environment. The training environs of police training institutions have been examined in depth. The various physical facilities existing in various police training institutions of the country have been enumerated. The present research study clearly indicates the utilisation of various training techniques and methods in police training institutions of the country and analysed the financial expenditure of various states on police training and identified the areas requiring financial support. He has touched on the trainee-trainer ratio and the various problems of training institutions and police trainers have been objectively identified and analysed.

Police research in India is still an unexplored field and existing research cells and centres have their own problems and difficulties. Limitations and handicaps to police research have been systematically discussed by the author. The author has carried out micro-studies of S.V.P. National Police Academy, Hyderabad and Internal Security Academy, Mount Abu to supplement his research findings and conclusions. In his concluding chapter, the author has made a number of valuable and useful suggestions for the improvement of the police training in India.

The author has developed a number of original concepts in his book and has done a real pioneering job in analysing the present state of police training. The future image of the police, as a whole, depends, to a large extent, on the proper attitude, professional skills and knowledge of the police officers and training is an important means in human resource development of the organisation. The need for continuous training effort is constantly increasing in view of the fast changing socio-political environment in which police have an important role to play. The author has covered a wide spectrum while analysing the structural and institutional problems of police training. Dr. Mathur has served the country as police officer for more than twenty years and learns that the seeds of this work were laid when he was on the staff of the Internal Security Academy, C.R.P.F., Mount Abu. I have known him as an avid student of police subjects. He has written a number of papers and essays which have been widely read and appreciated by police leaders all over the country. This volume bears testimony to the author's scholarship, wide reading, scientific research aptitude and comprehension of the subject in a most balanced manner.

I shall like to congratulate the author for making such a distinguished contribution to the field of police training. I have no doubt that this scholarly effort will generate a great deal of interest in police training and will be of immense use to the students of public administration, police officers at all levels and trainers from all walks of life. I strongly recommend the book to all police leaders, particularly those in training institutions. It will also be of immense interest to trainers and training institutions connected with management, industry and commerce.

J.F. RIBEIRO

Director General
Punjab Police, Chandigarh.

PREFACE

PERFORMANCE of an organisation depends largely on the quality of its members and the efficiency of the members in turn depends on the type of training which has been imparted to them for fulfilment of the organizational goals. Training is an effective tool for bringing about requisite professional skills, competence and attitudes. A study of administration of police training becomes a matter of primary concern to all those who are interested in the management of police organisation. The administration of police training in India has been a neglected area of public administration in the past. The idea to study the subject came to me when I was attending a course on Administration of Police Training at North-Western University, Evanston, Illinois U.S.A., Ford-Foundation Fellow in 1971. Later I found the subject very fascinating and my interest in the subject gradually resulted in my decision to take up the subject for research. Serious literature on police training in India has been scarce, unsystematic and even unpublished. The occasional writings by some scholars and police officers hardly touched the fringe of the problem in all its dimensions. Some of the brilliant ideas, embodied in the syndicate reports of senior police officers needed to be sorted out by objective research, leading to a restructuring of the training system and goal-oriented training of the police officers. The present study is a modest attempt in this direction. It represents a scientific research on some of the aspects of administration of police training in India. Administration of police training in India is carried out by the State Governments in respect of their own state police training colleges and institutions while the Government of India administers the national level institutions and academies. The scope of the subject being very vast, the researcher has selected a few areas for in-depth study. It is my humble hope that this book will contribute in some measure to a better understanding of the administration of police training in India.

The present book is an enlarged and revised version of my research work carried out under the inspiring and insightful guidance of professor P.D. Sharma of Rajasthan University. I am sincerely indebted to him for his generous kindness in giving me valuable suggestions, directions and constant guidance which enabled me to complete my work. He has been very kind in sparing his valuable time out of his busy schedule for occasional long academic discussions and taking the trouble of going through the entire manuscript and making constructive suggestions for its improvement.

I have great pleasure in expressing my deep felt and profound gratitude to Dr. B. Varma, Director, Internal Security Academy, Mount Abu whose sincere assistance and considerate help alone made it possible for me to complete my research work. He has been a source of great intellectual strength and has been instrumental in making most constructive and useful suggestions at every stage of the preparation of the book. Many new concepts and thoughts could be developed only through discussions with him. I am indeed grateful to him from the very core of my heart.

The librarians of several police training academies heaped the material on my desk and suffered the embarrassing queries with an ungrudging smile. Shri K.B. Ramchandani, Librarian of SVP National Police Academy Hyderabad deserves special mention. I thank all of them.

I am deeply indebted to Shri J.F. Ribeiro, Director-General, Punjab Police for writing the foreword of the book. My sincere thanks are due to the Director-General C.R.P.F., Director Training Division, Bureau of Police Research and Development, Directors-General and Inspectors-General of Police of various States who supplied valuable primary data for the present study. I am also thankful to the Director, S.V.P. National

Police Academy, Hyderabad, who permitted me to carry out in-depth study of the Academy and allowed me to see various records and files of the Institution. Principals and Heads of a number of police training institutions in India also deserve mention who supplied required data and responses to my various questionnaires. I am thankful to a large number of police officers of various ranks who responded to my questionnaires and gave me their opinions on various questions. I also owe gratitude to those serving and retired police officers who have been interviewed by me and who helped me by giving their considered views on various aspects of police training.

I am full of admiration for my large number of friends and colleagues who helped me in various ways at various stages of my research work.

It is extremely difficult for me to find words to express my thanks to Shri T.M. Sukumaran Nair and Shri K.P. Francis for their sincere and unstinted help and hard labour in typing out the present book with utmost care and excellence in spite of their other commitments.

I must also thank my parents, wife Prabha and children Shikha, Pragya and Shiv who gave strength during many moments of frustration and despair and encouraged me by sparing from all domestic liabilities for devoting full attention to complete this book.

7-6-1987 KRISHNA MOHAN MATHUR

Hyderabad

LIST OF MAPS AND DIAGRAMS

Plates

CONTENTS

APPENDICES

CHAPTER ONE

THE PRESENT STUDY : AN INTRODUCTION

TRAINING is a deliberate and planned process of teaching and learning wherein knowledge, skills, techniques, attitudes and experiences are acquired by the trainees with the help and guidance of the trainers in a given learning environment. Training is an integral part of the personnel function. Training activities, properly planned, conducted and evaluated, help to raise the effectiveness of the organisation through the more effective use of human resources. Training, according to the Chamber's Twentieth Century Dictionary, is the process of conscious, deliberate and planned efforts aimed at developing a particular type or types of aptitude, attitude, traits, skills, expertise or orientation in the trainees. Increasingly more attention is being given to the development of quality of persons in the organisations and utilising their potential talents, capabilities and skills. Human resource development system (HRDS) includes performance appraisal, potential appraisal, employee feedback and counselling, assessment of training needs of the various categories of people, designing and using special interventions, organisational diagnosis, organisational development, evaluation of various interventions and increasing the motivation of the people for the optimum effectiveness of the organisation. Human resources need to be developed at all levels, from the top executive to the lowest employee in the organisation. The need for training as one of the effective means for human resource development cannot be overemphasized. The importance of training goes beyond the need for new specialized skills or techniques ; training groups of public officials provide a forum for stimulating communication within the service or for motivating personnel of the organisation. The human resource has been defined as "the total knowledge, skills, creative abilities, talents and aptitudes of an organisation's work force, as well as the values, attitudes and beliefs of the individuals involved. It is the sum total of inherent abilities, acquired knowledge and skills represented by the talents and aptitude of the employed persons."[1] Training and development programmes foster the initiative and creativity of the employees and help to prevent manpower obsolescence. Training provides employees a wider awareness, an enlarged skill, an enlightened altruistic philosophy and makes enhanced personal growth possible. Training is a practical and vital necessity because it heightens the morale of the employees, helps in reducing dissatisfaction, complaints, grievances and indiscipline. Training helps in bridging the gap between existing performance ability and desired performance. Training generally aims at improved individual performance, improved job satisfaction and improved organisational effectiveness. Training, according to some traditional thinkers, is to transmit skills, attitudes and knowledge, with a view to fill the empty vessels and shape the trainees to a predetermined model. This traditional approach regards training as a lock-step content transmittal curriculum and didactic teaching methodology to human beings who are passive, empty and reactive organisms. This is traditional old concept of training which conceives the mechanical model of man. The modern approach to training conceives the organismic model of man and regards trainees as twing, growing and developing organisms. This pattern of training caters to flexible learning systems geared to competency—development of the trainees. The purpose of training, according to this modern approach is the continuous development of individuals towards their full and unique potential through their life span and thus the continuous development of human resources. According to the modern concept, training "is not teaching. It is, of course, learning."[2] The concept of human resource development has two main constituents.

(*a*) Personal growth and change through training, education and career development.

(*b*) Organisational growth and development.

The whole concept and range of human resource development have undergone a vast change over the last one decade, with it have changed the philosophy, methodology and strategy for training. "Training represents an intervention strategy with, *inter alia*, the following over-all objects, namely :

(*a*) arresting obsolescence, both individual and organisational (preventive) ;

(*b*) bridging pre-active insufficies of knowledge, and professional skill (curative) ;

(*c*) shaping adjustments with socio-technological, environmental changes (Adaptive) ;

(*d*) developing new outlook, an ethnological version of quality, excellence and accomplishment (promotive) ;

(*e*) making a total man with new cultural attributes (Transformative)."[3]

Training basically is an exercise of a reciprocal process of teaching and learning which aims at converting a human being into "a human resource" in an organisation and converting man into manpower by adding the required "power" to the "man" for the purpose of accomplishment of the assigned tasks. Training is admittedly an investment in organisational development and basically relates to and is part of the human resource development.

Training is a gradual process of change and has three main phases :

(a) The Unfreezing Phase

The first phase of the changing process involves motivating the trainees and making them ready mentally for change. It is achieved by,

(*i*) removing the trainees from their formal habits and routine and ultimately challenging the previous behavioural pattern

(*ii*) motivating the trainees to accept change and making them willing to change.

(b) The Remoulding Phase

Once the trainees are willing and motivated to change, new patterns of behaviour are accomplished through identification, internalisation or a mixture of both.

(c) The Refreezing Phase

The acquired new behaviour patterns are integrated into the trainee's personality for ever through constant reinforcement and feedback.

Thus any attempt to train means a "freezing-up" of relations between people which involves the three stages of "unfreezing", "moulding" and "refreezing". In all organisations unfreezing is necessary because individuals come with different habits, values, practices and pattern of behaviour. To affect them through training, their normal habits, styles, values and practices have to be questioned, disturbed and unfrozen. Later, trainees are indoctrinated and socialized with new patterns of behaviour, life style and working habits through a gradual process of identification, internalisation or a mixture of both. Identification refers to the acceptance of new styles or patterns of behaviour and response. Internalisation relates to the individual's development of internal responses in order to cope with new situations. Once new pattern of behaviour is learnt or internalised, there is a need for refreezing of the new acquired styles of performance.

Training is a learning-training activity which on one hand, aims at improving the capabilities of the individuals to meet the organisational needs in terms of their knowledge, skills and attitudes required in performing organisational tasks and functions and on the other hand, provides realisation of the personal aspirations of the trainees by enhancing their career prospects in terms of professional expertise, individual growth and self-actualisation. Training constitutes an integral part of the co-existence exercise where organisation cares for its personnel and members care for their organisational effectiveness and optimum performance. The fundamental postulates of training today are as under :

(1) Allow trainees to learn, create a suitable climate for learning with a bias for self-education, individual development and self-actualisation within a given environment.

(2) Through training, trainees inculcate broadened outlook with stress on professionalism and specialisation through liberal learning environment.

(3) Exposure to the organisational-environmental culture pattern, should be the primary concern for training.

(4) While other resources in the organisation depreciate with the passage of time, human resource is the only resource that appreciates with time.

(5) Training is admittedly an investment in organisational development.

(6) Training is the responsibility of three partners ; the organisation, the trainees and the trainers.

(7) Training is a continuous process of learning by the trainees and is a vehicle for consistently updating the skills, knowledge and attitudes of the individual human resources.

(8) Effective training calls for establishing relevant training objectives, defining training specifications, selecting the appropriate strategy, creating suitable structural arrangements and evaluating the training efforts on a scientific basis.

(9) Relevant training generates an innate capacity as well as demonstrable capacity to face the future, to overtake events and to tame turbulences that might torment men, organisations and societies of tomorrow.

(10) Training, which is ultimately learning, is a complex function of the motivation and capacity of the trainees, the norms of the training group, the training methods and the behaviour of the trainers, the general climate of the training institution.

(11) Training, Education and Development are though different words with different meanings and implications, many modern managers and experts use the word "training" in general parlance covering all the three concepts. The present author has used the word "training" in this broader context. Training like "broad-spectrum antibiotic" has a multi-coverage.

(12) Training works with human material ; it cannot create a wholly new man ; it can at best mould and manipulate man marginally.

(13) Training is an aid, it is not the end.

REFERENCES

1. Leon C. Megginson, *Personnel and Human Resource Administration*, 1977, p. 4.
2. Peter F. Drucker, *Management* ; *Tasks, Responsibilities, Practices*, New York, Harper and Row, 1973, p. 229.
3. Bata K. Dey "Training in the civil services. Plea for a Holistic construal". The Indian Journal of Public Administration—Oct.-Dec. 1982, Vol. XXIX, p. 4.

CHAPTER TWO

TRAINING ENTERPRISE AND ITS RELEVANCE

THE PROCESS of training of police officers as a conscious effort to impart professional knowledge and technical skills in a desired direction is largely determined by three factors, viz. (1) the importance of training as a cohesive force binding together large bodies in the organisation, (2) the impact of training in disciplining the minds and emotions of individuals, and (3) the effect of training enterprise on the field performance of the force. The need and relevance of Police Training, immediately after recruitment has been engaging the attention of authorities for more than a century now. A series of pre-promotion, specialised, advanced and refresher courses have been laid out and more and more Police Training Institutions have come up with the passage of time. Police Training is essentially an exercise in imparting instructions in police profession and inculcating discipline. Training helps to promote, maintain and enhance employee effectiveness in their job assignments and prepares them for future responsibilities of higher order. Naturally, Police training represents an integral part of development of personality of the policeman.

The police organisation is at the cutting edge of all governmental activities. The police are the visible symbols of authority. The quality and content of training are very important in the building up of an efficient modern police force. Duties of a police officer in India have been increasing day by day both in intensity and complexity due to increasing lawlessness, civil disorders, increasing crime, violence and offences against property and persons. New dimensions to traditional police tasks are arising due to changed role expectation which underscore the need for new knowledge, new skills and new attitudes for the future policeman. In view of these developing dimensions and emerging problems in police organisation, the entire approach to police training has to be pragmatic and exploratory. Police training in India is a very complex and big enterprise. The present study seeks to analyse only some aspects of training effort of Indian Police Organisation simply because it is too widely diffused to offer a complete overview in its entirety. Police training is a continuous process carried out formally and informally at various levels. In order to get the varied dimensions of police training efforts, relevant and reliable data alongwith scientific studies with respect to the following aspects of police training enterprise need to be collected, screened, analysed and scientifically studied :

(1) Number and nature of training institutions inside and outside the police organisation, that conduct training programmes for the police personnel.

(2) Number of courses of training programmes offered by the Training Institutions for the police personnel.

(3) Number of staff assigned to training activities in various Training Institutions.

(4) Number of police personnel trained annually by various training institutions.

(5) Training costs, salaries, materials, aids and equipments, maintenance and repair of facilities and their total costs.

(6) The physical facilities for training in terms of buildings available for accommodating staff and trainees, grounds for outdoor parade and games, class-rooms for indoor training, library facilities, recreational facilities and

welfare activities for the staff and trainees of training institutions.

(7) Number of personnel available for training in police organisation and a scientific analysis of their training needs in terms of their present jobs and future responsibilities.

(8) Periodicity by which police personnel require training at various levels of their career.

(9) Man-hours and man-days of training.

(10) Impact of training on the effectiveness of the trainees and its utility in the long run.

(11) Problems and difficulties of training institutions.

(12) Impact of research on training and co-ordination between training and police research.

An effort has been made in the present research to identify the training needs in the police organisation, to analyse the present training programmes and their course contents. The existing facilities for training for various ranks of the police have been examined. The present state of research done by police research centres and cells of training institutions have been studied alongwith follow-up action. Spread over an area of 32,97,782 square kilometers, the strength of 6,02,800 civil and 1,95,189 armed police in India totalled to 7,97,989 policemen in the year 1976. More than 120 police training institutions exist in the country to train these police personnel. There is an enormous information gap about police training efforts and police training results in India today. The studies made thus far offer little insight in understanding the problems of police training administration in India.[1] Police training in India does not find a place as a separate subject even in All India Police Science Congress.[2] In the context of democratic society and the nation's commitment for social, economic and political justice, "the new breed of policemen" are to be moulded and trained to fulfil their role expectations and this calls for an in-depth study of the police training in India. The police have to struggle hard to shake off the poor image they have acquired and image building can be achieved partially through a more effective and purposeful job of training the policemen. A scientific, objective and in-depth study and analysis of police training in India is needed to generate conceptual inputs in the formulation of training policy at national and state levels. Law enforcement being a major social problem in India, it is desirable that an objective and scientific study of police training is made available to the police organisation and to the people at large. The purpose of this study has been to describe, analyse and evaluate some of the salient features and structures of police training system in India. The field of police training in India is, by and large, a neglected one and little research has been carried out in the field. A few scholars, mostly serving police officers in India, have written some stray articles on some aspect of police training but serious, in-depth and detailed studies are sorely lacking.[3] Comparatively speaking, it is an unstudied field and there is ample scope for empirical research. To improve the existing police system and to enable it to keep pace with the fast changing social scene, police training research has to be an essential element in the evaluation of programmes and policies.

Research Design

The research design of the present study encompasses the entire training system of police of the country. The present research exercise proposes to stress upon the administrative aspects of this training. The research universe, being fairly wide, training imparted at two national level training institutions of the country has been picked up for in-depth study and micro-level analysis. The nature and impact of training on police officers of various ranks is the prime focus of present research. Training of Constables, Head Constables, Subordinate Officers and Gazetted Officers of various states of India comprises the scope of research. Both kinds of basic and follow up practical training programmes and inservice training courses have been included for purpose of studying the enterprise of police training in India. The specialist and technical courses like wireless operators course, driving and motor mechanic course, and bugler courses have, however, been excluded because of the limitations of space, time and resources of an individual researcher. Special attention has been given to police training programmes and techniques as obtained in Andhra Pradesh, Assam, Gujarat, Haryana, Karnataka, Maharashtra, Manipur, Nagaland, Orissa, Punjab, Rajasthan, Tamil Nadu, Uttar Pradesh and West Bengal. Union Territories of Delhi and Mizoram have been chosen for special reference. Police training in India broadly includes training activities at training centres including State Police Training Colleges, State Police Recruit Training Centres/Schools and National level Training Academies. Thus, research effort seeks to examine the working of Central and State Training Centres/Colleges/Academies where senior police officers are being trained at institutional campuses. The entire organisation of police training in India has been taken up at the macro-level for broad level generalisations but a micro-level analysis of some police training institutions has been included to make the study more meaningful in terms of its reliability, and validity of conclusions arrived at from the analysis of the data.

A hypothesis is a tentative assumption of the researcher postulated to draw out conclusions and test its logical and empirical consequences.[4] Being a tentative explanation or a proposition, it has been stated in testable form and attempt has been made to predict a particular relationship between two or more variables. The present study proposes to evolve and test the following hypotheses on the basis of data collected from the field operations of Police Training Institutions spread all over the Country :

(1) The police training institutions in India are inadequately staffed for purpose of administration of training of the police force of the country.

(2) The police training institutions in India are concentrating more on basic training programmes rather than on the refresher training courses for various ranks.

(3) The expenditure incurred on police training in various states of India is percentage-wise low in proportion to the total costs of police budgets of the states.

(4) The police training institutions in India are in a general state of neglect and more so in respect of the physical facilities obtained on their campuses.

(5) *Training tools and equipments for police training are out-dated in most of the training institutions of police.* Very little innovative effort has been made to render them functional.

(6) There is lack of co-ordination between police training and police research in India with the result that the training enterprise is non-goal oriented in terms of cost benefit ratio.

Some of these hypotheses have been postulated by the researcher due to his professional background of police service and, participant observation of police training institutions in different parts of the country. These hypotheses are based on the commonly held and widely shared beliefs of the serving police officers. The formulation of these hypotheses as stated provided a direction to the study and have assisted the researcher to limit the parameters of his enquiry.

The two national level police training institutions, namely, S.V.P. National Police Academy, Hyderabad and Internal Security Academy, Mount Abu have been selected as samples for an in-depth study. These two institutions have been selected purposely because of their national coverage and seminal characteristics. In addition, fourteen states, namely, Andhra Pradesh, Assam, Gujarat, Haryana, Karnataka, Maharashtra, Manipur, Nagaland, Orissa, Punjab, Rajasthan, Uttar Pradesh and West Bengal and two Union Territories, Delhi and Mizoram have been chosen to outline the nature of police training organisation and the training activities that go around in these states. A representative sample of the Central Reserve Police Force (CRPF) training institutions has been selected to study and evaluate the training programmes of the armed police organisations of the Union and State governments.

A stratified sample has been obtained by separating the trainer-trainee respondents into non-overlapping groups and a simple random sample from within each stratum has been picked up for the study. The police training institutions have also been stratified into three categories on the basis of the broad rank structure of the police personnel being trained i.e. senior IPS, Dy. S.P. and Subordinate Officers and Head Constables/Constables. Since the scope of the study extends to all the four corners of the country and the representative sample of various strata of police officers is too large to be handled. The method of purposive sampling has been employed for research analysis. The stratified sample has ensured representation to all ranks of the police trainees and has simultaneously covered the varieties of training institutions within the parameters of research universe which is being sampled.

"The administration of police training in India" is apparently a macro-level research. The unit of analysis is very broad. The study of police training efforts in a big country like India perhaps cannot help it. But to make the study meaningful, two micro studies of National Police Academy, Hyderabad and Internal Security Academy, Mount Abu have been included in the ambit of present research. Together they make the sample representative.

To test the hypotheses, statistical facts and figures have been collected from the field. In addition, opinion surveys through mailed questionnaires have been attempted. Two mailed questionnaires have been used to obtain opinions of different ranks of police forces in various states of the country. The tools employed for collection of data have been questionnaire, schedule, interviews, participant observation and the study of documents available at Police Headquarters and in the libraries and records of Police Training Institutions. Five questionnaires were used to elicit the required information for purposes of data collection.[5] The first questionnaire covered the organisation and administration of police training in the state. It dealt with the training of gazetted officers, subordinate officers, head constables/constables and training institutions. Various details, facts and figures given in this study on various pages have been compiled and collected on the basis of the primary data supplied by the various training institutions and

Inspectors General of Police by various states. Questionnaire second dealt with police research set up in the police training institutions under study. The third one attempted to discover the training techniques and other skill imparting methods employed in police training. Questionnaire four proposed to collect opinions about some of the relevant aspects on police training. It was an open ended questionnaire and was aimed at collecting views of knowledgeable individuals on some of the critical aspects of police training in India. The Fifth questionnaire aimed at collecting opinions of serving police officers. It was a closed end structured questionnaire. Besides these, several other methods were adopted to have an access to the facts and to collect data from police organisations in the states. As questionnaires are generally useful for data collection for studies that cover a wide ground, the present study used this tool quite extensively and that too in various forms. The mailed questionnaire was administered because of its obvious utility. It saved money, time and enabled the researcher to reach various units of his research universe. As many as 70 per cent of the respondents reacted and responded to the questionnaires and furnished valuable data for the study. Most of the police training centres also responded through their Inspectors-General of Police. Replies to Questionnaire No. 1 have been received from 25 police training institutions and researcher has used these replies as basis for comparative study of the administration of police training in India. Replies to Questionnaire Nos. 2 and 3 have been received from 20 police training institutions which enabled the researcher to analyse the general state of utilisation of training techniques and tools. Some of the replies to these questionnaires have been received directly from the training institutions, some through state Inspectors-General of Police and in some cases directly as well as from Inspectors-General of Police/Police Headquarters. This has enhanced the validity of the data which could be cross-checked. Schedule method of data collection as a tool of research has also been resorted to for the two case studies. Questionnaire No. 5 used in the present research could be filled only by personal contact with the respondents. It entailed great labour to motivate and prepare the constabulary to shed away their complexes and come out with their frank and honest opinions. 220 serving officers of various ranks have responded to Questionnaire No. 5 and this has enabled the researcher to assess the level of satisfaction of serving officers with the state of training in India. Serving officers from Haryana, Punjab, Uttar Pradesh, Maharashtra, Gujarat, Tamil Nadu and other states have responded, thus making the opinion survey broad-based. The fact that the name of the respondent was not to be filled in, enabled the present researcher to fill in the schedules with the requisite frankness and obtain honest opinions from the respondents. The study aimed to collect data from the various ranks of police officers about different aspects of police training. Hence, a number of retired and senior police officers were also interviewed by the researcher. More than a dozen heads of police training institutions were interviewed and formal and informal discussions were held with the respondents. The researcher attended the tenth symposium of the heads of Police Training Institutions in India held at Patna from October 22 to 24, 1981 and got the opportunity of listening to the proceedings of the symposium and discussed various aspects of training with 40 participants.

The researcher has interviewed more than one hundred serving police officers of various ranks for obtaining their opinions and views on various aspects of police training. About fifty police trainers of various ranks have also been interviewed by the researcher. These interviews have given insight into various facets of police training. Police trainees of various ranks were interviewed to elicit their views and assessments of training exercises. Initially very few trainees could open up but later on they could be persuaded to give their opinions on the assurance that their identity will not be disclosed. The interviews conducted with the respondents were primarily "direct interview" which were at times "focused" and converted into "depth" interviews. Besides being interesting, they generated a sense of realism and offered meaningful insights. As a member of the officer cadre of CRPF, the present researcher has been closely associated with the enterprise of police training during the last nineteen years. This association has provided him with closer and an indepth view of the entire police training system. On the spot visits to a number of training institutions have yielded a perspective. Personal observation as a trainer and a trainee, has contributed to the experience which becomes a useful input for the study in developing hypotheses. Documents, government reports and official records have been collected from varied sources. The case studies of S.V.P. National Police Academy, Hyderabad and Internal Security Academy, Mt. Abu are primarily based on the documents which were made available by the authorities of these institutions. The Committee Report on Police Training[6]. State Police Commission Reports and a number of other useful documents have been culled and utilized for carrying out present research which combines a descriptive, prescriptive approach and presents data for scientific field investigations. Physical facilities for training institutions have been examined on the basis of the criteria fixed by the working group of Annual Conference of Central Training Institutions, April, 1977[7]. Inspectors-General of Police and Deputy Inspectors-General of Police of various states have provided valuable data to the researcher for analysing different aspects of police training. Annual Administration Reports of the training institutions, feed back and evaluation of courses given by the trainees and syllabi of various courses were examined by the researcher during his visit to the training institutions.

However, the limitations of the study are very many and somewhat obvious. A great part of the study has been completed while serving in the police department. The leisure hours have been too scarce. The paucity of funds and non-availability of leave have handicapped the investigation. The research literature on the subject has also been bizzare and unsystematic. The police officers were reluctant to come out with their frank opinions due to the organisational police culture. Some aspects of police training had to be excluded from the scope of the study as requisite records and other materials were not available for scrutiny. The scope of the study being very extensive, it was quite difficult to give reasonable attention to discernible differences that exist in the training programmes and processes at the level of the states. The subject was too broad and administration of police training was quite inclusive. The study is a modest attempt to test only the relevant hypotheses postulated for present research. The two national level police training institutions have been picked up for micro-analysis because of their seminal importance. The other equally important training institutions could not be studied in detail. Police training for each rank has been analysed only at a broad level and the specialised courses have been purposely left out in the course of study. Computer training, wireless training, driving and mechanic training, armourer training, intelligence training and a number of several other specialised courses are being conducted for police officers of various ranks in the states but the present study could include basic training and refresher training courses only for purposes of analysis and evaluation. The study could not cover several other aspects of police training which were relatively of lesser significance. Much of the primary data received from various training institutions, could not be varified and cross-checked through other sources. However, efforts were made in several cases to recheck and verify the materials from published documents especially from the annual administration reports of the police departments. As much of the data was collected through mailed questionnaires, the respondents alone could ensure its correctness. As the offices of Inspectors-General of Police supplied this material, it can be assumed that information is reliable.

The feed-back of the trainees has been taken as a basis for analysis and evaluation. The occupational culture of police did inhibit the trainees in coming out with true responses to the questions mentioned in the evaluation sheets. Due to a high level of stress, particularly, in lower ranks, it is likely that some of them might not have given true responses in the evaluation sheets. However, care has been taken to reduce it to the minimum in the self evaluation of training programmes by the trainees. The study is circumscribed to limited aspects of evaluation of training exercise and several significant aspects of administration of police training have been left out. The use of statistical tools though tried, does not go far because of the obvious and logical implications implicit in rigorous analysis. The use of samples means may not ensure the representativeness of the data. Hence, the present study has only tried to explore the probabilities because it is always difficult to know how close the data have been to the universe parameters. The research conclusions are middle range generalisations tending to yield a low level theory. An empirical research study in order to be scientific must be verifiable, definite, objective, and predictable. To ensure these characteristics, the reliability and validity of the conclusions need to be tested and established. Reliability here means the stability of a test score on repetitions of the test. Similarly, the validity of the test implies the measurement of things which it proposes to measure. The questionnaires, schedules and interviews etc., undertaken for the study were designed to conduct tests and pilot surveys in the field. The utility and comprehensiveness of the questionnaires and the schedules were checked and ambiguous questions were redrafted. The contents of the questionnaires and the schedules were made specific, clear and comprehensive, and tests were also conducted to test reliability and validity of the responses received from the respondents. Quantitative analysis has been made to bring in objectivity in research.

A Schematic View

The present study has been divided into nine chapters. The first chapter outlines the methodology of research, including the statement of hypotheses, the parameters of research universe, the sample and the tools employed during investigation for collecting data and analysing their validity and reliability. The scope and limitations of the study have been stated in advance so that its conclusions may be evaluated in that context. The second chapter deals with the enterprise of police training and its relevance to police work. The training needs of the police organisation in India have been identified, and the general problems of police training organisations have been analysed and discussed. The next chapter attempts a historical retrospection of police training from 1859 onwards. The historical account has been subdivided into four phases (*i*) Police training from 1859 to 1902 ; (*ii*) Police training upto 1948 ; (*iii*) Police training from 1948 to 1974 ; and (*iv*) Police training from 1974 onwards. The fourth chapter of the study endeavours to work out the organisation of police training in India. The organisation of police training at the central and state levels has been analysed in detail. The fifth chapter deals with the police training programmes of senior level, subordinate level and constabulary level and their course contents, test system and general evaluation. In the sixth chapter a survey of the environs of police training institutions has been attempted. The physical facilities provided to the trainees and the trainers for their class room, accommodation and recreation have been surveyed and evaluated. The financial expenditure incurred on training has been studied in terms of cost benefit analysis. The seventh chapter deals with the progress and state of police research in India. It describes various organisations involved in police research activities and training courses on research methodology. It also surveys and mentions about various studies and research projects which have been completed or are under completion or are proposed to be taken up in future. The activities of research cells of the training institutions have been studied in this part of the study. A micro-study of two national level training institutions of the country, namely, The Sardar Vallabhbhai Patel National Police Academy, Hyderabad and Internal Security Academy, Mount Abu has been added to understand the problems in their depth and details. The epilogue presents an overview of the study including findings and suggestions offered by the researcher. These suggestions, it is hopefully believed can improve the quality of police training in India and produce functionally effective and socially useful policemen of future.

REFERENCES

1. Some of these police studies are :
   Bayley, David H., "*The Police and Political Development in India*", (Princeton University Press, New Jercey, 1969) ; Curry, J.C., "*The Indian Police*", (Mann Publications, New Delhi, 1977) ; Dias, S.M., "*New Dimensions to Police Role and Functions in India,*" (S.V.P.

National Police Academy Magasine Section, Hyderabad); Ghosh, S.K., "*Police Administration – Organisation and Procedure*", (Eastern Law House Calcutta, 1973); Gupta, A.S. "*The Police in British India—1861-1947*", (Concepts Publishing Company, New Delhi, 1979); Madan, J.C., "*Indian Police—Its Development upto 1905*", (Uppal Publishing House, New Delhi, 1980); Misra, S.C., "*Police Administration in India*" (National Police Academy, Nov., 1970); Misra, S.C., *State Policr Organisation in India*", (CRPF Press, New Delhi, 1975); Sharma, P.D., "*Indian Police—A Developmental Approach*", (Research Delhi, 1977); Shatma, P.D., "*Police Polity and People in India*", (Uppal Publishing House, New Delhi, 1981).

2. The five main heads of subjects for Police Science Congress are (i) Police Organisation and Administration (ii) Crime, Criminology and Criminal Law (iii) Application of Science and Technology in Police Work, (iv) Community Participation in Police Work, and (v) Victimology. "Agenda Papers for the XV All India Police Science Congress, Simla, 1980" (Bureau of Police Research and Development, 1980).

3. Bureau of Police Research & Development, New Delhi has brought out "*Selected Readings on Police*" (1978) in which a bibliography of 131 articles/papers/publications has been given covering "training and recruitment", out of which only 25 items deal with various aspects of police training in India. S. No. 302 to 433, pp. 26-37.

4. The function of the hypothesis is to state a specific relationship between phenomena in such a way that this relationship can be empirically tested, Goode, William J. and Hatt, Paul, K., "*Methods in Social Research*", (McGraw-Hill Kogukusha Ltd., Tokyo, 1952), p. 47.

5. These Questionnaires have been reproduced as appendices A to E at the end of the dissertation.

6. See Committee on Police Training 1971 Report, Government of India, Ministry of Home Affairs, 1974 (Chairman M.S. Gore), is generally referred to as "Gore Committee Report".

7. See Physical Facilities for Training Institutions Working Group of Annual Conference of Central Training Institutions, April 1977, (I.S.T.M. Training Monograph No. 22).

CHAPTER THREE

TRAINING ENTERPRISE AND ITS RELEVANCE TO POLICE WORK

Definition and Meaning of Training

TRAINING in the public service, according to The United Nations, is defined as :

> "Instruction in an art, a profession, or an occupation, consisting of teaching drill or discipline, by which powers of mind or body are developed......with particular reference to the civil service. Training is the reciprocal process of teaching and learning a body of knowledge and the related methods of work."[1]

Training implies imparting instructions, to make proficient by instruction ; to inculcate discipline, instruction, drill or practice designed to impart proficiency in a profession or an art or in any occupational work. In the context of police organisation, training generally means doing following four things :

(*a*) Imparting knowledge including its application to various different situations of law enforcement.

(*b*) Cultivating skills and techniques required in law enforcement work including that of appreciating different situations in different time frame.

(*c*) Building appropriate work habits necessary for doing the police work.

(*d*) And shaping attitudes, value orientations and behaviour pattern.

Training is what the trainer does to the trainees. Learning is what happens to the trainee after training. An effective training regimen must perform five basic acts, namely, stimulus generation, stimulus presentation, response acceptance, response comparison and feed-back presentation. For police trainees, it largely consists of organised opportunities to acquire requisite skills and understanding in a formalised training environment. Police training consists of a series of inter-related, interacting, precisely controlled teaching/learning experiences that are designed to achieve specific objectives in a well-knit unified dynamic whole for fulfilling the police roles. Police training will thus refer to the teaching/learning activities carried out for the primary purpose of enabling policemen to acquire and apply the knowledge, skills, abilities and attitudes needed by him to enact his roles effectively. Training can be on the job, in the class-room or even in informal situations. Training in training institutions can be termed as institutionalised training while guidance and instruction by the superior officers, peer groups and colleagues in informal or formal setting can be termed as non-institutionalised training. Non-institutionalised training besides on the job training also includes roll call training, training through circulars, orders and instructions by various authorities.[3]

Systems Approach to Training Process

Training is an integrated, comprehensive process in which development of job standards and job expectations, identification of training needs, determination of training objectives, development of course curriculum, selection of training methods and material, obtaining of instructional staff, conduct of actual instructional activity, evaluation and feed-back are the basic steps. For developing a training programme, development of job standards take the form of job analysis, job description and statement of various tasks. Identification of training needs is accomplished through observation, group self analysis, performance tests, interviews, questionnaires and organisational need analysis. The next step consists of formulation of training objectives which is the statement of terminal behaviour of the trainee under specific conditions and criteria of satisfactory performance. Thereafter, appropriate subject material is to be prepared and course-curriculum designed to achieve the training objectives. Application of appropriate training methods and techniques alone will ensure achievement of training objectives and hence selection of these techniques is an important phase of training process. Motivated and suitable instructional staff is a must in the training process. Without them all the steps described earlier will be reduced to empty rituals. Conduct of actual instructional activity is the interaction of the instructor and the trainees in a training/teaching environment. The evaluation and feed-back indicate the extent of success or failure of the training process in achieving its objectives.

The areas of training can be divided into skills, attitudes and knowledge which are built up not only through learning experience but also through an unlearning process. Thus, training in this sense has three stages : "unfreezing", "moving" and "refreezing".[3] Because the requirements of police role necessitate large scale revision of values, norms and usages prevalent in the society from which a policeman is recruited, this unfreezing assumes added importance in police training.

The Learning Process

Learning process is the process by which trainees acquire changes in their behaviour, improve performance, reorganise their thinking or discover new ways of behaving and new concepts and knowledge. Training is an overt process, a sequence of experiences, a series of opportunities to learn, in which the learner is exposed in some more or less systematic way to certain learning situations. Training is a set of procedures to facilitate learning by the trainees. Training can operate in the following six areas :—

(*a*) Knowledge ; (*b*) Techniques ; (*c*) Skills ;(*d*) Attitudes ;
(*e*) Experience ; (*f*) Development of sound judgement.

Learning is a process that takes place within the trainee. Learning is a relatively permanent change in behaviour of a trainee that occurs as a result of insight, experience or practice. Learning may be conscious or unconscious, it is such a complicated process that no one can really claim to know how it occurs. Learning can be assisted by improving the material arrangements and methods of training. Learning can be facilitated by improving the psychological conditions under which it takes place. There are following eight factors which bear upon the learning process.

(*a*) *Motivation*

Upto a point, the stranger the motivation, the more learning takes place, but beyond a critical level, the learner becomes too tense to learn. Motivation to learn can be intrinsic or extrinsic.

(*b*) *Stimulus, Response and Reinforcement*

A basic principle of learning is that the learner learns what he does because all learning requires activity on the part of the trainee. All training requires that the learner must learn correct response to a particular stimulus. Learning cannot proceed unless the learner has knowledge of results. Reinforcement and reward are important aspects of the learning process. E.L. Thorndike held that through learning the connection between Situations (S's) and Responses (R's) are strengthened.

(*c*) *Feed-back or Knowledge of Results*

The learner, in order to learn effectively, needs to know if he has learnt successfully. Effective feedback should be given to the trainees as soon as possible.

(*d*) *Practice and Participation*

Retention and transferability of learning depend on the amount and kind of practice the learner engages in. Learning must be practiced in a wide variety of situations with particular emphasis placed on situations like to recur on the actual job. Participation means practice or repetition of the behaviour to be

1. A view of the National Police Academy building from Officers Mess side.

2. Front view of National Police Academy building.

3. Smt. Indira Gandhi, Prime Minister with Shri S.M. Dias, Director, SVP, N.P.A. during her visit to N.P.A. in 1975.

4. Smt. Indira Gandhi, Prime Minister inspecting IPS Trainees.

5. Shri Zail Singh, President of India awarding Best Officer Cadet baton and pistol to IPS Best Cadet.

6. Shri Zail Singh, President of India inspecting IPS trainees during their passing out parade.

7. Shri Rajiv Gandhi, Prime Minister of India Visiting SVP, NPA.

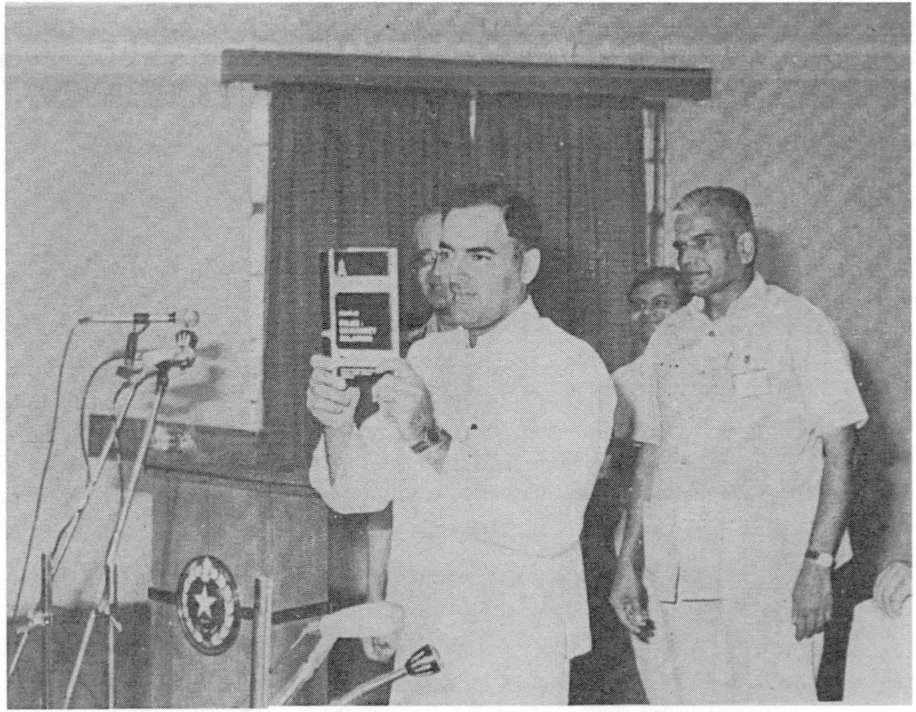

8. Shri Rajiv Gandhi, Prime Minister of India raleasing a Book on 'Police Community Relations'.

learned, which is necessary for transfer of the class-room learning to the real life situation.

(*e*) *Transfer or Application of Learning*

Learning is easier when trainees can see its relevance or applicability in their real life situations.

(*f*) *Perception*

Learners "perceive" when they (*a*) recognise (objects, sounds, tastes) ; (*b*) discriminate (between fallacies, facts and colours) ; (*c*) relate (parts to a whole, like objects to each other, a principle with its practice) ; (*d*) select (what interests them). Perception helps trainees to use the knowledge in an entirely different situation from that in which they learned it. Perception operates from the most concrete to the most abstract levels.

(*g*) *Sequencing of Material to be Learnt*

Better learning can be achieved if instructional material can be so arranged that trainees can build up a coherent structure in their minds. Trainees can be given a comprehensive structure by,

(*i*) moving from the known to the unknown ;

(*ii*) progressively from the simple to the complex ;

(*iii*) relating the material to the present tasks.

(*h*) *Individual Differences*

Trainers must have full knowledge about the individual differences with respect to the trainee's skills, motivation, previous experience, intellectual capacity, working habits and physical capacities.

There are various theories of learning which seek principles to explain how learning occurs. Stimulus-Response (S-R) theories are derived from the work of Pavlov in Russia and E.L. Thorndike in the United States. B.F. Skinner represents a major school of thought with S-R psychology. This theory relies on the concepts of stimulus, response and reinforcement. The foremost Gestalt psychologists, Wertheimer, Kohler and Koffka were less directly interested in learning than in perception but these men exerted strong influence on Kurt Lewis and E.C. Tolman. According to Tolman, the learner's activity is always directed towards some goal. When he learns, he does so by finding what leads to what. He develops a "cognitive map" of his environment. According to modern thinking, teachers and trainer must know how the trainees learn. There are a number of different theories of instruction. Some important theories are enumerated below :

(*a*) *Maieutic Theory of Instruction*

Socrates advocated this theory and held that all knowledge emanates from within the learner.

(*b*) *Communication Theory of Instruction*

Herbart originated this theory and held that all knowledge, skills, attitudes and experience are communicated by the instructor to the trainees.

(*c*) *Moulding Theory of Instruction*

John Dewey advocated this theory. The theory emphasizes the shaping, forming and moulding the behaviour of the trainees.

(*d*) *Mutual Inquiry Theory*

This theory emphasizes that true knowledge is inquiry. It assumes that each learner has the capacity to discover new knowledge with mutual inquiry.

(*e*) *Description Theory of Instruction*

It is based on theory of empirical evidence and observations. Bruner held that a theory of instruction must encompass :—

(*i*) Learner's predisposition to learn ;
(*ii*) Structure of knowledge ;
(*iii*) Effective sequence in presentation of learning material ; and

(*iv*) Reinforcement of learning.

(*f*) *The Cognitive Theory of Instruction*

This has been propagated by N.L. Gage. It is derived from the principles of cognition and principles of perception.

(*g*) *The Theory of Teacher Behaviour*

Teacher behaviour consists of those acts that the teacher performs typically in the class-room in order to induce learning. D.G. Ryan advocated this theory.

(*h*) *The Psychological Theory of Instruction*

It emphasizes the contractual relationship between the instructor and the trainee. This theory explores the psychology of learning and makes instructors acquainted with various psychology concepts like interest, motivation, learning curves, retention power etc.

(*i*) *The General Theory of Instruction*

It has been formulated by Clarke and is based on the assumption that through teaching, changes in the behaviour of the students are produced.

Even today there is no comprehensive theory of instruction which can help instructors in planning their instructional strategies.

Principles of Learning

Learning has been defined as more or less permanent modification of an individual's activity in a given situation, due to a process of acquiring the appropriate responses. It implies cumulative improvement in psychological factors. The psychological factors and the environmental factors are involved in the learning process. The learning process involves a motive or drive, an attractive goal and a block to the attainment of goal. Some well-known principles of learning are as under :

(1) The capacities of learners are important in determining what can be learned and how long it will take.

(2) Trainees learn more effectively when they learn at their own pace.

(3) Different kinds of learning require different training processes.

(4) The order of presentation of materials to be learned is very important.

(5) Learning with understanding is more permanent and more transferable than learning by some memorized formula

(6) Learning is aided by active practice rather than passive reception.

(7) The frequency with which a response is reinforced will determine how well the response will be learned by the trainee.

(8) Belongingness and satisfaction lead to effective learning.

(9) Knowledge of results leads to increases in learning because learning proceeds most effectively when the learner's correct responses are immediately reinforced.

(10) Continuous repetition of the learning message is desirable because the rate of forgetting tends to be very rapid immediately after learning.

(11) Learning can be more effective when identical and varied repetitions are carried out.

(12) No one learns without some motivating force or urge to learn.

(13) Showing errors in how to do something can lead to increases in learning.

(14) Learning is influenced directly by environment and surroundings.

(15) Learning is easy and more effective when certain methods and aids are applied to aid learning.

(16) Leaning is a cumulative and complex process and learner learns many things at a time.

(17) There are upward spurts in understanding, followed by plateaus in the curves of learning.

(18) Learning is more effective when learners shed their prejudices, bias, likes and dislikes.

(19) Practice in a variety of settings can increase the range of situations in which the learning can be applied.

(20) The larger the number of human senses involved, the more effective is the learning.

(21) Learning process requires a great deal of time for assimilation, testing, acceptance and the development of confidence.

(22) New learning sometimes can interfere with the remembering of something learned earlier.

(23) The rate of learning decreases when complex skills are involved.

(24) A message is more easily learned and accepted if it does not interfere with earlier habits and experiences.

(25) Four important dimensions of learning are :

(*i*) Level of performance

(*ii*) Rate of learning (speed)

(*iii*) Retention and

(*iv*) Generalisation and application of learning.

The Psychology of Adult Learning

Adult learners are different from children and in all professional training, adults are given opportunities to learn. It is a well accepted fact that with age, the speed of perception declines and the reaction time increases. For professional training, it is pertinent to remember that there are some distinct characteristics of adults as compared with children. Adults are more realistic because they see life as a set of realities. Adults have had more experience than children and develop a sort of accumulated wisdom. Adults attend training often with a mixed set of motives. Adults have needs which are more concrete and immediate and like to see theory applied to practical problems. Adults are generally impatient with long discourses on theory and do not comprise a captive audience. Adults want themselves to be treated as mature persons by the instructors and trainers. Generally, all adults enjoy having their talents and knowledge made use of in a training situation. Adults in professional courses come from a wide variety of backgrounds and intelligence level and adult groups are therefore generally heterogeneous. Adults can learn at any age but their physical responses may become dull with age. Adults appreciate teaching devices which add interest and a sense of liveliness. Some of the main characteristics of adult learners are as under :

(1) The adult learner is generally more rigid in his thinking because he acquires a set pattern of behaviour in due course of time.

(2) Adult learner requires a long time to perform learning tasks because his reaction-time is slow.

(3) He is more impatient in the pursuit of learning objectives.

(4) Adult learner requires more and better light for study tasks.

(5) Adult learner requires a more constant and ideal environmental condition in order to learn effectively.

(6) Adult learner has greater difficulty in remembering isolated facts because memory starts decreasing with age than a child.

(7) Adult learner can easily relate new facts to experience and gets reinforcement in his learning from his past experience.

(8) Adult learner wants to be treated as adult in learning situations.

(9) Adult learners develop various responsibilities in life and thus have mental distractions at the time of learning.

(10) Adult learner has better understanding and can learn even complex subjects if properly presented.

(11) Based on a finding of his study on adult learning, E.L. Thorndike held that "the influence of intellect upon the curve of ability to learn in relation to age is slight. The ablest man and the ordinary man show very nearly the same curve."

(12) Active involvement of the older learner in learning situations may produce improvement in performance and recall.

(13) With age the speed of perception declines and the reaction time increases.

(14) According to Thorndike, inner growth in the adult goes on at least upto the age of fifty which helps them to learn better than adolescents or younger ones. Thorndike's stress is on the "quality of learning rather than on speed of learning rather than on speed of learning or retention."

(15) Adults learn better those things which are reinforced by their previous experience.

Goals of Training

The basic goals of police training are to make lasting improvement in his role enactment capacities as a policeman and to develop his capacity for assuming higher levels of responsibility. Thus, police training is an effort to fit men for police life and to make him think, act and live like a police officer. However, in view of all embracing nature of a policeman's role, police training *ipso facto* results in development of his total personality including building up of physical fitness, development of *espirit-de-corps* and imbibing of general police ethos. Training not only aims at improving his existing enactment and capacity to adapt to changing situations but also prepares him for the future role in the fast changing social milieu. It enables the policeman to develop precision of thought, analytical clarity and holistic approach to the problem.

Role of Police

Traditionally, duties of police are to enforce law and order, regulate traffic, and act as organisation of social control. The police functions provide the security base upon which the polity rests and sustains its support for growth. The traditional duties assigned to the police seem to be out of place in modern India today. The economic, political and social conditions in India have rapidly changed after Independence. The democratic and welfare nature of our polity has added new dimensions to police work not only by involving changes in the quality, approach and methods of police work but also by incorporating within the range of police duties safeguarding the fundamental rights of the citizens. Today, the police role can be broadly categorised under five major headings :

(*a*) Police as a law enforcement agency.

(*b*) Police as an arm of the executive government.

(*c*) Police as the protector of rights and liberties of citizens.

(*d*) Police as a social service and agents of social change.

(*e*) Police with a role in political development.

Police as law enforcing agency become agents of law answerable only to the courts. Enforcement of law involves detection, investigation, judgement and punishment. Thus, police, judiciary and correctional authorites are the primary agencies involved in the process. The police force is organised on the assumption that at least 99 per cent people want laws to be enforced against a criminal minority of, at the most, one per cent. One major difficulty in enforcement of law is the multiplicity of laws themselves. Law enforcement by the police is also limited by some factors which are beyond its control i.e. the inadequate and defective laws, ambiguous interpretation of the laws by the courts and public apathy. Police as the executive arm of the government, have to act in accordance with the directives and instructions of the senior executives. They are called upon to help the government in the implementation of family planning programme can be cited as an example when such role is resented by the people if the government programmes are not popular with the people. Arrest of political leaders at the behest of the politicians in power can be another instance. So long as the police have to work under the directions of the executive government, it may not be reasonable to expect it to act independently. However, they have to keep in mind the principle of accountability both to the law and to the people. While they have to conform to the basic policies and programmes of the government, they have to keep the ground perspective of public interest in view. Certain actions must be performed, certain acts are prohibited but in between the two extremes there is a large area where individual discretion and judgement has to be exercised. It is this area of flexibility of action that is governed by the principle of accountability, maximal at policy levels and minimal at action levels. The police role as protector of rights and liberties of the citizens emerges out of its role as law enforcing agency and as executive arm of the government. In a welfare state where the government is to ensure the rights and liberties of citizens, this role of police gets added impetus, putting the responsibility of protecting citizens especially the weaker sections of the society—minors, women, minorities and handicapped persons—squarely on the shoulders of the police. It is for the police to ensure the dictum propounded in the Mahabharata that in a well governed state, a fully bejewelled unescorted maiden should be able to go from one end of the realm to the other in the middle of night unmolested and unhindered. The rights and liberties of the citizens cannot be isolated from the totality of the social context, hence police as protectors of their rights and liberties also become a social service. Police have the tasks of developing, sustaining and strengthening of democratic institutions and processes thus, contributing to economic growth and helping in acceleration of social change. Political development is closely related to social change and, therefore, police gets a role in political development of the country.

Police play a critical role by maintaining the balance between order and violence, security and insecurity, lawlessness and order thereby determine to a large extent the fortunes of any developmental effort. Police affect the political life of the nation by directly participating in the top-level policy making and by supporting the implementation of policy decisions. There is considerable gap between role enactment, role perception and role expectation of police. In the case of role expectation different categories of the society have different views. This further widens the gap between role expectation and role enactment. The role enactment, and the role perception of the members of the police force, however, is determined by the overall socio-political system that constitutes their operational environment, the criminal justice system under which they function, the public support they receive in the performance of their duties, the policies of the government in the context of emergence of welfare state ideals and the occupational sub-culture and ethos of the police force. For some, the role of police is a mechanism for the distribution of non-negotiably coercive force, others consider police as an agency for social service and managers of socio-politico-economic change.

The Relevance of Police Training

Police training is to prevent the police officers' obsolescence because without the support of planned training, they both at individual and group levels may keep on applying the tools of yesterday for the problems of today and tomorrow.[4] The rapidly increasing political consciousness among the people, and the technological explosion resulting in mass education, speedier means of transport require an up-to-date policeman to handle them. In a democracy police officers are also to be trained in the art of handling their political "masters"—the public. The individual's adjustment is dependent on his emotional factors, psychological built up, training and on the set of expectations he has of the job, his superiors, peers and subordinates. This process can be termed as "occupational socialisation" of an individual in an organisational context. The occupational socialisation process requires the individual to blend his personality, his views, self expression and his behaviour in a manner that is acceptable to the organisation.[5] Training is one of the most important factors in building and sustaining this socialisation process. Training is specially relevant for police officers because of the presence of three elements in police organisations—danger, authority and efficiency. Many hazardous and dangerous situations have to be tackled by the police officers and lack of adequate response may cost them their lives or limbs. Policemen have to face public violence, armed criminals, decoits and other anti-social elements and they are required to be trained in sensing the danger ahead.

TABLE 3.1

Showing rank-wise police personnel killed or injured in India during 1976

S. No.	Rank	Killed	Injured	Total
1.	Constables	89	789	878
2.	Head Constables	16	147	163
3.	Assistant Sub-Inspectors	8	37	45
4.	Sub-Inspectors	20	132	152
5.	Inspectors	2	21	23
6.	Other Gazetted Police Officers	3	17	20
	Total	138	1,143	1,281

Figures given above indicate that all ranks face danger in police life. State-wise figures are as follow :

TABLE 3.2

Showing state-wise number of police personnel killed or injured on duty during 1976

S. No.	State/Union Territory	No. of persons killed	No. of persons injured	Total strength of police force	Casualty per thousand of strength
1	2	3	4	5	6
1.	Andhra Pradesh	3	39	35915	1.17
2.	Assam	6	9	11877	1.26
3.	Bihar	11	13	41513	0.57
4.	Gujarat	5	30	37001	0.94
5.	Haryana	5	21	11225	2.31
6.	Himachal Pradesh	—	—	5442	—
7.	Jammu & Kashmir	3	36	6429	6.06
8.	Karnataka	3	59	31542	1.96
9.	Kerala	4	49	18012	2.94
10.	Madhya Pradesh	10	100	35805	3.07
11.	Maharashtra	11	170	73755	2.45
12.	Manipur	—	12	2927	4.09
13.	Meghalaya	—	—	3014	—
14.	Nagaland	2	1	3545	0.84
15.	Orissa	6	32	19843	1.91
16.	Punjab	16	16	21174	1.51
17.	Rajasthan	3	143	33723	4.32
18.	Sikkim	—	—	738	—
19.	Tamil Nadu	6	54	39017	1.53
20.	Tripura	—	—	2533	—
21.	Uttar Pradesh	33	198	82713	2.79
22.	West Bengal	1	42	50544	0.85
	Total	128	1024	568287	2.03

Union Territories

1	2	3	4	5	6
23.	A. & N. Islands	1	8	1264	7.12
24.	Arunachal Pradesh	—	—	641	—
25.	Chandigarh	—	2	1091	1.83
26.	D. & N. Haveli	—	—	73	—
27.	Delhi	8	106	15367	7.41
28.	Goa, Daman & Diu	1	2	1444	2.07
29.	Lakshadweep	—	—	241	—
30.	Mizoram	—	—	1269	—
31.	Pondicherry	—	1	660	1.51
	Total	10	119	22050	5.85
	Grand Total	138	1143	590337	2.8

Source : Crime in India 1976, Bureau of Police Research and Development, MHA, Govt. of India, 1980, pp. 97-98.

These two tables clearly show that policemen face danger of getting killed or injured in all areas of the country and all ranks share this danger equally.

Police officers are transformed into authoritarian personalities by virtue of the police role.[6] Police stand before the public as the symbol of government authority. The police officer is a symbol not only of law but also of the entire system of law enforcement and criminal justice. Thus, police authoritarianism arises out of his role as agent of social control and law enforcement. A police constable on a traffic junction, expects instant obedience to his signals and at that time there is no question of permitting individual freedom of judgement and thereby he acts authoritatively. However, because there is considerable scope of personal discretion in law enforcement, police must know how to exercise this personal discretion. This cannot be learnt by trial and error and hence adequate training becomes

Diagram No. 1

POLICE PERSONNEL KILLED OR INJURED ON DUTY DURING, 1976

KILLED (50 40 30 20 10 0)	STATES	INJURED (0 100 200 300 400 500)
3	Andhra Pradesh	30
6	Assam	6
11	Bihar	13
3	Gujarat	30
5	Haryana	24
Nil	Himachal Pradesh	Nil
3	Jammu & Kashmir	30
3	Karnataka	50
4	Kerala	40
10	Madhya Pradesh	100
11	Maharashtra	150
Nil	Manipur	15
Nil	Meghalaya	Nil
2	Nagaland	
6	Orissa	32
16	Punjab	16
3	Rajasthan	143
6	Tamilnadu	54
Nil	Tripura	Nil
Nil	Sikkim	Nil
33	Uttar Pradesh	168
1	West Bengal	58
	Union Territories	
8	Delhi	173
2	Other Union Territories	13

imperative. Efficiency and effectiveness in police work can alone provide needed sense of security to the common man. Training is relevant to the police in the context of increasing its efficiency and effectiveness. Efficiency and effectiveness have to be learnt before a policeman is put on duty because society cannot risk the chaos and confusion that may arise from an inefficient and ineffective performance by the agents of law enforcement. Police officers have to take on the spot decisions and therefore, they have to learn art of decision-making and problem solving. The police training has to be such that it prepares a policeman to be flexible and cognizant of "cross-functional ripple effect". The major responsibilities of the police lead them to pursue contradictory and hence unattainable ends and training is also expected to prepare them for managing this role conflict.

Identification of Training Needs

Training needs of police organisations can be categorised in terms of those which can individual has ; a group has ; must be met immediately ; can be met in the future ; call for formal training activities ; call for informal training activities ; call for on the job instructions ; call for off the job instructions ; the police organisation can meet best within itself, the organisation can meet best through "out-house" resources ; a police officer can meet in concert with others and as police officer can meet only by himself.[7] Training needs can be determined through a three faceted approach of organisational analysis, operational analysis and man analysis.[8] These analyses can be made on the basis of articles, books, case studies, complaints, crises, experience of others, factual data, grievances of people, future plans and policies of the organisation. The effective police training has to meet the training needs at the individual, group and organisational level aiming at effectiveness in the personal, inter-personal, team and organisational effectiveness. The organisational analysis involves a study of the entire organisation, its objectives, its resources, and the total economic/political social and technological environment within which the police organisation operates. Operational analysis of the police involves a study of jobs within the organisation in as much detail as possible determining the constituents of the job ; techniques and methodology of performance and expected behaviour, attitudes, skills and knowledge of the individuals. Man analysis in police organisation is a tool for determining through appropriate observation, supervisory evaluation and diagnostic testing to decide whether or not individual performance is upto standard and whether any training is needed. In order to determine the training needs of organisations, most training theorists[9] use the equation which can be stated as standard or desired performance minus present and actual performance equal training. However, in the conttext of police set up performance discrepancies should not be automatically interpreted as training needs because police have to function in a situation where economic, social, political and cultural environment factors play an important role in shaping an incident. Hence police training needs must be determined only after taking into account extraneous and socio-politico-economic factors which impinge upon the performance of police officers.

For identification of group (rank) needs for each "cluster of individuals" job contents of each group are to be analysed ; job performance may only indicate actual levels of performance as against the expected levels and hence environmental appreciation of the job contents alongwith the gap between job performance and job expectation would clearly indicate the needed input to be met by training. These gaps can be categorised as :

(*a*) Specific discernible gaps in certain distinct functional areas of police work like investigation of economic offences.

(*b*) Specific gaps in terms of individual performance and behaviour as noticed in certain individuals like harsh behaviour of individual policeman with poor people.

(*c*) Specific noticeable gaps in senior, middle and junior level functionaries of the police organisation with special reference to the functional areas like personnel management training for senior level officers, (*d*) Specific performance to expectancy gaps in the police organisation as a whole.[10]

Various police commissions appointed by the state governments during the post-independence era have indicated specific areas where training is needed for the police officers. In police organisation, the groups can be divided into three distinct levels on the operational basis :

(*i*) Policy level ;

(*ii*) Supervisory level ;

(*iii*) Action level.

The training needs of these three levels will obviously be different. A survey conducted by the researcher shows that in the opinion of police officers training is needed for different levels in the following areas :

1. For Policy level ;

   (*i*) Policy formulation and implementation ;

   (*ii*) Cost benefit analysis and financial resource allocations ;

   (*iii*) Organisational analysis and organisational development ;

   (*iv*) Issues in police philosophy, methodologies and techniques ;

   (*v*) New horizons in management and behavioural sciences ;

   (*vi*) Concepts of career planning and human resources development ;

   (*vii*) Research methodology and techniques ;

   (*viii*) The dilemma of police accountability.

2. For Supervisory level

   (*i*) Analysis of the working environment (social economic, political and cultural) ;

(*ii*) Problem solving and decision-making ;

(*iii*) General management training consisting of areas like planning, organising, directing, motivating, controlling and budgetting ;

(*iv*) Functional areas as such police-public relations, personnel management, organisational analysis ;

(*v*) Behaviour sciences and its application in police work ;

(*vi*) Management of human resources ;

(*vii*) Supervision of training ;

(*viii*) Police accountability in a democratic society.

3. For Action level

(*i*) Techniques of interrogation ;

(*ii*) Latest criminal legislative enactment ;

(*iii*) Crime prevention techniques ;

(*iv*) Confrontation management techniques and crowd control ;

(*v*) Poilce behaviour in non-situations and contact situations and behaviour modification techniques ;

(*vi*) Role of police in pluralistic society ;

(*vii*) Police and polity and areas of individual accountability ;

(*viii*) Protection of weaker sections, women, minorities and minors ;

(*ix*) Handling of politicians

(x) Police-public relations.[11]

In view of the quantitative and qualitative tasks involved in the process of identification of training needs, it is imperative that this function should be carried out in each state at the highest level by a team of experts.

Another opinion survey of serving police officers shows most of the officers of all the three levels are of the opinion that there is greater need to train subordinate ranks and constabulary than training superior officers.

TABLE 3.3

Showing opinion survey of serving police officers that there is greater need to train subordinate ranks and constabulary than training superior officers

Rank	OPINION				Total
	Totally agree	Partly agree	Somewhat disagree	Totally disagree	
1	2	3	4	5	6
Is.G.P./D.Is.G.P.	8	4	4	4	20
Ss.P.	14	14	2	10	40
Dy. Ss. P	17	14	3	6	40
Inspectors	24	11	1	5	40
Sub-Inspectors	18	5	5	2	30
Constabulary	30	6	7	7	50
Total	111	54	22	34	220
Percentage	50.45	24.54	10.0	15.0	—

In a democratic society, issues like police image, police accountability, relations with politicians, police role in political development and as agents of social change are in-determinate and nebulous. In a welfare state especially in a developing democratic nation-state the demand on the police are multifarious varying from psychiatric help, first aid and settlement of domestic disputes to capturing dacoit gangs and combating guerrillas. There are big gaps between role-enactment and role-perception on one hand and role-expectation and role-perception on the other besides the gap between role-expectation and role-enactment. These gaps can not be filled in by police training alone howsoever elaborate and complex it may become. These limitations of police training must be realised. Training can not neutralise the deficiencies in administration especially those due to mismanagement, nor can it make up the lack of motivation and resources inadequacy. Malfunctioning of the system of criminal administration can not be compensated by training alone. Administrative failure usually are undeserved promotions, bad placement policy, poor recruitments and other administrative lapses. Lack of motivation is due to negative role image. Resource inadequacy is inadequate number of police personnel, inadequate finances and insufficient and obsolete equipment. The malfunctioning of criminal justice system is due to the fact that its four limbs i.e. legislative, police, judiciary and correctional services are not well coordinated and except for police the other three are not held directly responsible for its effect on the society. This assigning of responsibility without power and power without accountability is a major cause of failure of the system of criminal justice in India.

Conclusion

Training is to enable a police officer to perform his present role adequately and also to prepare him for higher responsibilities. Inadequate or improper enactment of the roles of police viz. law-enforcement agency, executive arm of the government, protection of rights and liberties of citizens, agent of social change and facilitator of political development, would result in chaos and break down of social system and hence the importance of police training. Training needs are identified through a three faceted approach by analysing organisation, operations and the man. These training needs are to be identified for three different levels i.e. policy level., supervisory level and action level separately. The inherent constrains and limitations of police training have to be understood and taken into account while formulating training policy. In addition, administrative deficiencies, role dilemma, systems defects and resources inadequacy are four maladies which can not be cured by police training alone.

REFERENCES

1. The United Nations, Handbook of Training in the Public Service (New York, United Nations, 1966), pp. 1-10,

2. For similar views, see Singhvi, G.C., Police Training Perspective ; C.B.I. Bulletin Vol. VI, No. 9, p.6.
3. Whisenand, Paul M., "*Police Supervision—Theory and Practice*" (New Jersey—Prentice Hall in, 1976, Second Edition), p. 258.
4. For similar views, see Saxena, A.P., *Training and Development in Government*, (The Indian Institute of Public Administration, New Delhi, 1974) pp. 27-28.
5. For similar views, see Monappa, Arun and Sanyadam, Mirza's Personnel Management, (Tata McGraw Hill Publishing Company Ltd., New Delhi, 1979) p. 140.
6. Niederhoffer, Arthur, Behind the Shield—*The Police in Urban Society* (Garden City, N.Y., Doubleday and Company, 1976), p. 118-119.
7. For similar views, see Johnson, B.R., *Determining Training Needs*, in Training and Development Handbook American Society for Training & Development (Ed. Craig), New York, McGraw Hill Book Co. 1967), p. 17.
8. For similar views, see Mc Gehee N. and Thayer, P.W., *Training in Business and Industry*, New York Wiley, 1961.
9. Rose, H.C., "*The Development and Supervision of Training Programms*", N.P.P. American Technical Society 1964 ; Gilbert, T.F. Poraxeonomy—Management of Personnel Quarterly, 7 Fall 1967, pp. 20-30 ; Warren, M.W., Training for Results, Reading Mass, Addison Wesley, 1969.
10. For similar views, see Saxena, A.P., The Training Function—Identification and Implementation ; Training Monograph No. 6, Training Division, March 1970, New Delhi, p. 8.
11. Indentifying the specific area for training, Madhya Pradesh Police Commission emphasised "training of constables in police public relations, crowd control, management, beat duty and scientific aids to investigation so far as they relate to presentation of scene of crime and of articles left on the spot",—Report of the Madhya Pradesh Police Commission, 1965-66 (Government of Madhya Pradesh, Home (Police) Department, Bhopal) 1967, p. 231

CHAPTER FOUR

HISTORY OF POLICE TRAINING IN INDIA

HISTORICAL background provides a balanced perspective for appreciating some of the unique features of police training in India. This history of police training in India though not very old, has four distinct phases of evolution and development. The first phase commences with the establishment of first regular police training school in the year 1859. The second landmark in the history is the publication of the report of the All India Police Commission of 1902. The establishment of Central Police Training College at Mount Abu in the year 1948 marks the beginning of the third phase and the report of the Committee on Police Training, Ministry of Home Affairs, with Prof. M.S. Gore in 1974 symbolises the beginning of the fourth phase. Though there is remarkable continuity and each stage slides smoothly into the succeeding one yet each stage has characteristics which distinguish it from the rest.

The Seminal Phase

The first police training school for police constables was started at Vellore in Madras Presidency[1] in the year 1859. The Police Commission of 1860, with Mr. M.N. Court as its President, recommended that the police force should be so constituted and trained that it may be thoroughly relied upon for the performance of all duties of a preventive and detective police. But the Commission failed to lay down specific or any hard and fast rules for the training of the police force available after Mutiny of 1857. The Commission used very delightful but vague words about the need and relevance of training. Later in 1863 Col. H.D. Taylor, the First Inspector-General of Police in Central Provinces and Berar took the idea further and established a chain of 13 police training schools at various district headquarters in central provinces. Six years later, training schools for station writers were opened at Sagar and Nagpur in the year 1869. The district police training schools were generally manned and run by senior head constables and sometimes by court Inspectors although formally these schools were under the administrative control of the district Superintendent of Police. The training programme in these schools included regular drill and emphasised upon the importance of sound discipline. In these police schools, men were taught to read and write and were trained in their day to day duties as police officers. The men were made to learn their lessons like parrots without understanding them. Little attempt was made to train the faculty of observation. In the early phase, the recruits who joined as police constables were mostly illiterate. They were taught alphabets only during their training in the district schools. The police training was of a very rudimentary kind. Quarterly reports were submitted on the Inspector's work until he was finally confirmed in his post. The success of the system depended on the qualification of the Superintendent and the Inspector under whom the probationers had to work in the first instance. In the early days of the police in India, the Asst. Supdts. of Police were either seconded from the army or nominated from among young men closer to the India Office. They were all Europeans. In 1865 instructions and orders regarding the nature of training for Asst. Supdts. of Police were issued as under :

> "The Assistant Superintendents should be directed to attend parade and office daily; in the latter he should be employed in keeping up the registers and English correspondence

> generally. He should also be instructed to hear the reports of certain stations and be allowed to pass orders on the same under the guidance of district Superintendents. He should occasionally be instructed to attend the Magistrate's Court both to watch and to take notice of the progress of several police cases. The Dist. Supdt. should insert daily in his order book the duties on which the Assistant Supdt. is to be employed on the following day. Such duty is to be performed with military regularity and no Asst. Supdt. will be excused of such attendance until he is reported to be thoroughly fit to take charge of a sub-division or a district.[2]

Most of the training schools in India at that time were temporary as the Government was reluctant to create permanent institutions. In 1890, a Committee of Police Officers recommended that the investigating staff should be recruited directly and the recruitment of the subordinate ranks should be separated from that of investigating officer. A central police training school was proposed to be established to train the newly recruited investigating officers. A curriculum for their training was also drawn up. The recommendations of this committee were accepted by the Local and Central Governments. As early as 1881, the former Mysore state had four police training schools one each located at Bangalore, Hassan, Chickamanglur and Shimoga. Here instructions were imparted in criminal law, police procedures, drill and musketry. In October, 1892 a regular police training school was opened at Bangalore. It was ordered that the officers of Imperial police should undergo practical and theoretical training when first appointed. The training of the police constables was to be carried out in districts as before with the object of training investigating officers in legal knowledge and procedure. The first school was established in Uttar Pradesh at Allahabad in the year 1893. By the year 1892, it was decided that a certain proportion of officer of the Indian Police should be recruited through the competitive examination. The training of probationers whether appointed in England or in India, was to be carried out by placing them under the personal supervision of Superintendents of Police, specially selected for the purpose. These probationers were to qualify by passing the prescribed examinations within or at the first examination held after two years from the date of joining the police force. The first competitive examination was held in the year 1893 for this purpose. Probationers were required to pass the prescribed departmental examinations and the riding tests within two years of their arrival in India. On passing the above examinations they were first appointed as Asst. Supdts. of Police. Different methods were adopted in various provinces for recruitment and training of the subordinates ranks from inspector down to the constable. In North Western Provinces and Oudh, there were four grades of Inspectors. The constables were appointed through a system of direct recruitment by the District Superintendent of Police in all the Provinces. In the first phase of their police training the constables were required to pass a medical examination which used to be conducted by a civil Surgeon and had to learn the elements of squad drill, general police duties and the law of the land. As a sequel to the recommendations of the Police Commission of 1860, all the ranks of Police were required to be trained in drill exercises and use of fire arms. However, the training of subordinate police ranks was prescribed at more rigorous and intensive scale as compared to the training of officers appointed to the superior grades.[3] The Indians who were directly recruited for the post of Sub-Inspectors were sent to a training school for a strenuous course and severe tests in several allied subjects. Some of them were weeded out either during the first six months or during the remaining twelve months of the course for want of suitable character or desired capacity. They were trained at the School in Departmental rules and regulations and law course. It embraced the whole of Indian Penal Code, the Code of Criminal Procedure, the Indian Evidence Act and the sophisticated niceties of the law of evidence in relation to the criminal law together with some training in drill in accordance with the infantry drill Manual. After completion of training at the training school, they were posted to a district where they were imparted practical training in varied kinds of police work.

Directly recruited Head Constables and Constables were also required to receive appropriate training in law and drill. During the British rule, there were very few police training schools in the country and the police officers had to be sent for training to far distantly located police schools. The Principal of the police training school was the official of the rank of an Asst. Supdt. of Police of the 1st grade for an officiating appointment as District Superintendent. He was entitled to a local allowance of Rs. 150/- per month in addition to his grade pay and free quarters.[4] Originally, recruitment to all superior grades in the police department from the I.G. down to the Asst. Dist. Supdt. was made only from amongst Europeans and no Indian could go beyond the 5th grade (the lowest) of the Dist. Supdt. of Police carrying pay of Rs. 500/-. Most of the Indians were thus appointed to the subordinate ranks only.

In 1892, Punjab opened a police training school at Phillaur for purpose of training the S.Is and the Inspectors. Later a police training school was established at Bhagalpur in Bihar in 1895. The object was to impart suitable police training to investigating officers especially to the probationery S.Is. Madras opened another police training school in 1896 at Vellore. The school provided for the training of 70 probationery officers at a time selected for appointments in the investigating branch of the police. The general curriculum of study provided for adequate acquaintance with English, a sufficient knowledge of law for police purposes and a reasonable grasp over departmental procedures like plan drawing and system of interrogation. This course was linked with the scheme for reorganisation of the subordinate ranks of police which has already been sanctioned by the Secretary of State for India earlier. The other numbers of teaching faculty consisted of Assistants to the Principal who were required to reside in the premises of the school and had to assist the trainees in the preparation of their work after class hours. They helped to explain the practical application of law and official procedure to police work. Besides, two Drill Instructors, a Survey Teacher, a Law Lecturer and a small ancillary staff were also sanctioned. Later similar police training schools were opened for each major province though their administration and staff strength varied in details from province to province. In due course of time, specific rules were framed for superior grades in each province requiring all uncovenanted officers of the higher grades serving in the police to pass an examination criminal law and procedure in its various branches. After one year of appointment, the officers were required to pass an examination in the vernacular language of the district to which they were appointed. Examinations were held in each province for superior posts in (*a*) civil law and procedure, (*b*) criminal law and procedure and vernacular Indian languages and each such subject was to be passed separately by the examinees. Before appointment to the subordinate ranks by direct recruitment, the subordinate officers in each province was required to pass an examination in reading and writing the vernacular Indian language to the satisfaction of a nominated gazetted officer. After induction, the appointees were required to pass the departmental examination in the six subjects. Thus, prior to 1895 there was no formal police training as such in India. Only examinations were conducted for superior and subordinate ranks. There was no rule authorising an extension of time prescribed for passing these departmental examinations and the rules were not strictly observed in practice. The Enquiry by the Police Sub-Committee of 1887 has revealed that an officer appointed in May 1883 had not passed his examination in vernacular, in penal code or departmental paper till August 1887. Similarly, in another case an officer appointed in November 1882 had not passed the vernacular test till January 1887. The system of training made the police officers well disciplined and amenable to the orders of their seniors. This pattern continued for four decades and proved quite effective in coming with various sorts of problems caused by the growing volume of work, the intricacies of organisation and development of police administration during the 19th century. It did lay a solid foundation for a police training system which is still being followed even after three decades of Indian Independence. The training school also imparted appropriate training to the directly recruited head-constables and constables. The training of subordinate ranks was comparatively more rigorous and intensive than that of the superior grades. Though the local variations existed in each province, rules and instructions for the initial training of Imperial Officers were by and large uniform throughout the country. Only basic training for all ranks was envisaged and very few training institutions could emerge for the job all over the country.

The Expansion Phase

The Police Commission of 1902-1903 appointed by Lord Curzon visited all the provinces, the police training schools at Bhagalpur, Moradabad, Vellore and Phillaur and came to the conclusion that :

> "Police force is far from efficient ; it is defective in training and organisation ; it is inadequately supervised and it had utterly failed to secure the confidence and cordial co-operation of the people."[5]

The system of training of superior police officers, introduced towards the close of the 19th century was different from the system which had preceded it but they found that there was room for considerable improvement in the overall system. The Commission observed that some of the officers lacked proper education and training as they were unable to reflect and lacked a sense of personal dignity and responsibility.[6] The Commission, therefore, recommended that the candidates selected as superior officers should undergo a two years probationary course of training and this course of study should include criminal law and practice (including taking of notes of cases in the criminal course), Indian History and Indian Vernaculars, Geography, Ethnology and Horse Riding. They were to be attached to one of the provincial police training schools for one session where they had to pass a departmental examination. The training schools were to be located in non-presidency towns. They were to undergo suitable course of study under qualified instructors at a training school for not less than 18 months. The Commission pointed out that training of Sub-Inspectors and Inspectors in the post had been inadequate, unsystematic and entrusted to an inferior agency. The Commission recommended that a well-equipped provincial training school should be established in every province. The training syllabus was to include, among other things, instruction in criminal law and law of evidence, police procedures and practices and a practical training under efficient supervision.[7] The Commission suggested outlines of a curriculum for this provincial police training school. The Commission pointed out a number of defects in the training of constables and recommended that the constables should be trained at central police training schools and each such school was to be located in a town accessible to several districts belonging to a common division, speaking common languages and having other similar characteristics and conveniences.[8] The Government accepted the recommendations of this commission regarding training of subordinate and lower ranks. Though the commission recommended a two years' probationary course of training for Asst. Superintendents at an English residential university, the Government of India did not agree and instead decided that the training of probationary Asst. Supdts. shouid be carried out in India. The reforms recommended by the Report of the Police Commission on training, however, formed a distinct landmark in the history of police training in India. The Police Commission desired that all the members of the police force should be taught the use of arms and instructed in drill and that this knowledge must be kept up by periodical training at headquarters or by regular drill and target practice at the police stations or by both the methods. The concept gave birth to refresher training in the police organisation. It was decided by the government that matters of training in arms, drill, exercise and internal discipline should be put under the control of the district Superintendent of Police in each district. The Commission were of the view that the most important element in this reform should be an improved system of selecting and training Superintendents. This was one of the most important recommendations of the Commission made in 1902-1903.

In the year 1905, it was decided to establish a Provincial training school for police in each province and all the police officers were to be provided institutional training in law, administrative procedures, drill, horse-riding, Indian vernaculars, Indian history and geography. Next year a training school was established in Bhamburde in Bombay province and another at

Saugar in Central provinces (now Madhya Pradesh). Early in 1907 the police training school at Vellore was reorganised as a training centre for A.Ss.P., Inspectors and S.Is and was placed under a Supdt. of Police. In the same year, the Secretary of State's Officers were directed to wear the letters "I.P." on their epaulettes to distinguish them from Deputy Superintendents and other officers not recruited by the Secretary of State. Till 1912, they were referred to as members of the Imperial Branch of the Police Service. The Islington Commission (1912) used the term "I.P." for the first time.[9] Entry into the then Imperial Police was thrown open to Indians in the year 1920 and the following year entrance examinations for the service were conducted both in England and India. The U.P. Government anticipated most of the recommendations of the Police Commission and in the first year of the present century the buildings were acquired at Moradabad for shifting of P.T.S. and officers of Imperial Police Service were sent there for training. Sri G.H. Dem Coutiere was appointed as the first Principal of Police Training School, Moradabad and he worked there from March 5, 1905 to March 9, 1909. In 1906, a new set of rules for the selection of candidates was formulated, which, it was hoped, would bring forward a better type of recruit. In 1906, a project for enlarging the Police Training school was launched.

By 1908, there were improved facilities for the training of Gazetted Officers at Moradabad. The rank of Dy. Supdts. had been created in 1905 and officers of this rank were also trained at the Police Training school, Moradabad. In 1908, a central training school was established for the training of recruit constables in Assam and later this school was shifted to Dibrugarh in the year 1916. It was designated as provincial police training school. A scheme of sending constable trainees out on tour for a month or two with district Superintendents was approved by the Government. In 1909, a system of dividing the students into companies was instituted. The popularity of the school was so widespread that Indian States began to send their own police personnel for training. In the year 1910, the Bengal Government opened three new police training schools for the training of constables and head constables. The year following witnessed the opening of four training schools for constables in Madras,

The course of training in these schools was only of six months duration. In 1909, the Bombay Government issued orders for the shifting of police training school from Bombay to Nasik. In the same year the training school for officers and the two schools for constables in Eastern Bengal and Assam were amalgamated into a combined training school.

On August 31, 1912, the British Government appointed a Royal Commission on Public Services in India with Lord Islington as the Chairman. The Commission visited all the provinces and invited memoranda and recommendations from various departments of government including that of the police, on methods of recruitment, system of training and probation and other service conditions of public service in India. In the year 1912 Mr. G.W. Gayer, Principal of the Police Training School at Saugar developed a new system of tracking criminals through their foot prints left on the scene. Crime photography as an aid to investigation got started since 1917 a small photographic unit in the HDrs of C.I.D. in Central Provinces (now Madhya Pradesh) was established. In Bengal the police training school, Serdah was raised to a College in 1913 and schools for the training of constables were opened in five towns namely : Serdah, Dacca, Rampur, Boalia and Berhampur. A Fingerprint Bureau was established at Shillong (Assam) in 1913. Thereafter, the Gezetted officers were sent to Bengal for training and the probationary S.Is were trained at the districts. By the end of the year 1916, the P.T.S. Silchar got removed to Dibrugarh and its status was also raised. In 1914, a Constables Training School was established at Cuttack for the training of constables of Orissa Province which was created in 1912. In 1918, the Bengal Government started a Detective Training School to train S.Is and constables in investigation on work. From 1912 to 1915, 77 superior Indian Police Officers were trained in the Police Schools of India after their recruitment through a system of competitive examinations. The province-wise break-up of these Trained Superior Officers was as given in the table that follows.

Only five Indian could be appointed to senior police posts during this period—one each in Bombay, Bengal and Assam in 1913, one each in Bihar and Orissa in 1914 and one in Punjab in 1915. Upto 1914, the examination was the same as that for

TABLE : 4.1
Showing state-wise superior officers trained

S.No.	Province	1912	1913	1914	1915	Total
1.	Madras	3	3	2	1	9
2.	Bombay	3	3	2	1	9
3.	Bengal	5	5	4	2	16
4.	United Provinces	4	3	5	2	14
5.	Punjab	3	4	4	3	14
6.	Bihar & Orissa	1	3	1	—	5
7.	Central Provinces	2	2	2	—	6
8.	Assam	2	1	1	—	4
	Total	23	24	21	9	77

admission to the British Army through Sandhurst. When Imperial Police was first constituted, no minimum educational qualification was prescribed for admission to this service.[10] Later when admission to the police service came to be governed by a competitive examination to be held in England, the minimum education qualification was prescribed at senior Cambridge or its equivalent. A minimum age limit of 19 years was also insisted upon. Later on, the recruitment rules were amended to raise the minimum educational qualification to the degree of the University. The present buildings of the officers mess and residential quarters of PTS Moradabad were acquired in 1920. A large number of officers, who were appointed on demobilisation from the army, came for training at Moradabad. Classes for sergeants were also opened in 1924 and refresher courses for Armed Police Sub-Inspectors, other recruits and remounts for the Mounted Police were concentrated at one place. Sir S.V.L. Dem Gordon, Principal, PTC, Moradabad reported in 1926 to the government that the resources of the school were being utilised to the optimum. As the Police forces keep developing new courses of instruction were added to the curriculum of PTC,

Moradabad. By the year 1934, the position about training courses conducted at Moradabad School was as under :—

(1) Initial course of training for probationary A.Ss.P. and D.Ss.P. and direct appointed Sub-Inspectors of Civil Police.

(2) Refresher courses for Head Constables of the Armed Police approved for promotion and for physical training instructors.

(3) Qualifying courses for Mounted Police recruits and Sergeants.

(4) Specialist courses for physical training instructors.

(5) Training of Remounts.

A provincial Police Committee had been appointed in the Punjab in November 1925 under Mr. Lumsden, with Sir Sikandar Hayat Khan, Cocks and Gauri Dayal as members to examine the adequacy of the police establishment in each district. They reported in 1926 and observed that the training of constables in the districts left much to be desired. There was no provision for proper instructors on the recruit schools and insufficient reserves made systematic training impossible. In view of this Committee, the constables were "foisted on the public" without any real knowledge of the elements of the duties they were supposed to perform and recommended the opening of Recruit Training Centres in selected places. In 1934, a thorough overhaul of the system of police training was proposed. It was felt that the expansion of training facilities had not proceeded along the planned lines. A committee of police officers under the presidency of Mr R. H. Williamson, I.C.S. evolved a new syllabus for training and examinations were designed to arrive at a comprehensive estimate of all round development of the cadets. The P.T.S. Moradabad was recommended for elevation and converted into a "college". Prior to 1936, the recruit constables were trained in the districts of their enlistment for a period of six months at district police lines. In actual practice, it was found to be too short a period and was increased to one year in 1936. The Superintendents of police of the districts were expected to supervise and look after their training establishments. These officers could not supervise police training properly and hence Recruits Training Centres were opened in the districts in 1942 with better facilities of accommodation and training. In 1941, a police training school at Sitapur (U.P.) was started for the training of lower ranks. The emphasis here was on the promotion courses for constables in both civil and armed police. The P.T.C. Moradabad gradually became more popular and police officers from Hyderabad, Kotah, Jaipur, Jodhpur, Gwalior, Kashmir, Nepal, Delhi, Sikkim, Andaman and Railway Board were sent here regularly for police training in general areas of work. Two constables training schools were established in Central Provinces one at Nagpur in 1934 and the other at Jabalpur in 1937. Another training schools for constables was established at Angul in 1937 for the province of Orissa which was constituted by separation from Bihar on April 1936. This was raised to the status of a police training school in 1941. An advanced course of Sub-Inspectors was introduced here in 1936, it included instruction in Scientific Aids to investigation. In 1938, Law graduates were recruited for the first time to man the prosecution branch and they were imparted training specialised in police prosecution work.

In the year 1937, there came provincial autonomy to the provinces under arrangements made by the Government for a gradual transfer of authority to Indian hands. Police training till now was merely to orient the young officers to the conditions of the country and no specialisation was intended as superior police work was counted as the sphere of the generalist. The ideas was to avoid over centralisation.[11] The training included education in Criminal Law and Procedure, proficiency in local language, work on the parade ground and visits to trial courts and police officers of various denominations. The imperial police service officers were also given a short course in survey and settlement operations. This was thought desirable because a considerable time of the senior police officers was expected to be spent in solving confrontations caused by land disputes which often erupted into violent riots.[12]

In May 1939, a conference of senior officials was held at Simla and was attended by the Chief Ministers of Punjab, the N.W.F.P. and Orissa. The Home Ministers of Bombay, Bengal and Sind and the Parliamentaıy Secretaries of U.P., Bihar, Orissa attended it. The Govt. of India was represented by the Home Minister and the Director, Central Intelligence Bureau. The conference mooted a proposal for the establishment of an All India Staff College for Police Officers with a Central Finger Print Bureau and Laboratories of Serologist, Chemical Examiner and the Examiner of Questioned documents. The local Governments were consulted and they were all for the establishment of this staff college.The conference also recommended a scheme for the creation of a Research Institute with the object of imparting instructions to selected officers. However, these proposals ultimately got postponed due to the outbreak of World War II in the year 1939. During the outbreak of 1942 movement, U.P. raised three battalions of special armed constabulary with a strength of about 2500 in all ranks and trained them to relieve the military of certain internal security duties. 1202 additional police was enrolled and trained in U.P. when the figure for the preceding year 1941 was 65 only. In Punjab from 1936 to 1939, 10 Inspectors, 23 S.Is., 56 A.S Is., 78 H.Cs and 464 Constables were trained. In 1939, the Angul school was expanded to train S.Is in Orissa. The war commitment increased the enrolment of police in India and the problem of training them on emergency basis had to be accepted. As a part of war effort, 15,000 men were trained to perform the duties of armed police. By the end of Sept. 1943, the strength of the Armed Police as compared to that of the beginning of the war had almost doubled. The additional police force in India raised and trained from pre-war days to 31 December 1943 is shown in the table at p. 60[13]

In 1944 a G.R.P. Recruits Training Centre was opened at Moradabad for improving the training of GRP Constables. By the middle of 1945, the total strength of the unarmed police in India had increased to 1,76,808 sanctioned and 1,66,181 actual and that of the armed police came down to 1,20,228 sanctioned and 1,13,657 actual.

TABLE 4.2

Showing Additional Police Force Raised and Trained (1939-1943)

S. No.	Provinces	Pre-war Armed	Figures Unarmed	As on 31-12-1943 Armed	Unarmed
1	2	3	4	5	6
1.	Madras	5027	23609	12973	27541
2.	Bombay	7805	15871	16583	21376
3.	Bengal	7138	26255	12485	29435
4.	U.P.	8000	27078	18948	28976
5.	Punjab	23231	2027	25033	10650
6.	Bihar	2518	11320	11096	15080
7.	C.P. & Berar	932	10707	2814	14063
8.	Assam	1324	3227	4265	5132
9.	N.W.F.P.	6842	Nil	16199	38
10.	Orissa	824	3263	2023	4291
11.	Sind	3336	2849	7800	5318
12.	Delhi	2149	Nil	3111	Nil
	Total	69126	126206	133330	161900

Post-Independence Centralisation Phase

The Central Police Training College was established at Mount Abu on 15th September, 1948 with Shri P.L. Mehta (IP) as its first Commandant. On September 15, 1948 the pioneers of the Indian Police (I.P.) service assembled at Mount Abu to seek a fresh orientation to respond to the challenges of free India. The Central police training college, Mount Abu was designed to provide adequate and advanced kind of training to senior police officers and officers of the Indian Police Service. The college, started under the direct control and supervision of the Ministry of Home Affairs, Govt of India, was conceived as an all-India training institute catering to the national needs and providing training facilities conducive to development of an all-India outlook among the senior officers of the police administration.[14] In the year 1948 the Govt. of Assam decided to establish a police training college at Salonibari. A central recruits school was opened at Bihar in 1950. The Indian Constitution which came into force on January 26, 1950, puts police and law and order in the state list of the VII schedule (No 7 list II item 2) but simultaneously it includes police training, fire arms and explosives and several union police agencies in the Union list of subjects which permit the Ministry of Home Affairs of the Government of India for ensuring uniformity and co-ordination.[15] The first batch of regular IPG officers completed their initial training on September 14, 1949.[16] The merger of princely states in 1948-49 with the union created the task of integration and training of the police received from these merged states. The reorganisation of states in 1956 again required further orientation and streamlining of the police personnel and restructuring of the training organisation of the states. In 1959, the Kerala Government appointed a "Police Reorganisation Committee" which emphasized the need for a fundamental transformation in the role of police in view of the attainment of political independence and the emergence of a democratic system based on adult sufferage inspired by the objective of the steady uplift of the common man. During 1960-62 the state governments of U.P., West Bengal, Punjab and Bihar appointed police commissions. In 1963, the Govt of India created a Research Division in the C.B.I. with a skeleton staff under the charge of a Deputy Director for developing and stimulating police research work in India. These state police commissions made several useful recommendations for improving the quality of police training in India. Maharashtra had a police commission working from 1964-65, Madhya Pradesh from 1965-66 and Delhi from 1966-68. The Assam state government appointed the state police commission in 1966. The Tamil Nadu Commission submitted its report in January 1971. All these commissions had made very useful recommendations pertaining to improvements in police training but only a very few states have implemented the recommendations fully.[17] A committee of Inspectors General headed by Shri B.N. Mullik had gone into the deficiencies of training of the IPS probationers at Mount Abu and had called for a much wider curriculum than the intensive doses of infantry training, horsemanship and dry-as-dust law with a handful of other topics dealt with cursorily. The Committee recommended upgradation of the posts of instructional staff and introduction of police principles and administration, common standing orders, investigation procedures, criminology in the Indian setting and the scientific, medical and technical aids to policemanship. Consequent upon the recommendations of the B.N. Mullik Report and the commencement of the Advanced Course, the post of a Deputy Commandant was created in the rank of a DIG in 1957 and there was an increase in the strength of directing staff from June 1960. Advanced course of six months duration was started in June 1960 for IPS officers of six to eight years of service in the field. The course was redesignated as the Senior Officers Course in the year 1969. From April 1973, the duration of the course had been cut down to 14 weeks only.

The conference of Inspectors-General of Police (1956) recognised the need for police research again when it recommended the establishment of Research Centres in the C.I.D. of each state and a similar institution at the Centre as a coordinating agency. In the year 1963, a research division was set up in the Central Bureau of Investigation. The Central Detective Training School was started in 1956, with the objective to train investigating officers of the rank of sub-Inspectors to deal with advanced and scientific methods of crime. In 1958, the idea of a Police Science Congress was mooted in the conference of the Inspectors-General of Police. The First Police Science Congress was held at Patna in 1960. The Police Science Congress is in the nature of a seminar where officers who have done original work on any particular matter related to the various facets of police administration and duties may read their papers with the object of eliciting opinions and views of others. So far 16 All India Police Science Congresses have been held. Beginning in 1969-70, the Govt of India, with the intention of modernising the police force of the country, started a funding scheme to purchase equipments in the areas of communication, transport, scientific aids and police training to be provided by the state governments. This is now called modernisation grant of Central Government. With a view to discuss problems of police training institutions in India, Symposium of heads of the police training institutions are held from time to time under the arrangement of National Police Academy in collaboration with Bureau of Police Research and Development, Govt of India. So far ten symposia have been organised and the last one was held at Patna from 22 to 24 October, 1981.[18]

The Central Government established the Central Training Detective Schools at Calcutta and Hyderabad in 1958. These schools have been organising course of training for fourteen weeks for S.Is of police of all states in modern methods of investigation. In 1962, a Central School of Weapons and Tactics was created by the Central Government for training the police officers in weapons and tactics. The Bureau of Police Research and Development was established in the year 1970 as a separate organisation under the auspicies of the Ministry of Home Affairs, Government of India. The Institute of Criminology and Forensic Science headed by an Inspector General of Police designated as Director was established in Delhi in 1972. Currently the Institute has been organising a number of orientation and professional courses for in-service training of police personnel drawn from various states and specialised wings of state police departments. Inspectors-General of Police of various states were requested by the researcher to furnish the figures showing numbers of S.Is who have been given basic and refresher training in various states and are presented here.

Specialisation Phase

The fourth phase of History of Police Training in India starts from 1974 when the recommendations of the Committee on Police Training were submitted to the Govt. of India. Several states took to the revision of their training programmes and included new subjects which were recommended by the Gore Committee. The National Police Academy was rechristened

TABLE 4.3

Showing State of Refresher and Basic Training for Sub-Inspectors

Sl. No.	State	1966		1967		1968		1969		1970		1971		1972	
		B = Basic Trg.; R — Refresher Trg.													
1	2	3		4		5		6		7		8		9	
		B	R	B	R	B	R	B	R	B	R	B	R	B	R
1.	Assam	77	—	35	—	35	—	104	—	45	—	135	—	199	—
2.	Gujarat	41	—	46	—	41	—	78	—	62	—	—	—	48	—
3.	Karnataka	54	—	78	—	33	—	59	—	59	30	79	50	71	51
4.	Maharashtra	136	—	67	—	97	—	112	—	110	—	250	—	113	—
5.	Orissa	75	—	46	—	58	—	50	—	—	—	28	—	33	—
6.	Punjab	—	—	—	—	149	—	55	—	113	—	85	—	43	—
7.	Tamil Nadu	75	—	143	—	59	—	—	—	147	—	—	—	113	—
8.	Uttar Pradesh	—	—	—	—	—	—	618	100	88	32	—	35	394	105
9.	West Bengal	79	—	69	—	101	—	111	—	70	—	31	—	76	—

(The figures show that almost np refresher training was imparted to sub-inspectors during this period).

as "Sardar Vallabhbhai Patel National Police Academy". The new campus has gradually developed various physical facilities for trainers and trainees at Hyderabad. Similarly, in Rajasthan the Police Academy was shifted to its present location at Jaipur from Kishangarh in August, 1975. The Gore Committee on Police Training submitted its comprehensive report in 1974 and its recommendations have broadly been accepted by the Govt. of India. The recommendations of Gore Committee paved the way for the introduction of the revision of syllabi of various training courses in the states. The introduction of behavioural science, management, socio-economic problems of modern India and application of science and technology to police work has almost revolutionised the training contents of various basic and in-service courses. The Report has a new awareness about new training techniques, instructional methods and other aids in the police organisation. The Internal Security Academy, Mount Abu started three in-service courses for police officers of India in the year 1977, one of 6-days' duration for D.Is.G., the second of 10 days' duration for D.Ms. and Ss.P. and the third for 18 days' duration for Dy. Supdts. of Police. In 1979, the first two week Top Management Development Programme for D.Is.G. was started at N.P.A. Hyderabad. The first Training Terminal Course for I.P.S. probationers was also started in March 1979 at N.P.A. Hyderabad. The fourth phase has ushered in an era of specialisation in police training and at the national level a number of new in-service courses were started. The number of trainees in various in-service courses increased since 1973. The Institute of Criminology and Forensic Science has been conducting the following specialised in-service training courses in criminology for various kinds of police officers drawn from the centre and the states :

(*a*) Advanced course in Criminology ;

(*b*) Police-community Relations ;

(*c*) Research Methodology ;

(*d*) Behavioural Orientation ;

(*e*) Methodology of Behaviour Modification and ;

(*f*) Role of Police in dealing with Delinquents.

In the specialised field of forensic science, the following varieties of courses are organised by the Institute of Criminology and Forensic Science for varieties of durations ;

(*a*) Diploma Course in Document Examination ;

(*b*) Special Course in Document Examination for the Customs and Revenue Intelligence Officers ;

(*c*) Diploma Course in Forensic Ballistics ;

(*d*) Certificate and Diploma Course in Police Photography ;

(*e*) Forensic Toxicology and ;

(*f*) Forensic Biology.

The figures of trainees trained at the Institute of Criminology and Forensic Science, M.H.A., New Delhi are as under :

S. No.	Officers Trained	1973	1974	1975	1976	1977	1978	1979
1	2	3	4	5	6	7	8	9
1.	D.Is.G.	22	—	—	—	15	6	6
2.	Ss.P.	126	86	118	160	125	180	127
3.	Dy. Ss.P	123	71	84	105	164	143	86
4.	Inspectors	20	13	12	18	14	11	15
5.	S.Is.	27	25	35	27	23	17	12
6.	A.S.Is.	—	—	—	—	—	—	1
7.	A.P.Ps.	—	—	—	—	—	—	24

Good research work has been carried out by the faculties of Criminology and Forensic Science at the Institute. Under the guidance of the supervisory staff of the Institute of Criminology and Forensic Science, various kinds of researchers are invited to conduct courses i.e. small research projects are also undertaken by whole time police researchers at the Institute.

Internal Security Academy, Mount Abu has also been organising varieties of in-service courses in internal security since its inception. The data about the number of officers who have been benefited by these courses are as under :

S. No.	Courses	1977	1978	1979	1980	1981
1	2	3	4	5	6	7
1.	Internal Security Seminar for Dy. Inspectors General (six days)	12	53	21	9	8
2.	Internal Security Courses for Dist. Magistrates and Superintendents of Police (10 days)	11	35	48	32	49
3.	Internal Security Courses for Dy. Superintendents of Police	14	90	115	111	85

Dy. Supdts. of Police, especially the direct recruits are generally trained at two levels in their respective states. In most of the states, the administrative training institutions of the state provide the foundational training and later on, they are sent to police training colleges of the state for intensive institutional training. Training in physical endurance, basic laws of the centre and the state and socio-economic framework of the country from the core of institutional training. In July, 1981, the Union Home Ministry decided to revive the scheme for modernisation of police forces in the states and planned to spend Rs. 100 crores on this scheme upto the end of this decade.[19] According to the scheme 50 per cent of the money will be given to the states as loans and 50 per cent as grants-in-aid. The Centre held the view that police training institutions are generally heavily over-crowded and in some places expansion of training facilities has not taken place at all although the intake of police trainees has gone up considerably. Training centres have been upgraded without any addition to physical or faculty norms and it has resulted in lowering of standards of training. Improvement of training facilities is one of the objects of modernisation grant. During October, 1981 the Bureau of Police Research and Development (BPRD) has recommended a concerted country-wide effort to introduce certain changes in the training of the policemen to improve the efficiency and image of the police forces.[20] The changes are proposed to be introduced in phases during next ten years. The Bureau has suggested that at least 50 per cent of the police instructors in the police training colleges and schools should be replaced by civilian instructors. S.V.P.N.P.A., Hyderabad and I.S.A., Mt. Abu are already making extensive use of university academicians to support the existing faculty and utilise their expertise in various fields.

There has been qualitative and quantitative development of police training in India after 1974 as a result of implementation of the recommendations of the Committee on Police Training (Gore Committee). In 1976, the State Reserve Police Training Centre was established at Choki in Junagadh district of Gujarat for providing training to the recruits of State Reserve Police Force w.e.f. 8.4.1976. In September, 1980, Police Training School was opened at Pondicherry. In Jammu and Kashmir, Sheri-Kashmir Police Training College was started in 1981 at Udhampur. In September 1981 R.T.C. Sitapur in U.P. was upgraded and converted into U.P. Police Training College III. State Armed Police Subsidiary Training Centre for recruits of Manipur Rifles was opened w.e.f. 1.10.1986 at Jiribam. In Andhra Pradesh on 15th May 1986 the Chief Minister of Andhra Pradesh laid the foundation of a prestigious A.P. Police Academy at Hyderabad. At National Police Academy Hyderabad three new courses, Junior Management Course of 6 weeks, Senior Management Course of 4 weeks and Top Management Course of 2 weeks, were started during 1986. These courses have been started as recommended by the Sixth Report of the National Police

Commission 1981 Chapter XLV for training and Career development of Indian Police Service Officers. The Fifth Report of the National Police Commission was published in November 1980 and it has wholly endorsed the recommendations of Committee on Police Training 1973 in their totality and reiterated that the Government should implement the same under a time bound programme. The research findings of the author reveal that although the syllabus and training format prescribed by the Gore Committee on Police Training have been accepted by the states yet no perceptible improvement has been noticed in the organisation of training, training of trainers, motivation for trainers, preparation of training material and use of audio-visual aids in police training.

Concluding Remarks

There has been gradual evolutionary development of police training enterprise in India. The first phase—seminal phase—brought about establishment of a number of training institutions for the police laying the edifice for the training systems. The second phase—expansion phase—witnessed expansion of various training efforts on the basis of the recommendations of Police Commission, 1902 followed by subsequent reviews by a number of committees. In the post-independence phase, centralisation of a number of central training institutions was started bringing uniformity and co-ordination in police training effort. The fourth phase—specialisation phase—began with the acceptance of the Gore Committee Report on Training and the resultant emphasis on specialised training. The first two phases laid a solid foundation for a police training system which is still enduring with some modifications even during the subsequent phases. However, the training aspect of police development has not evoked the same support and emphasis in the later phases.[21] From the very beginning. police training in India has been organised essentially as an in-house exercise with very little outside support as is the practice in U.K. which opposed to that obtained in U.S.A. where police training is primarily imparted by universities in consultation and collaboration with police specialists.[22] All the states have gradually built up their own training institutions for basic and refresher training. Outside support is taken only for specialised and advanced courses like unarmed combat, weapons and tactics, internal security intelligence and like and even for these officers are deputed to other training institutions managed by police or para-military organisations. As recommended by Indian Police Commission 1902-03, training centres were located in non-metropolitan towns of the states where they are still functioning. During recent years, there has been a knowledge explosion particularly in the fields of management and behavioural and social sciences all of which are essential for police. The training institutions of police cannot build up and keep pace with this increase in knowledge by themselves and, therefore, must seek support of specialised agencies and institutions outside the police organisation. Thus, it is necessary to evolve a system of training in which the outside support is blended and harmonized with the in-house approach in vogue so far.

REFERENCES

1. The earliest police training institution in a foreign country was the one started in France in 1883. Coatman, J., 'Police London' (Oxford University Press, 1959), p. 131.
2. Quoted in Jayavant, A.R., "*A Century of Police Trg.* The Indian Police Journal—Century Issue", p. 170.
3. Madan, J.C., "*Indian Police : Its Development' upto 1905—An Historical Analysis*", (Uppal Publishing House, New Delhi, 1980) p. 102.
4. Madan, J.C., *op. cit.*, p. 103.
5. Quoted in Gupta, Anand Swarup—*The Police in British India 1861-1947* (Concept Publishing Co., New Delhi, 1979), p. 201.
6. Report of the Indian Police Commission, 1902-3, p. 64.
7. Report of the Indian Police Commission, 1902-3, p. 59.
8. Ibid., p. 55.
9. Sir Griffiths Percival—To Guard My People—The History of the Indian Police, p. 97.
10. Lahiri, B.N., "*Before and After*", (Chugh Publications, Allahabad, 1974), p. 5.
11. Nath, "*Forty Years of Indian Police*" (Concept Publishing Co., New Delhi, 1981), p. 23.

12. Commenting on the general utility of the training of Imperial Police Service, Sri Trilok Nath has observed : "At the end of the training, I found that I had little grasp of the job that would present itself before us. But with the machinery running and letting things take their pre-determined course, little difficulty was expected in accomplishing the task ahead."
13. Home Department, *History of Congress Rebellion*,, Part I, 1942-43, p. 88
14. Jayavant, A.R., "*A Century of Police Training*", (Indian Police Journal Centenary Issue 1961), p., 169-94.
15. See Union List I, VII Schedule, item Nos. 5, 8, 9, 27, 31, 61, 65, 73 and List II concurrent, items Nos. 1, 3, 13, 19, 33, 35 and 39 of the Constitution of India. Publication Division, Govt. of India, 1981.
16. For Reminiscences of first batch officers, See Sri S.C. Chaudhari—Sept. 15, 1948 ; Sri K.N. Prasad—In Retrospect, National Police Academy Magazine (Vol. XXIII, Nov., 1973).
17. A useful study on the subject has been made by a syndicate group of N.P.A. Hyderabad of the gap between recommendations and their implementations, see Transactions, Vol. XXII, April, 1976, pp. 1-34.
18. The First Symposium of the Heads of Police Training Institutions was held at Mount Abu in April, 1968. The second symposium at Mysore from 25-28 Sep., 1969. Proceedings are sent to all the training institutions and Inspectors-General of Police of States but no watch is kept on implementation of recommendations.
19. Chawla, G.S., "*Police Forces in States*" Centre to spend Rs. 100 crores for modernisation, Indian Express, Monday, July 27, 1981 (Ahmedabad Edn.), p. 4.
20. Changes in Police Training Proposed—Staff Correspondent, *Times of India*, October 30, 1981 (Ahmedabad Edn.).
21. In Working Paper of Seminar on Police Training held in 1961 at C.P.T.C., Abu, it has been asserted that the increased emphasis on the quality of training to be imparted to various ranks have evoked highest measure of interest only after independence. See Proceedings of Seminar 23-24 Oct., 1961, p. 114.

    This view is not based on facts. Moreover, in the later phases, there is failure of the state and the central governments to implement fully the recommendations of various committees and commissions on Police Training.
22. Bcolsen, Frank, Directory of Colleges and Universities offering programmes in Law Enforcement Criminalistics and Corrections May 1961.—Germann, A.C., "*Police Personnel Management*" (Springfield, Thomes, 1958) Gammage, Z. Allen, "*Police Training in United States*" (Charles, 1963).

CHAPTER FIVE

ORGANISATION OF POLICE TRAINING IN INDIA

THE ORGANISATION of police training in India is much more diverse and plural than in Japan and Great Britain. It is certainly better knit than the one obtained in U.S.A.[1] The constitution of India leaves enough scope for this desired plurality.[2] It enumerates police as an item in the state list of the seventh schedule, yet the central government has been assigned a definite role in terms of policy co-ordination, personnel control, police research and modernization of police training in the country. The organization of police training is largely in the hands of the government agencies of the state which is one of the unique features of Indian polity. The Government of India also do maintain a wide set-work of forensic science laboratories and other training institutes to conduct research and serve as clearing houses for various kinds of scientific aids to detect criminals and law-breakers. The Directorate of Police Wireless is conducting initial and up-grading training courses in radio telecommunication for wireless operators of the state police. The National Police Academy, The Bureau of Police Research and Development and the Institute of Criminology and Forensic Science are other important Union Government organisations which undertake functions of training police officers and co-ordination of research activities. Police training is generally institutionalised in the police training colleges and Recruit Training Centres at the state level. In districts, the Superintendents of police organise routine training courses and annual training programmes for district reserves. Due to shortage of staff and other commitments, there is hardly any training in police stations. The structural pattern of training in various states differs according to the size and nature of duties of the police force. Moreover, this organisation and structure of police training institutions have undergone noticeable changes in the pattern of staffing and structure in most of the states. Several posts of heads of training institutions have been upgraded during the last decade. The present study proposes to outline the organisational structure of training as obtained in most of the states of the Indian Union.

Police Training Organisations of the Union Government

After independence when the Indian Police Service Cadre came into existence alongwith the constitution of the Indian Administrative Service, the Ministry of Home Affairs became responsible for the training of all Indian services. The Ministry of Home Affairs has jurisdiction over a number of Union subjects. These subjects include "matters relating to the National Academy of Administration, the Central Police Training College (now National Police Academy), the Central Detective Training School, the Central Forensic Science Laboratory, the Central Finger Print Bureau, the Central Emergency Relief Training Institute and the National Fire Service College" and other "matters relating to the Indian Administrative and Police Services".[3] The functions of the Ministry of Home Affairs of Union Government are organised in several divisions. The "police division" and the "training division" are the two wings of the ministry that directly concern with the training of police officials of the government. In the central secretariat, there are two positions of deputy directors looking after training. The two attached offices of the Home Ministry viz. the National Academy of Administration, Mussorrie and the Secretarial Training School, Delhi directly supervise the tasks associated with training. The

National Police Academy, Hyderabad, the Directorate of (Police Wireless) co-ordination, the National Fire Service College, Nagpur and the National Civil Defence College, Nagpur are some of the important subordinate offices of the Ministry that look after allied matters. The Training Division, M.H.A. was established in the year 1968. Prior to that, the Planning Commission of India had recommended the appointment of a Director of Training to organise systematic training programmes for different grades of employees of the Government. The Chanda Committee also went into the question of training and made several recommendations. On the recommendations of the Administrative Reforms Commission's Report on personnel administration, the Training Division as part of the Department of Personnel and Administrative Reforms, came under the cabinet secretariat in 1970. However, the Department of Personnel and Administrative Reforms including the training division again became part of Ministry of Home Affairs in 1977. Some of the functions of the training division of the Ministry include :

(*a*) Tendering advice on training matters to the government at the Centre and in the states as well as to the Public Enterprise Managements.

(*b*) Making training plans long term as wall as annual for the Government of India and providing assistance to the state governments and major training institutions in the matter of plan preparation.

(*c*) Providing support to all training organisations and institutions.

(*d*) Designing training programmes tailored to the specific requirements of personnel in the development agencies and other organisations.

(*e*) Conducting seminars, conferences, and other programmes relating to training for special groups of development administrators and trainers.

(*f*) Ensuring co-ordination of training activity between Central Government training organisations, between training institutions of the Centre and in the states and among the other various training institutions.

(*g*) Identifying appropriate training programmes of training abroad for Civil servants from a wide range of disciplines and arranging for their training under the various technical and other programmes.

(*h*) Promoting research relating to training and development and production of training materials for wide use.

(*i*) Monitoring and evaluating training to see that it conforms to the pre-determined plan priorities and contributes to the overall development of staff and organisation.

The Training Division acts as a clearance house on all information pertaining to training. The training division sponsors several training programmes including Advanced Professional Training Programmes, Programme for Development Personnel, Management Development Programme and Executive Development Programme. The institutions where such programmes are conducted for government servants include the Indian Institute of Public Administration, New Delhi ; The Administrative Staff College of India, Hyderabad ; Indian Institute of Management at Ahmedabad and Bangalore and many other universities and institutions.

Sardar Vallabhbhai Patel National Police Academy, Hyderabad

The Central Police Training College was started in 1948 at Mount Abu on the initiative of the late Home Minister Sardar Vallabhbhai Patel. Later, it was rechristened as National Police Academy. On its shifting to Hyderabad, it has been given a new name of "Sardar Vallabhbhai Patel National Police Academy". The Academy organises basic course for I.P.S. probationers, Basic Terminal Course, Senior Officers' Course, Top Management Course and Crime Prevention Course for officers of senior ranks. It also conducts a basic course for C.B.I./I.B. cadets. The Academy organises a number of seminars and workshops every year as a part of its normal academic activities.

A case study of this Academy has been undertaken by the recent researcher and has been included in this study as a micro level analysis. The National Police Academy, hyderabad has been responsible for organising symposium of heads of the police training institutions of India. The problems of training institutions and police trainers are discussed in these forums and recommendations are formulated and processed for implementation by the states. The National Police Academy (N.P.A.) has served as a Brain Trust to improve the espirit-de-corps of the senior police officers class in India. It seeks to eliminate the risk of avoidable divergence of administrative theory and practice as well as the lack of co-ordination which is inherent in any scheme of devolution of powers in a federal system of government such as ours.

Central Forensic Science Institutes

The Government of India has established a wide network of Forensic Science Institutes to conduct research and to serve as clearing house for various kinds of scientific aids necessary to examine, compare and evaluate physical evidence with a view to link a suspect to the victim or to the scene of crime.[4] Training facilities are now available for investigating officers in the practical application of scientific aids at forensic science laboratories. Under the modernisation grants and other technical assistance programmes, facilities for training the personnel of forensic science laboratories, and aids for purchase of equipment from abroad are being made available. Some of these institutes have highly specialised functions and assist the state police forces in detecting organised crime such as forgery of documents, counter-feiting of currency and manufacture of explosives. The organisation has its three major units at Calcutta, namely The Central Forensic Science Laboratory, The Central Detective Training School and the Central Finger-prints Bureau. The Serologist to the Government of India at Calcutta, the Govt. Examiner of questioned documents at Simla, the Masters of the Mints are Calcutta and Bombay, The Indian Security Printing Press at Nasik and the Inspectors of Explosives at Calcutta, Bombay, Madras, Agra and Gwalior are some of the specialised services in the country to which states refer their cases for the establishment of scientific proofs with a view to detect crime.

Central Detective Training Schools

The first Central Detective Training School was started in 1956 with a view to train investigating officers of the rank of Sub-Inspectors and above to deal with advanced and scientific methods of crime. The central detective training schools are located at Calcutta, Hyderabad and Chandigarh. These schools are conducting courses on advanced scientific methods of crime investigation. The total intake capacity of these schools is limited.[5] Efforts have been made in recent years to increase the capacity of the existing schools, but the problem persists. According to sample survey, majority of the trainees who attended these courses in the past found this training very useful. During interview with the trained officers, it was discovered that in some cases, the services of the trained S.Is. are not being properly utilised and their expertise remains unexploited. The organisational set-up is given below :

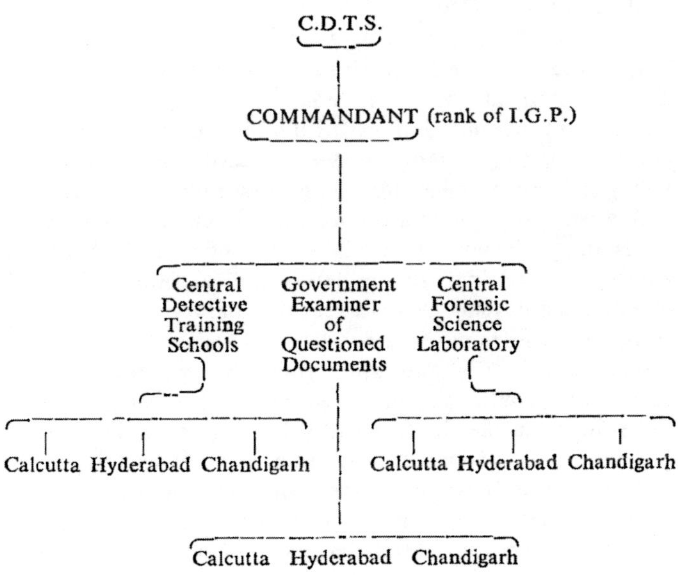

Institute of Criminology and Forensic Science

In 1968, the University Grants Commission appointed a Committee to look into the applied aspects of education, training and research in Criminology and Forensic Science commensurate with the needs of the country. The committee recommended the establishment of an autonomous institution at the national level with the objective of imparting-inservice training to functionaries of criminal justice system and to undertake research in the fields of Criminology and Forensic service. In 1972, the Government of India established the Institute of Criminology and Forensic Science headed by an Inspector-General of Police who is designated as Director. The institute is currently organising a number of orientation and professional courses for the inservice police personnel/members of judiciary and correctional services.[6] The Institute has so far trained 2,821 personnel and this list includes judicial officers, police officers, officers from correctional services, prosecutors, forensic science experts and 14 foreign trainees from Iran, Iraq, Malaysia, Nepal, Thailand, Phillipines and Singapore. The chart given below shows the training activity of the I.C.F.S. at Delhi :

The Bureau of Police Research and Development

The Government of India took a decision to create an independent organisation called the Bureau of Police Research and Development in the year 1969. The Bureau considers the policy and programme for police research and development with a view to promote a speedy and systematic study of the needs and problems of police in a changing society. It provides advice in initiating, stream-lining and co-ordinating police research and development work in the country and encourages research on various aspects of police administration by the state research cells and other research agencies devoted to such work. With the intentions of modernising the police forces in India, the Government of India since 1969-70 started a funding programme for purchasing equipments in the areas of communication, transport, scientific aid and training. The Bureau, apart from doing research and development work, also administers the Central Forensic Institutes and discharges

Institute of Criminology and Forensic Science

Criminology		Forensic Science	
Research Oriented Courses	Inter-actional Courses	Orientation Courses	Professional Courses
1	2	3	4
1. Research Methodology	1. Advanced Course in Criminology	1. Crime & Justice	1. Ballistics
2. Orientation to research	2. Police-community relations	2. Orientation to Forensic Science	2. Document examination
3. Methodology of Behaviour modification	3. Behavioural orientation	3. Orientation to document examination	3. Biology
	4. Role of Police in dealing with juvenile delinquents		4. Serology
			5. Toxicology
			6. Photography

the role of a consultant for the Ministry of Home Affairs to understand, tackle and solve problems of state police organisations. It disseminates information on crime, criminology, weapon system, transport, traffic control, scientific aids, training and other technical matters so that the police forces in the country can constantly be kept informed of the developments and progress made in police science in India and abroad. Initially the B.P.R. & D consisted of two divisions viz : (i) The Research Division and (ii) The Development Division. As a result of the recommendations of the Committee on Police Training, a Training Division was added to the Bureau in 1973 to formulate police training policies and to provide an element of co-ordination at the national level. The research and development effort of the Bureau is reviewed and guided by a Police Research and Development Advisory Council. The Council meets twice a year, under the chairmanship of Union Home Secretary. The following seven standing committees constituted by the Government assist the Bureau in discharging its functions. These committees are in the areas of :

(*i*) Police Research ;

(*ii*) Police Training ;

(*iii*) Weaponary and Riot Control ;

(*iv*) Police Transport ;

(*v*) Traffic Equipments ;

(*vi*) Forensic Science and ;

(*vii*) Forensic Medicines.

The committees function under the overall guidance of the Police Research and Development Advisory Council. The Bureau is the convening authority of Police Science Congress, All India Forensic Science Congress and the Conference of Directors of Forensic Science Laboratories. These annual conferences provide useful forum for exchange of ideas. The administrative organisation of the Bureau can be presented as under :

Organisational Chart of the Bureau of Police Research and Development, Ministry of Home Affairs, New Delhi

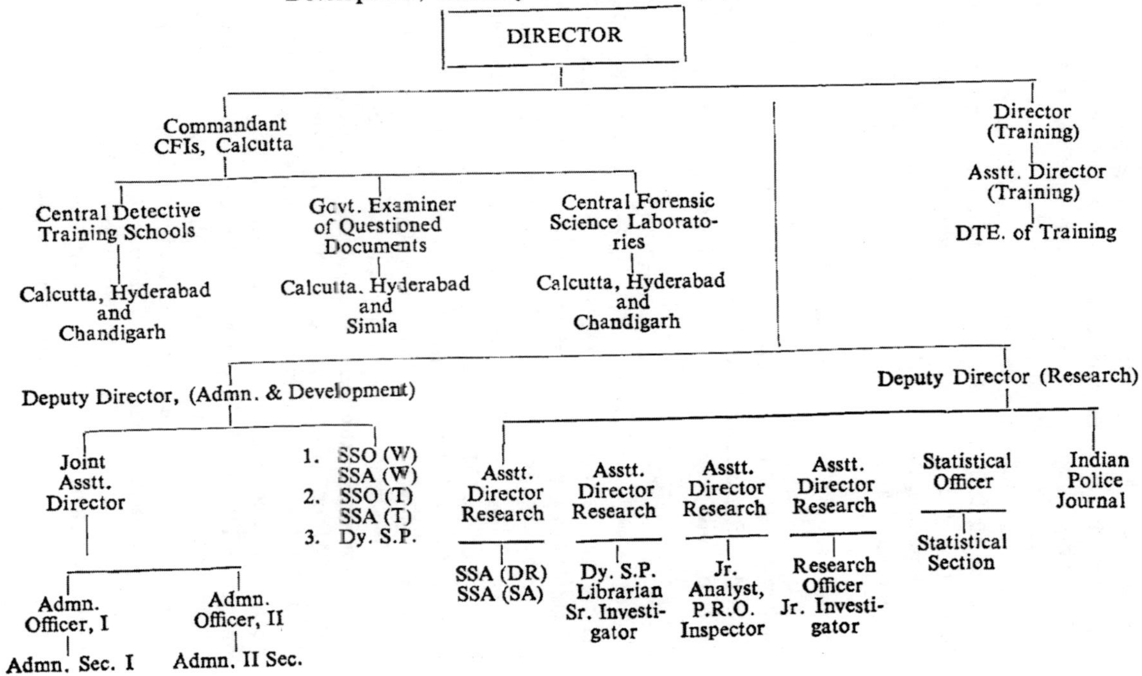

The existing staff pattern is considered as inadequate and a proposal is pending with the government for enhancing the number of staff.[8] One of the reasons for the stunted growth of the Bureau has been the fact that police as such stands placed in the non-plan sector. The expenditure on police has severely been graded down and adequate funds are not available. There has been an enormous shortage of qualified, competent and motivated staff in the Bureau. Some of the reasons are beyond the control of the Director. In the judgement of majority of the respondents, the B.P.R.&D. needs a through reorganisation for its revitalisation.

Organisation for Training in C.R.P.F.

The Central Reserve Police Force came into existence on 27th July, 1939 as Crown Representative's Police Force. Subsequently, after independence it was converted into the Armed force of the Union by Central Reserve Police Force Act (No. LXVI of 1949) and since then has been doing duties of a reserve police force. The responsibility cast on the centre to prevent threatened internal disturbances and protect states against such disturbances necessiated the elevation of police policies above and beyond the limits of states.[9] The C.R.P.F. Act was enacted in the year 1949 and Members of the Central Reserve Police Force have been assigned general duties under section 7 of the C.R.P.F. Act. The Force is commanded by a Director-General assisted by a Directorate General and six Inspectors-General of Police. The Central Reserve Police Force has five major para-military training institutions and one Signal training institution. The Internal Security Academy, C.R.P.F., Mount Abu is commanded by a Director of the rank of I.G.P. Internal Security Academy which was established in the year 1975 conducts in-service courses of internal security for police officers of the states. It also conducts a number of C.R.P.F. Courses for the gazetted and the non-gazetted ranks. In addition, it conducts seminars of six days' duration for Deputy Inspectors-General of Police of the states. The Academy offers internal security course of 10 days for District Magistrates and Superintendents of Police of state police forces. Internal security courses of 16 days are conducted by the Academy for Dy. Supdts. of Police and other officers of equivalent ranks drawn from public undertakings.[10] The C.R.P.F. has two Central Training Colleges located at Neemuch and Avadi and two Recruit Training Centres at Barwaha and Avadi. The Central Training College Neemuch conducts courses on Unarmed Combat for police forces of the country. Similarly, Central Training College, Avadi offers specialised courses on Tear Smoke/Gas and crowd control for the non-gazetted ranks of the police forces from various states. The Recruit Training Centres are (in addition to the training of C.R.P.F. Constable recruits) also providing basic training to the constables of C.I.S.F./S.S.B. and other police organisations. The C.R.P.F. training is basically the armed police training and has been patterned on the lines of para-military training. The sanctioned strength of C.R.P.F. training institutions is given in table below :

In the C.R.P.F. Directorate General, there is one officer of the rank of Dy. Director (D.I.G.) who is assisting the Director-General in supervision and co-ordination of training. The Dy. Director (Training) is assisted by one Assistant Director and other administrative staff. For training of police wireless personnel of C.R.P.F., there is one Central Training College (Telecommunication) at Neemuch. In view of increase in the sanctioned strength of the force and to meet the increasing requirements of the force, the reorganisation of training institutions is regarded as necessary. Proposals for expansion have been pending with the Government of India for consideration.

Border Security Force

Border Security Force was created by the Border Security Force Act 1968 with a view :

(*a*) to police and patrol the Indian borders and to give a sense of security and high morale to the people living in border areas by providing special protection to their person and property against depredations from across the border ;

TABLE 5.1

Showing Sanctioned Strength of C.R.P.F. Training Institutions

S. No.	Ranks	ISA	CTC-I	CTC-II	RTC-I	RTC-II	Total
1	2	3	4	5	6	7	8
1.	Director	1	—	—	—	—	1
2.	Dy. Director	1	—	—	—	—	1
3.	Asst. Director/ Principal	2	1	1	1	1	6
4.	Jt. A.D./Vice-Principal	1	1	1	1	1	5
5.	Dy. A.D./Asst. Principal	6	4	3	6	6	25
6.	Inspectors	5	5	7	11	11	39
7.	Sub-Inspectors	7	18	19	34	34	112
8.	Hd. Constables	14	115	109	113	115	466
9.	Naiks	12	41	39	117	75	284
10.	Lance Naiks	6	9	9	4	57	85
11.	Constables	52	73	73	80	71	349
12.	Medical Officer	1	—	—	2	2	5
13.	Office Supdt.	1	—	—	—	—	1
14.	Head Clerks	—	1	1	1	1	8
15.	Hindi Translator	1	—	—	—	—	1
16.	Asst. Librarian	1	—	—	—	—	1
17.	U.D. Cs.	3	2	2	2	4	13
18.	L.D. Cs.	2	8	9	11	12	42
19.	Stenographers	4	1	1	1	1	8
20.	Other staff	27	76	72	78	79	302
	Total	148	355	346	464	468	1781

(*b*) to deal effectively with minor border incidents of intrusions, infiltrations and trans-border smuggling in the sensitive areas of the Indo-Pakistan and Indo-Bangladesh borders ;

(*c*) to co-ordinate the activities of various laws and order agencies involved in the prevention and detection of crime in the border areas.

The Border Security Force has established a number of training institutions for training its personnel. The available facilities of training have been extended to other police forces of the country. The various training institutions of B.S.F. are shown below :

TABLE 5.2

Training Institutions of the B.S.F. and the Courses Being Run Therein

Name of the Institutions	Courses
1. B.S.F. Academy, Tekanpur	(*a*) Recruits Training Course
	(*b*) Battalion Commandant Course
	(*c*) Dy. Commandant (TAC) Course
	(*d*) Company Commanders (TAC) Course
	(*e*) Field Engineering Course for Officers and NGOs
	(*f*) Commando Course
	(*g*) Dy. Commandant (D.E.) Course
	(*h*) Asst. Commandant (D.E.) Course

Name of the Institutions	Courses
	(*i*) Instructor Technical Course
	(*j*) Asst. Commandant Technical (D.E.) Course
	(*k*) SI/ASI-Radio (Mech) Course
	(*l*) Radio Operator's Course
	(*m*) C.I.S.F. Constable Course
	(*n*) Drill Course for N.C.Os.
	(*o*) Junior Leader's Course.
2. B.S.F. Training Centre & School, Hazaribagh	(*a*) 3-m Mortor Course
	(*b*) M.M.G. Course
	(*c*) Jungle Course
	(*d*) Camouflage and Concealment Courses
	(*e*) Field Engineering Courses
	(*f*) Physical Training Courses
	(*g*) Anti-extremist activity Course
3. B.S.F. Training Centre, Jammu	(*a*) Recruit Training
4. B.S.F. Training Centre, Jullundur Cantt.	(*a*) Recruit Training
5. B.S.F. Training Centre, Kadamtala	(*a*) Recruit Training

Name of the Institution	Courses
6. B.S.F. Training Centre, Jodhpur	(*a*) Recruit Training
7. B.S.F. Training Centre, Shillong	(*a*) Recruit Training
8. C.S.W.T., Indore	(*a*) Basic Recruit Training (*b*) Weapons and Tactics Course (*c*) Platoon Weapons Course (*d*) Sniper Course (*e*) Armourer Basic Course (*f*) Armourer Refresher Course

Organisation of Police Training at the State Level

Each state has its own organisational set-up of police training institutions. The governing factors are :

(*i*) its police strength

(*ii*) its training needs and

(*iii*) the finances available.

In view of this, training centres in the states have different patterns of staffing. There is a noticeable variation in the strength of various ranks which are engaged in training enterprise at the various training centres. The duration and course contents of different training institutions also indicate major variations. The federal character of the Indian constitution is well reflected in the organisation of police training institutions of the federating states. To get a closer view of these variations, the organisation of police training of states has been examined in the present study. The names and locations of the police training institutions of India are listed in Appendix 'P'. A map of India showing training institutions is also given.

Andhra Pradesh

In Andhra Pradesh, there is one Dy Inspector-General of Police who supervises training of police personnel. There is one Police Training College and Police Recruits School at Anantpur which is commanded by a principal of the ranks of Superintendent of Police. The principal is assisted by a vice-principal. The institution has two wings. The Police Training College wing and the Police Recruits School wing. There are two other training institutions namely Police Recruits School, Amberpet, Hyderabad and Police Recruits School, Vizianagaram for imparting basic training to police recruits and conductory promotion course for constables. Courses conducted in various institutions are given in the chart below :

Name of Trg. Institution	Courses
1. Police Training College & Police Training School, Anantpur	(*a*) I.P.S. Probationers Orientation Course
	(*b*) Basic course of Sub-Inspectors
	(*c*) Basic course for Armed Reserve Sub-Inspectors
	(*d*) Basic course for Dy. Ss.P.
	(*e*) Refresher course for Constables
	(*f*) Refresher course for Hd. Constables.
	(*g*) Radio Technician course

Name of Trg. Institution	Courses
	(*h*) Course for Band Constables
	(*i*) Refresher course for Circle Inspectors and S.Is.
2. Police Recruits School, Amberpet, Hyderabad	(*a*) Basic course for recruit constables
	(*b*) Promotion course for constables
	(*c*) II grade operators course
3. Police Recruit School wing, Vijayanagaram.	(*a*) Basic course for recruit constables
	(*b*) Promotion course for constables

On 15th May 1986, the Chief Minister of Andhra Pradesh laid foundation for Andhra Pradesh Police Academy at Hyderabad. The Academy is being organised in three wings :— (*i*) the academic wing, the field training wing and the schools wing, each of which would be headed by a Deputy Director as a higher level training facility. The Academy is being planned to organise. (*a*) Induction courses (*b*) Orientation courses (*c*) Promotion courses (*d*) Supervision courses (*e*) Professional courses and (*f*) Advanced professional courses. The first course in the Academy "Personal computers and their applications" was organised in the last week of October 1986 for senior I.P.S. Officers. At present, three police recruits schools are functioning on adhoc basis at Hindupur in Anantpur district, Kuruchendu in Prakasam district and Pochampadu in Nizamabad district to train a large number of constables recruited in 1983 onwards to fill the vacancies caused by the retirement of a large number of policemen. Kona Ramchandra

Organisation pattern of the P.T.C. is as given below :

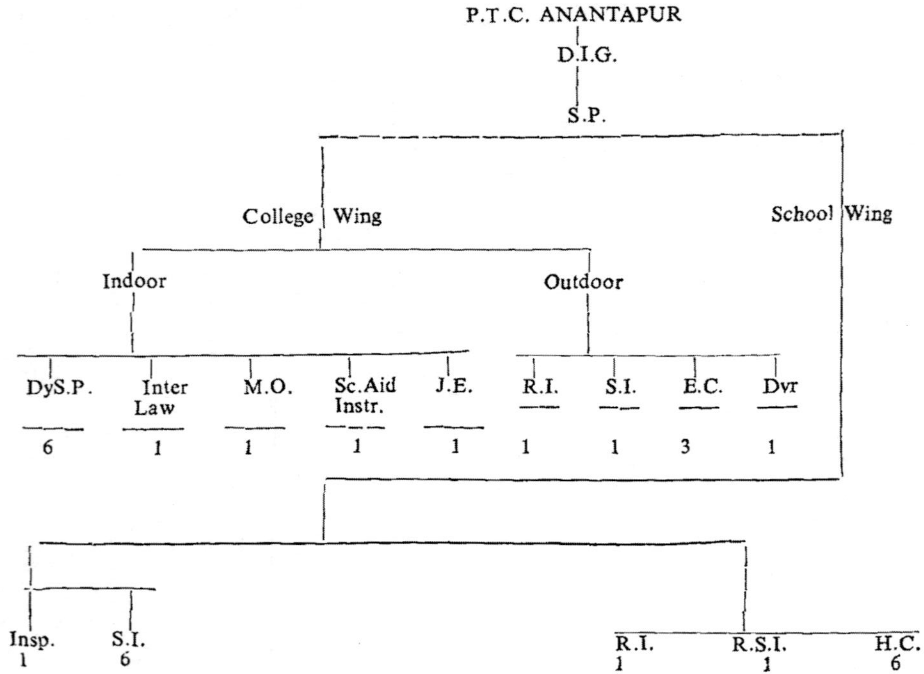

Reddy's Report of the Police Commission published in April 1984 has given a very factual state of the police training in Andhra Pradesh and has made many useful recommendations on training.

Expenditure of Police Training College, Anantapur for the last six years was as under :

Year	Amount (Rs. ps.)
1975	490041.90
1976	750800.00
1977	828101.32
1978	843033.78
1979	1002725.40
1980	1126918.68

The table shows a rising trend of expenditure on training institution.

Assam

In pursuance of the recommendations of the Gore Committee on police training, a Director of Police Training at the state level with headquarters at Dergaon functioned during the year 1979-80. However, since May 1980, the post of Director, Training has been kept in abeyance and there has been a D.I.G. (Training) with headquarters at Dergaon responsible for supervising and administrating training in the state under the overall guidance of Director-General of Police, Assam. Under the D.I.G. (Training) Assam there is supposed to be a staff officer known as the A.I.G. (Training) whose services are being utilised these days in working under the Additional I.G. (Armed Police and Technical wing). There are three training centres for the state police located at Dergaon namely : (*a*) the Police Training College for the training of police officers of the rank of A.S.I. and above and also all ranks of women police (*b*) the Recruit Training School is responsible for training of District armed branch and unarmed branch constables and also conducting refresher and cadre courses for district constables and (*c*) the Armed Police Training Centre (A.P.T.C.) which is responsible for the training of constables of the Armed Police Battalion and for conducting refresher and cadre courses upto the rank of A.B.S.I. All these three training centres located at Dergaon, are directly supervised by the D.I.G. (Trg.) whose headquarters is located at Dergaon. Police Radio Training School, Gauhati is responsible for conducting various courses for the wireless staff. Various courses conducted in training institutions are given below :

Name of the Trg. Institution.	Main Courses
1. Police Trg. College	(*a*) Basic training course for Probationer Dy.S.P.
	(*b*) Basic course for cadets S.Is.
	(*c*) Basic course for A.S.Is.
	(*d*) Basic course for women S.Is/A.S.Is. Constables
	(*e*) Refresher course for S.Is.
	(*f*) Refresher course for A.S.Is.
2. Recruit Trg. School	(*a*) Basic training course for district U.B. constables.
	(*b*) Basic course for district armed branch constables
	(*c*) Refresher course for constables
	(*d*) Junior N.C.Os. pre-promotion course for senior constables
3. Armed Police Trg. wing	(*a*) Basic training course for constables of armed police Bns.

Name of the Trg. Institution.	Main Courses
	(*b*) Junior N.C.Os. pre-promotion course for promotion from Constable to Naik
	(*c*) Senior N.C.Os. pre-promotion course for promotion from Nk to Hd Constables.
	(*d*) Pre-course for U.A.C., Tear Smoke, Map reading, weapons and Tactics and other courses.
4. Radio Trg. School, Gauhati	(*a*) Grade III Operator course
	(*b*) Grade II Fitter-cum-Electrician course
	(*c*) Grade III Radio Mechanic course
	(*d*) Grade II Operator course for ASIs.
	(*e*) Grade II Radio Mechanic course for A.S.Is. and S.Is.

The expenditure on training increased during last few years was as under :

Year	Expenditure (Rs. ps.)
1975-76	14,73,332.00
1976-77	19,14,759.00
1977-78	19,66,170.00
1978-79	18,02,793.00
1979-80	18,94,399.00
1980-81	20,32,708.00

The above figures indicate gradual increase in expenditure over the years.

Bihar

At present, the Principal of Police Training College, Hazaribagh is an officer of the rank of Dy. Inspector-General of Police. In Bihar, there is one constable training school at Nathnagar and advanced training school at Patna. A self-contained proposal in the shape of a blue print for the establishment of a Police Academy in Bihar, prepared on the basis of Gore Committee Report has been submitted to the Bihar government for consideration and sanction. The Bihar Police Academy will be headed by a principal/Director of the rank of Inspector-General of police with a Dy Director of the rank of Dy I.G. To have effective control over administration and training. the proposed Academy will have two wings, each headed by a S.P. The proposed scheme is likely to be sanctioned by the government and it will provide sufficient executive staff for effective conduct of training of police personnel of all rank of the state. Courses conducted in various training institutions are shown below :

Name of the Trg. Institutions	Main Courses
1. Police Trg. College, Hazaribagh	(*a*) Trg. course for A.S.Is.
	(*b*) Trg. course for Inspectors
	(*c*) Trg. course for Sergeants
	(*d*) Trg. course for Dy.Ss.P.
	(*e*) Trg. course for Asst. Dist. Prosecutors
2. Constable Trg. School, Nathnagar	(*a*) Basic Trg for Recruit constables
	(*b*) Section Leaders' Course.
3. B.M.P. Trg. School, Patna	(*a*) Trg. for B.M.P. Recruits
	(*b*) Trg. for District Armed Police Recruits

Name of the Institution	Main Courses
	(*c*) Section Leaders' Course
4. Advance Trg. School, Patna	(*a*) Course of Criminology & Scientific Aid to Investigation for S.Is. and Inspectors.

Gujarat

In Gujarat, there is one Additional Inspector-General of Police who overall supervises the training of Gujarat Police. The Police Training College, Junagarh has one Principal of the rank of Dy. I.G. Police Training School, Baroda conducts basic training for the recruits. Police Wireless Training Centre, Ahmedabad is headed by one S.P. Courses conducted in these training institutions are given below :

1. P.T.C., Junagarh	(*a*) Basic course for directly recruited Dy. S.P.
	(*b*) Institutional course for A.Ss.P.
	(*c*) Basic course for P.S.Is.
	(*d*) Refresher course for H.Cs.
	(*e*) Qualified H.C.s course
	(*f*) Excise officer course
	(*g*) M.V. Inspector course
2. P.T.C., Baroda	(*a*) Basic Trg. course for U.P.Cs.
3. Police Trg. Centre Chowkey, Junagarh	(*a*) Basic course for S.R.P. Constables
4. Police Wireless Trg. Centre, Ahmedabad	(*b*) Trg. courses in Wireless-telegraphy.

Total amount of police budget and amount spent on training for last five years are given below :

Year	Total amount of Police budget (Rs. ps.)	Amount spent on training (Rs. ps.)	Percentage
1976-77	32,70,14,000/-	41,09,000/-	1.26
1977-78	31,05,15,000/-	39,90,000/-	1.38
1978-79	34,82,91,000/-	51,51,000/-	1.48
1979-80	40,99,91,000/-	63,88,000/-	1.55
1980-81	52,42,25,000/-	66,93,000/-	1.27

The above figures indicate a rising trend of expenditure on training.

Haryana

In Haryana State, the Dy Inspector-General of Police (Administration & Training) is the senior most officer who is supervising and administering training. In Madhuban, there is one police training college in which 30 various types of courses are conducted for various ranks. The organisational chart is as seen at page no. 97. There is also one Armed Police Training Centre at Madhuban for training of District armed branch personnel and Haryana Armed Police battalion personnel.

P.T.C. Madhuban started functioning on 16.1.1976. The expenditure incurred on training during three years is as under.

Year	Expenditure (Rs. ps.)
1977	20,13,40.00
1978	43,200.00
1979	15,21,50.50

Organisational Chart of P.T.C. Madhuban (Haryana)—(Ref. p. 96)

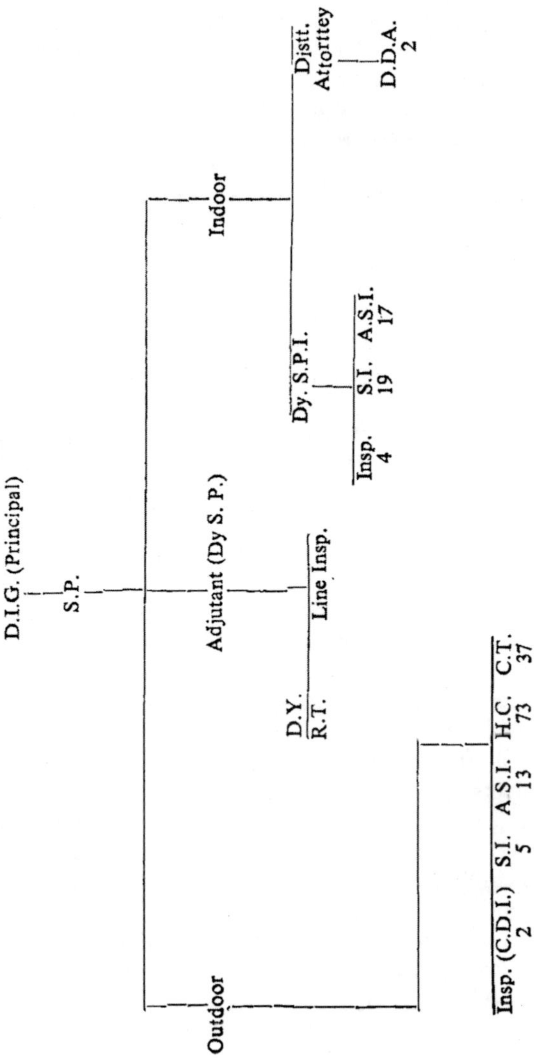

Karnataka

In Karnataka state, special I.G.P. (Training & C.I.D.) Bangalore, is the senior most officer supervising the police training. There is one Police Training College at Mysore for training of K.P.S. probationers, Dy.S.P. and police inspectors/ S Is. The Karnataka State Police Training School, Channapatna conducts basic training course for civil police constables. In addition, there are temporary police training schools at Mysore and Gulberga for conducting basic course for civil police constables. There is one Armed Police Training School at Rayapura for training armed police constables. Karnataka State Reserve Police I Bn. at Bangalore conducts training for K.S.R.P. men (recruits). Police Driving and Maintenance School at Yolahanka, Bangalore conducts special training to drivers and mechanics. Special Branch Training School at Bangalore conducts training in special branch matters. The Police Training College at Mysore is headed by one Principal of the rank of Dy.I.G. Main courses conducted in various training institutions are given on the page that follows.

Kerala

Additional Inspector-General of Police Training and Special Units is in-charge of police training in the state. D.I.G.P. (Training) is the senior most police officer directly supervising and administering police training in Kerala. In Kerala state, there is police training college at Trivandrum and police training school at Tamavaramapuram. The police training college conducts I.P.S. probationers orientation course, Dy. Supdt. of Police basic course to sub-inspectors (General executive), basic course to A.P.Is., basic training to R.S. Is./M.T. R.S.Is. and qualifying/refresher course for head constables fit for promotion as assistant sub-inspectors. Police training school, Tamavaranapuram conducts basic training for recruit police constables and drivers. The P.T.C./P.T.S. has a permanent skeleton staff and the strength is augumented when there are more trainees. There are sanctioned civilian posts of two part-time law lecturers and one criminologist. The D.I.G. (Training

Institution	Main Courses
1. P.T.C., Mysore	(*a*) Post N.P.A. Trg. for I.P.S. probationers (*b*) Basic course for Dy.Ss.P. (*c*) Basic course for S.Is. (Civil) (*d*) Basic course for Prob. Jemadars/P.G.Is. (*e*) Basic course for women police constables (*f*) Police community relations course for Dy. Ss.P./ P.Is. (*g*) Role of police in dealing with juvenile delinquency for R.S.Is. (*h*) Trg. of trainers course for instructors (*i*) Orientation course for Dy. S.P./P.Is.
2. Karnataka State Police Trg. School, Channapatna	(*a*) Basic course for constables (Civil)
3. Temporary Police Trg. School, Mysore and Gulbarga	(*b*) Basic Trg. for constables
4. Armed Police Trg. School, Rayapur	(*c*) Trg. of armed police constables
5. K.S.R.F. 1st Bn., Bangalore	(*d*) Trg for K.S.R.P. recruits
6. Police Driving and Maintenance School, Yelabanka	(*e*) Trg. of drivers & mechanics
7. Special Branch Trg. School, Bangalore	(*f*) Special branch trianing.

Staff Pattern of Police Training in Kerala

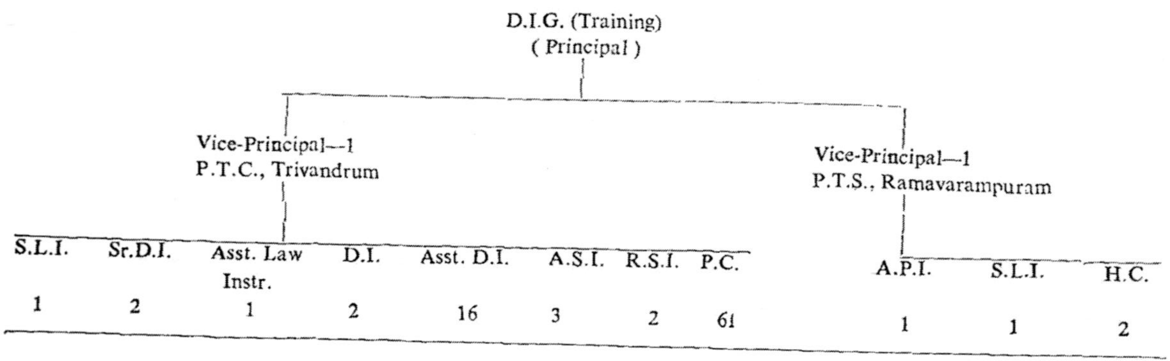

is the training co-ordinator of the Kerala police and has overall control and supervision of the police training in the state.

Maharashtra

In Maharashtra state, Police Training College, Nasik is the only institute for training of senior police officers. The training of recruit police constables is conducted at four places in police recruits training schools at Khandala, Nagpur, Jalna and Akola. The organisational set-up of the training institution is as under :

Chart Showing Organisation of P.T.C., Nasik

PRINCIPAL
(D.I.G.)

Indoor subjects		Outdoor subjects	
10	Dy S.P. Instructors	1	Hd. Const. Drill Instr.
1	Law Instructor	3	Reserve Police S.Is.
1	Police Prosecutor Selection grade	30	Asst. Drill Instrs.
6	Police Prosecutors for law subjects	1	H.C. Armourer
1	Reader Social Sciences	3	P.Cs. Arms Branch.
2	Lecturers in Social Sciences		

P.T.C., Nasik is conducting courses for I.P.S. probationers, Dy. S.P. Police instructors, sub-inspectors and Hd. constables. The expenditure incurred during the last six years is given below which shows that there is an increasing trend of expenditure on training institutions.

Year	Expenditure (Rs.ps.)
1975	11,79,580/–
1976	10,48,740/—
1977	15,98,005/—
1978	15,39,221/—
1979	16,03,295/—
1980	18,32,172/—
1981 (upto May)	6,58,614/—

Madhya Pradesh

In Madhya Pradesh, Additional Inspector-General of Police (Trg.) is overall in-charge of training. There is one D.I.G. (Trg.) at police headquarters. P.T.C., Sagar and A.P.T.C., Indore are also headed by Dy.I.G.P. Police training of gazetted officers and subordinate officers is conducted at M.P. P.T.C., Sagar. There is one officer of the rank of D.I.G. who supervises the overall training activities of the armed police. There are five constable training schools at Tigra, Indore, Rewa, Rajnandgaon and Pachmari. There is a Radio Training School at Indore. A full-fledged training section has been established in the police headquarters to coordinate the training of police personnel of various ranks under D.I.G. (Trg.) hqrs. with one A.I.G. (Trg.) to assist him. For armed police personnel, there is Armed Police Training Centre at Indore. 1st Trg. Battalion S.A.P., Indore and 6th S.A.F. Trg. Bn. are conducting courses for armed police personnel. Circle inspectors and sub-inspectors who are on the teaching faculty of training institutions receive instructions in pedagogy at the Government Training School, Khandwa. The organisational pattern of training institutions in Madhya Pradesh is as given on the following page.

Chart showing Organisational set-up of Training Institutions in Madhya Pradesh

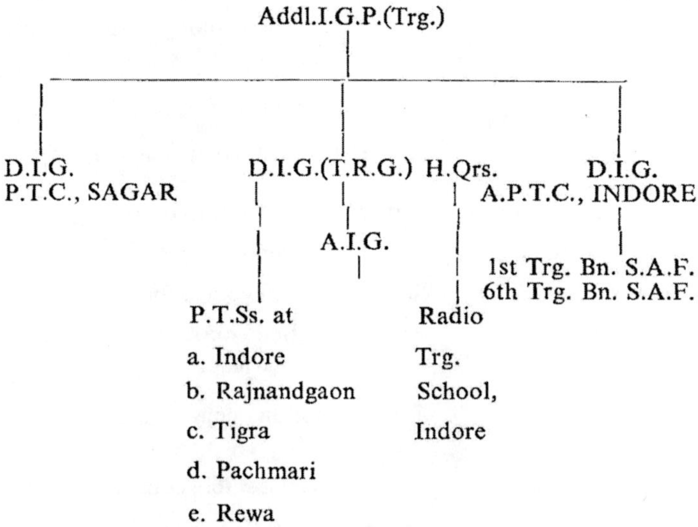

Various courses run in the training institutions of Madhya Pradesh are as below :

Trg. Institution	Main Courses
1. P.T.C., Sagar	(*a*) Orientation course for I.P.S. probationers
	(*b*) Basic course for S.Is.
	(*c*) Promotion course for S.Is.
	(*d*) Diploma in criminology and forensic science

Trg. Institution	Main Courses
	(*e*) Mob psychology and crowd control
	(*f*) Asst. police prosecutors course
	(*g*) G.R.P. officers' trg. course
2. P.T.S., Pachmari, Tigra, Indore, Rajnandgaon & Rewa	(*a*) Basic course for constables
	(*b*) Promotion course for Cts.
	(*c*) Promotion course for traffic Cts.
	(*d*) Promotion course for Hd. constables (unarmed)
	(*e*) Promotion course for Hd. Cts. (armed)
	(*f*) Traffic constable course
	(*g*) City constable course
	(*h*) Traffic Hd. constables advance Course
	(*i*) G.R.P. officers course.
3. Armed Police Trg. Centre, Indore	(*a*) Basic Trg. of armed Bn. S.Is. and other ranks
4. Ist Bn. S.A.F. Indore	(*a*) Basic Trg. course for recruit Cts.
	(*b*) Refresher/promotion course for Hd. Cts.
	(*c*) Refresher/promotion course for platoon commanders
	(*d*) Promotion course for S.Is.
	(*e*) Pre-course trg. for various courses

5.	6th S.A.F. Trg. Bn.	(*a*) Basic course for recruit Cts.
		(*b*) Basic course for direct havildars
		(*c*) Basic course for direct platoon Comdrs.
		(*d*) Course for direct Subedars
		(*e*) Tear-smoke course
		(*f*) Jujitsu course
6.	Radio Training School, Indore	(*a*) Basic radio operators course
		(*b*) Radio operators course grade III
		(*c*) Refresher course for radio staff.

Manipur

Manipur Police Training Centre, Pangei was sanctioned on 2nd January, 1967. Manipur Police Training Centre, Pengei is located on Imphal Pukhro Road about 12 kms. from Imphal towards the north. It has an area of 103 acres and has been sanctioned with a view to centralise basic collective and advance training of both civil police and Manipur Rifles Bns. A senior officer is the head of the institution under the direct supervision of D.I.G.P. (A.P. & Training). The M.P.T.C., Pangei, conducts refresher courses upto head constables and basic course for constables only. The organisational set-up, rank-wise of the training centre is as under :

Principal	1	
Asst. Comdt.	1	
Subedar	2	Administrative wing
Jemadar	4	
Havildar	6	
Subedar	1	
Jemadar	1	
Havildar	3	
Naik	12	Outdoor instructors

Rifle-man	22	
H.C.	1	Adm. duty
Constables	2	
Inspectors	1	
Sub-Inspectors	2	Indoor instructors
Asst. Sub-Insps.	1	
Accountant	1	
U.D.C.	1	
Steno	1	Ministerial staff
L.D.C.		
Safai Karamchari	6	
Washerman	2	Followers

The members of instructional staff are on attachment basis and are not given in the authorisation of the M.P. P.T.C., Pangei.

Meghalaya

Police Training School, Maghalaya was started on 18th April, 1977. P.T.S. is headed by one Principal of the rank of S.P. S.Is, A.S.Is. and constables are imparted basic and refresher training in this institution. Deputy Inspector-General of Police (Range and Training) is the senior most police officer who directly supervises the training. The training school also organises 3 months' course on unarmed combat (Judo, Karate and Kongfu). Wireless training is given to the trainees at Meghalaya Police Radio Organisation. There is no specific intelligence branch training in the state. Diving and maintenance training is given in District Executive Police Force and Police Armed Battalions. The Police Training School has trained following number of trainees so far.

TABLE 5.3
Showing Number of Trainers trained at
The Police Training School, Shillong

Year	Basic Trg. of Cts.	Refresher Trg. of Cts.	Basic Trg. of S.Is.	Refresher Trg. of S.Is.
1	2	3	4	5
1978	60	–	18	—
1979	24	—	25	—
1980	134	4	—	4
1981	57	11	22	11

Above table indicates that refresher training for constables and sub-inspectors has been started in 1980 and very small number of trainees have been given refresher training.

Nagaland

In Nagaland, there are two training institutions for conducting training of police personnel. Police Training School caters to the needs of civil police and Nagaland Armed Police Training Centre (N.A.P.T.C.) caters for the training needs of the armed constabulary. P.T.S. and N.A P.T.C. both are located at Chumukedima.

The present staff is inadequate for training and administrative purposes. The organisation of training institutions in Nagaland was started in November, 1966 and a number of new courses are now being conducted by P.T.S. The organisational set-up is as under :

Orissa

Additional Inspector-General of Police (Trg. and Development) is the senior most officer supervising training of the state police.

Organisational set-up of P.T.S. Nagaland

PRINCIPAL

ASSTT. PRINCIPAL

INDOOR

Insp. 1 S.Is. 4A. S.I. 1
(CL-1) (L-1) L-1)

OUTDOOR

Insp. 1 S.I. 2 Hav. 14 Nk. 14 L.Nk. 7 Ct. 26
(CDI) (D.1)

In Orissa, Police Training School was started at Angul with effect from 1st Sept. 1937 and subsequently, it was sanctioned as a police training college with effect from 1st January, 1948. A separate police training school at Nayagarh was started under the direct supervision and administrative control of Principal, Police Training College, Angul, with effect from onwards. P.T.C., Angul is conducting 11 courses for various ranks. Till the end of 1980, P.T.C., Angul has imparted training to 25,934 officers and men of various ranks. Based on recommendations of Gore Committee on Police Training, various course syllabi have been revised and 7 Dy.Ss.P., 533 S.Is., 29 sergeants, 55 A.S.Is., 2677 constables and 482 drill instructors have received training so far. The total expenditure incurred on P.T.C., Angul for the past five years is given below :

Punjab

Police training in Punjab state is conducted by three training institutions. Police Training College, Phillaur is one of the oldest training centres in the country and was started with effect from 1st January, 1882. A.D.I.G.P. is the Principal of the P.T.C., Phillaur which is training gazetted and subordinate

Year	Expenditure (Rs. ps.)
1975	21,28,585/-
1976	21,31,978/-
1977	24,49,934/-
1978	22,50,774/-
1979	26,84,758/-
1980	27,32,081/-

officers of Punjab and many smaller neighbouring states. Police Recruits Training Centre, Jahan Khelan, Distt. Hoshiarpur is headed by an S.P. The Refresher Training Centre, Fort Bahadurgarh is commanded by a Dy.S.P. The strength of staff sanctioned on various training institutions of Punjab is quite adequate to cope with the training and administrative needs of the institutions. During the year 1978-79, total number of 2720 trainees from various states viz. Punjab, Haryana, Jammu & Kashmir, Himachal Pradesh, Union Territories of Chandigarh and Delhi were trained in P.T.C., Phillaur as against 2472 in the previous year.[11] The college has also been imparting training to various officers of Railway Protection Force, Central Industrial Security Force, C.B.I., Manipur and Assam police personnel. It is approximately conducting 24 different types of courses for various ranks of police personnel. P.T.C., Phillaur has organised a number of refresher and specialised training courses and has done pioneering work in the field of training in tear-gas.

The expenditure on state police and P.T.C., Phillaur from 1975 to 1979 is given as :

Year	State Police Budget (Rs. ps.)—thousands	P.T.C., Phillaur budget (Rs. ps.)—thousands
1	2	3
1974-75	11,32,22/-	1388/-
1975-76	13,43,98/-	1509/-
1976-77	16,40,81/-	1691/-
1977-78	17,05,68/-	1887/-
1978-79	18,40,54/-	2451/-

Rajasthan

In Rajasthan, there is one Additional Inspector-General of Police (Training) who is the co-ordinator and directly responsible for training of police personnel in Rajasthan. Rajasthan is one of the pioneer states in modifying the various training programmes on the lines recommended by the Gore Committee on Police Training. Rajasthan Police Academy, Jaipur covers nearly 378 bighas of land (approximately 5.2 square kms.). The academy has a well-planned administrative and academic block, large well furnished class-rooms with modern sound system.

In Rajasthan, there are three police training schools located at Kishangarh, Jodhpur and Udaipur. The staff at each police training school is as given on the following page.

At times additional staff is attached on a scale of one Sub-Inspector civil police for 30 trainees and one H.C. (Armed Police) for 20 trainees. For training of armed police personnel R.A.C. and A.P. Training Centre, Jodhpur has been started in Rajasthan. At the time of integration of princely states and the formation of the state of Rajasthan, the new state inherited the illiterate, ill-equipped and untrained police personnel from the integrating princely states. But during the last ten years, it has now built up a well-equipped, literate and well-trained

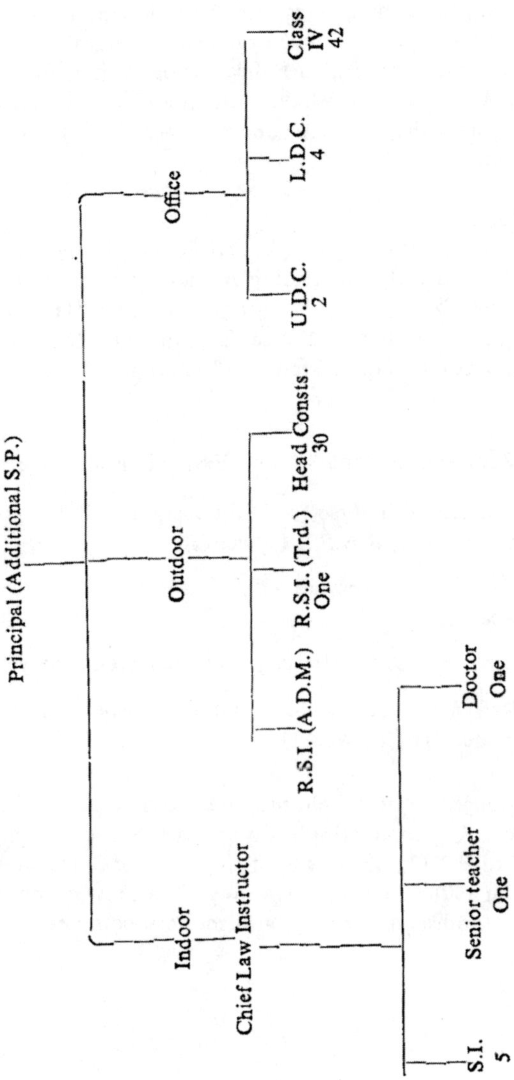
Principal (Additional S.P.)
Office
Outdoor
Indoor
U.D.C.
2
L.D.C.
4
Class
IV
42
R.S.I. (A.D.M.)
R.S.I. (Trd.)
One
Head Consts.
30
Chief Law Instructor
S.I.
5
Senior teacher
One
Doctor
One

police force. The organisation chart depicting training enterprise in Rajasthan, given on the following page, indicates the efforts made by the police organisation to train its personnel on proper lines. Rajasthan Police Academy has started a pilot project to bring about behavioural modification and development of personality by introducing Yoga and Meditation in police training.[12]

Tamil Nadu

In Tamil Nadu, the I.G.P. (Armed Police) is the senior most police officer directly supervising and administering the training. He is assisted by Dy.I.G. (Training). There are three training institutions in the state. Police Training College Madras is situated at Ashok Nagar, Madras-83 and conducts the following courses :

(*a*) Reorientation course for I.P.S. probationers (3 months).

(*b*) Condensed course for Hd. constables fit for promotion to the rank of A.S.I. (9 weeks).

(*c*) Basic course for directly appointed Dy. Ss. P. (one year).

(*d*) Basic course for directly recruited S.Is. (one year).

(*e*) Refresher courses for deputy inspectors and sub-inspectors (six weeks).

The police recruits schools are located at Vellore and Coimbatore for conducting training of the constabulary. The principal of P.T.C., Madras is of the rank of Superintendent of Police. In 1976, the Police Training College was moved from Vellore to Madras in a newly built modern complex.

Organisational chart showing training enterprises in Rajasthan

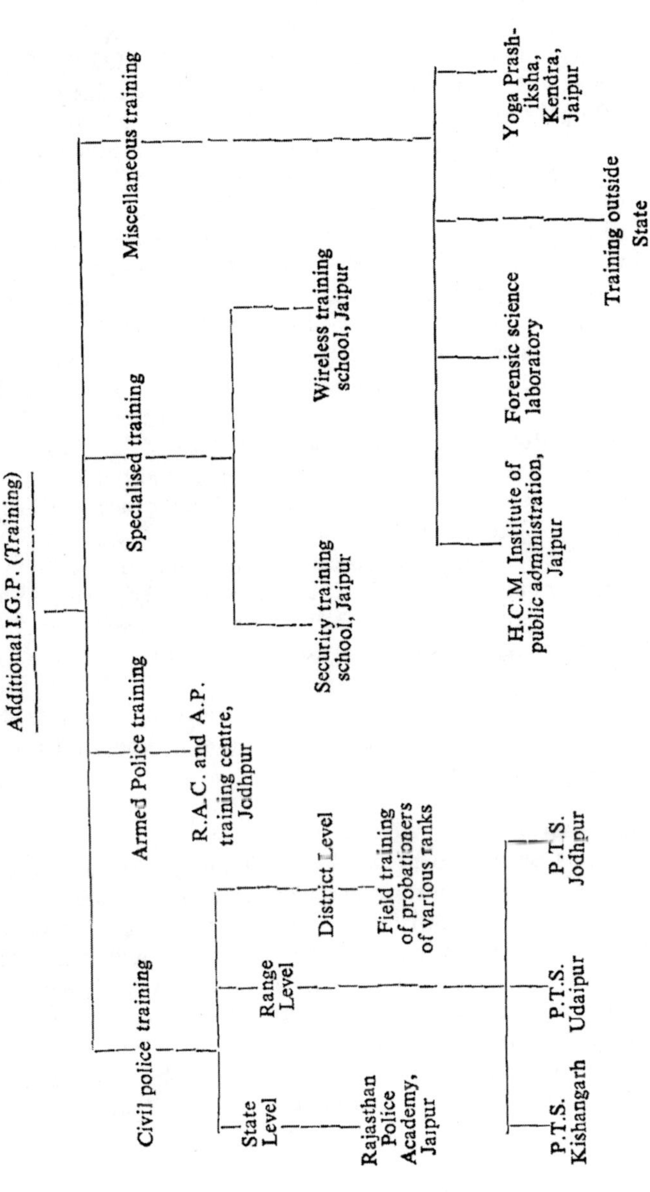

Uttar Pradesh

In Uttar pradesh, Additional I.G.P. (Trg.) is overall incharge of training enterprise, office of the I.G.P. (Trg.) is located at Lucknow from where he co-ordinates the training of U.P. police personnel. In U.P., there are three police training colleges ; two located at Moradabad and one at Sitapur. Police Training College I, Moradabad is one of the oldest training institutions of the country. At PTC-I, Moradabad, post N.P.A. training of three months for I.P.S. probationers, basic course for Dy.Ss.p. (12½ months duration), refresher course for Dy.Ss.P. (two months duration) and basic course for S.Is. (direct recruits) are held. At P.T.C. II, Moradabad and P.T.C. III, Sitapur basic course of sub-inspectors direct cadets and rank cadets are held. The Armed Police Centre, Sitapur conducts various training courses for armed Bns. personnel of U.P. police. Recruit training schools are located at Moradabad, Sitapur, Shahjahanpur, Gonda, Ghazipur and Fatehgarh. For specialised training in intelligence, Intelligence Department Training School is located at Lucknow. Police Motor Transport Centre, Sitapur conducts motor transport training for various ranks of police. In U.P., there are 18 recruit training centres at different D.I.G. range HQrs. of the state. In Police Headquarters, there is one A.I.G. to assist I.G. Police training colleges at Moradabad and Sitapur are headed by three D.Is.G.P. with Vice-principals of the rank of Superintendents of Police. There are ten other training institutions for training of constable recruits.

West Bengal

In West Bengal, the D.I.G.P. (Training), Police Training College, Barrackpore is the senior most police officer of the state directly supervising training. It has two wings, the college wing which imparts training to S.Is. and other senior ranks of police and the school wing that imparts training to recruits constables. The school wing also conducts refresher courses for the drill certificate. The P.T.S., Calcutta conducts training in weapons, unarmed combat and drill besides giving recruits training to the constables. P.T.C., Barrackpore also

Organisational set-up of P.T.C. 1 Moradabad

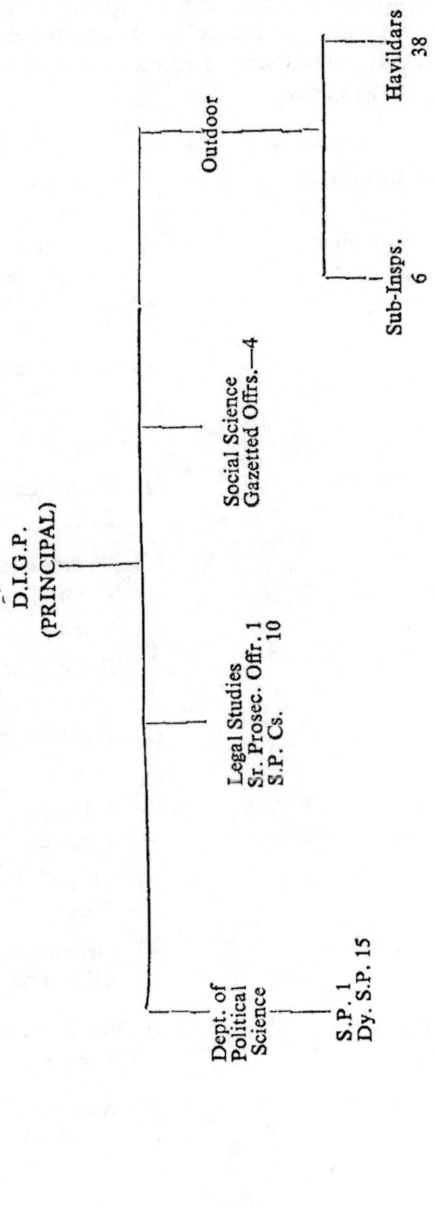

conducts detective training for S.Is., wireless operator course, drill certificate course and promotion course for constables and Asst. S.Is. Important training institutions and the main courses run therein are as under :

Name of the Institution	Main Course
1. Police Trg. College, Barrackpore	(*a*) Basic course for Recruit Constables
	(*b*) Basic course for A.S.Is.
	(*c*) Basic course for S.Is.
	(*d*) Basic course for Sergeants
	(*e*) Basic course for Dy. Ss.P.
	(*f*) Promotion course for Cts and A.S.Is.
	(*g*) Refresher course for Probationary and officiating S.I.s.
	(*h*) Drill Certificate Course N.G.O.s.
	(*i*) Wireless Operator Course
	(*j*) Detective Training for S.I.s.
	(*k*) Orientation course for I.P.S. Probationers
2. Police Trg. School, Calcutta	(*a*) Basic course for Recruit Consts.
	(*b*) Refresher course for Const. Drivers

Name of the Institution	Main Courses
	(*c*) Refresher course for H.Cs.
	(*d*) Refresher Course for S.Is. and Sergeants
	(*e*) Drill Course Part I
	(*f*) Drill Course Part II
	(*g*) Weapons Course

Note : (Unarmed Combat Training is compulsory for all the courses)

Delhi

The Additional Commissioner of Police (Armed Police and Training) of the rank of Dy. I.G.P. is overall in-charge of training in Delhi Police. There are two training institutions for Delhi police : Police Training School, Malviya nagar and Recruit Training Centre, New Police Lines, Delhi. P.T.S., Malviya nagar was set upon the recommendations of Khosla Commission in 1967. Recruit Training Centre is conducting advance mob control course and tear smoke gas training course for head constables and constables. Organisational set-up of P.T.S., Delhi and R.T.S., Delhi are as given at page nos. 118 and 119 respectively.

Jammu & Kashmir

There was only one police Training School in the State prior to 1962. During 1962, it was shifted to Udhampur and was basically meant for constables training. In 1981, it has been upgraded to the level of College. At present, it is conducting 21 different courses including basic courses for Dy. Ss. P. P.S.Is./A.S.Is./ and other ranks. It is conducting a refresher training of one month for G.Os. and a number of promotional courses for S.Is./A.S.Is., head constables and constables. One administrative block, three blocks of

Organisational set-up of P.T.S., Delhi

- PRINCIPAL (D.C.P.)
  - Vice-Principal (A.C.P.) — Indoor staff
    - Sr. Prosecutor Chf. Law Instr.
    - Asst. Pub. Prostir-3
    - Insps. 10
    - S.Is. 10
    - H.Cs. 27
    - Cts. 71
  - Adjutant (A.C.P.) — Outdoor staff
    - Insps. 1 (CDI)
    - S.Hs. 3
    - H.Cs. 17
    - Cts. 5

Organisational set-up of R.T.S., Delhi

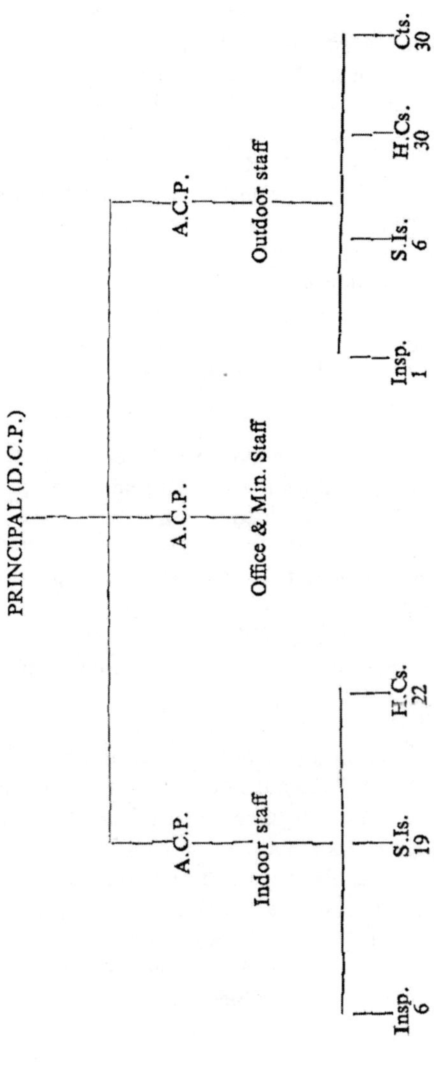

residential accommodation of 24 flats each, five barracks with mess facilities which could accommodate about 700 men have been constructed so far in the sprawling campus of 1036 kanals, 7 marlas at the foot of a hillock. The College has a transport fleet of one bus, 3 trucks, one water tanker, one matador, one car and 4 motor cycles. Approximately, 1353 trainees passed out from the College during 1984 and about 1344 trainees including 53 Dy. Ss. P. passed out during 1985 from the College. Police Training College Journal was launched in April 1984, 5 basic courses, 3 promotional courses, 2 refresher courses and 11 specialised courses were being conducted in the College during 1986-87 as per the calendar of the courses. Two police training schools one in Kathua, Jammu and other in Manigam, Kashmir have been opened in the State for training of constables.

Pondicherry

The Police Training School was opened in September, 1980. About 490 constables have undergone nine months' basic training and 31 S.Is./A.S.Is. and 60 Havildars have attended Refresher course. About 500 Police constables have attended promotion course upto November 1986. The training College is following the recommendations of the Gore Committee report in imparting training as far as syllabus is concerned. During 1982, new barracks and administrative block were constructed.

Goa

One Police Training School is functioning at Valpoi in north Goa for training the constable recruits. 30 percent of the total emoluments has been sanctioned to the training personnel as an incentive. Gore Committee Report is being fully implemented. There has been twenty percent increase in the training staff. The financial allocation on training institution from 1976-77 to 1985-1986 is Rs. 24,61,25000. 20 'A' type and an equal number of 'B' type quarters have been constructed upto 1986. 218 head constables underwent refresher course in batches of 40 each. Nine jail guards and 16 Excise guards have also been trained by the P.T.S. A batch of 24 A.S.Is./P.S.Is. have undergone Refresher course at the P.T.S. during 1986.

Mizoram

In Mizoram, there is no training set-up sanctioned by the government. Police Training Centre, Lungverh has been set up on ad hoc basis and presently manned by 1st Bn. Mizoram Armed Police. It is conducting recruit basic training and refresher training of constables. The P.T.C. at Lungverh started functioning on 1st April, 1974 and it has so far trained 1050 constables. D.I.G.P. (Range) is supervising the training of police personnel of the Union Territory. As P.T.C. is not a sanctioned institute for police training, no funds are allotted to it. There is no research cell and physical facilities are available in 1st Bn. Mizoram Armed Police.

Chandigarh

This Union Territory has no training institution and officers and men are getting training from the Police Training Centre, Phillaur, Recruits Training Centre, Jahan Khelan (Punjab) and other institutions of Government of India, including one located at Chandigarh.

Andaman and Nicobar Islands

The total police force of Andaman and Nicobar Islands as on 31st December, 1976 was 10 gazetted officers, 45 inspectors and sub-inspectors, 1209 other ranks making a total of 1264 policemen. There is no police training institution in this union territory. A proposal for the establishment of a training institution is under consideration of the administration. At present, police officers of this union territory are getting basic and refresher training from P.T.C., Phillaur, P.T.C., Moradabad, C.S.W.T., B.S.F. Indore, C.T.C.I. C.R.P.F. Neemuch, C.T.C. II C.R.P.F. Avadi, C.D.T.S., Chandigarh and other training institutions of the country. During the last five years, eight S.Is, 20 H.Cs., 14 L.H.Cs. and 9 P.C.s. have received basic training in these training institutions. During the last five years, one I.G.P., two Ss. P. one A.S.P., five Dy. S.P., four inspectors, 29 S.Is., five A.S.Is., ten H.Cs., five lower head constables and 27 police constables have attended refresher and specialised training courses in these institutions. However, recruit training for police constables and bush police constables and refresher training for lower subordinates (Police constables, lower head constables, head constables bush police constables and bush police juniors) has been conducted in the police lines under the supervision of Dy Supdt. of Police (Armed Police). The number of people trained is given below :

S. No.	Year	Basic Recruits training	[Refresher Bush police	training of] Civil police	Total
1	2	3	4	5	6
1.	1977	75	171	35	271
2.	1978	110	166	—	276
3.	1979	89	16	—	106
4.	1980	32	39	31	102
5.	1981	104	141	105	350
	Total	410	523	171	1104

The figures indicate that refresher training is being given due attention in this union territory.

The total expenditure on police during the last five years and the amount spent on police training on mainland police training institution and percentage thereof is as under :

S. No.	Year	Actual expenditure on police	Expenditure on Police Training	Percentage
1	2	3	4	5
1.	1977-78	1,30,39,323	30,110.95	0.23
2.	1978-79	1,27,59,958	16,889.70	0.13
3.	1979-80	1,45,92,442	23,356.45	0.17
4.	1980-81	1,67,63,750	38,172.40	0.23
5.	1981-82	1,80,31,218	29,389.90	0.16

The table shows that percentage of expenditure on police training is very low.

Police Training in the District

After completion of institutional training, it is desirable that police officers get practical training at the level of the district. The I.P.S. probationers are given practical district training as per recommendations given in the D.P. Kohli Report (1970) and the Gore Committee Report. In Madhya Pradesh, Orissa, West Bengal, Punjab and Uttar Pradesh, the duration of this practical district training varies a good deal.[13] A general break-up of this practical training in the districts is somewhat as follows :

First and Second month	in State Police Training Colleges or I.G.P. office to learn local laws and language ;
Third month	Headquarters of District of posting —familiarisation with the district officials and conditions ;
Fourth month	Training in police stations (Rural and Urban) ;
Fifth month	Station House Officer ;
Sixth month	Attachment to Circle Officer/ Office ;
Seventh month	Attachment to prosecution branch ;
Eighth, Nineth and Tenth months	Attachment to Dist. Police and Dist. Headquarters ;
Eleventh month	Attachment to Crime Branch and State C.I.D.;
Twelfth month	(i) First two weeks at HQrs. of Armed Police battalions and ; (ii) second two weeks miscellaneous, if any, state government considers necessary to augment the period under item first upto two weeks, miscellaneous last two weeks can be adjusted.[14]

In pursuance to the recommendations of the Gore Committee on Police Training, the Home Secretary, Govt. of India, passed orders to states for the conduct of practical training of I.P.S. officers in the respective states. But the data of present study show that in most of the cases, the I.P.S. probationers have not been able to keep their programme in order due to multi-farious commitments and diversions. The practical training in various offices remains a codel formality and does not serve the desired purpose. It has been suggested time and again that the sandwich pattern of training[15], wherein trainees can be put for eight months' training at N.P.A. in the first leg and then two months and one week can be utilised for first leg of practical training at rural and urban police stations and attachment with Circle Inspector/Sub Divisional Officer should be implemented in India. Later on, the I.P.S. probationers can go to N.P.A. for seven months again which may be followed by practical training of eight months and three weeks. But there are practical difficulties and this suggestion of sandwich pattern training too has remained unworkable. However, with the introduction of Basic Training Terminal Course for I.P.S officers, the mothod of integrated teaching linked with concurrent field exposure to be followed by rounding off at the academy has been partly achieved. After shifting of N.P.A. to Hyderabad, facilities for field exposure are available and are being used to a large measure.

For directly appointed inspectors, sub-inspectors, Head constables and constables of the state, practical police training is imparted at the level of the district. The duration of this practical training of directly recruited sub-inspectors differs from state to state. In Karnataka and Gujarat, it is year and a half. Uttar Pradesh, Maharashtra and Haryana have it for one full year. In West Bengal, the duration of practical police training for the constabulary is just six months. In Punjab, the duration is two years. Orissa and Nagaland do not follow any system of practical training, once the basic training programme is complete. The practical training programmes of sub-inspectors in all the states of the country include attachment to police stations to learn about the duties of different ranks and to build up confidence to get involved in real life of work of a police station. In Uttar Pradesh, the S.Is. get one year, long practical training at police stations, district police lines, P.A.C. units and S.P. office. Practical training programmes are not similar for direct S.Is. and departmental promotees. Rajasthan prescribes three month attachment to rural police stations in varying capacities, three month attachment to urban police stations, one and half month attachment to S.P. office, N.O.B., Special Branch Confidential Branch and Reserve lines, one month attachment to circle office and two weeks attachment to D.I.G. office. The Gore Committee on police training has recommended one year practical training for S.Is.[16] at the level of the district. This practical training programme for H.Cs. and constables also differ from one state to another. Its duration also varies from nine months to two months.

Besides these practical training programmes to new entrants, every police line in the district carries regular short training courses to available staff there. Annual musketeer firing is carried out in many states after a short period of refresher training. The Dist. S.P. is held directly responsible to ensure that district police personnel carry out routine training at police lines. Similarly, in Armed Bns., training is carried out as daily routines by the staff available. All police lines and units of armed Bns. keep conducting routine field training as a matter of normal course.

The table at page 126 shows certain clearly visible patterns of staffing. Out of 18 central training colleges, 10 Colleges have Dy. Inspector-General of Police as head of the institution. Eight C.T.Cs. have civil staff lecturers/public prosecutors/ district attorneys to teach specialised subjects. P.T.C. I Moradabad (U.P.) has a good number of Dy. Ss. P. who take all indoor classes. Andhra Pradesh and Karnataka have seven Dy. Ss. P., each for training purpose. Seven institutions have more than 75 constables who form infrastructure for administration of the training-institutions. Six institutions have adequate supporting staff consisting of ministerial staff and followers while other institutions have not reported about availability of supporting staff. Seven institutions have adequate number of inspectors and S.Is. who form the core of training faculty. P.T.C., Phillaur (Punjab) and P.T.C, Madhuban

Staffing Pattern of Central Training Colleges

The staffing pattern of 18 central training colleges has been given in the table below :

S. No.	Trg. College & State	D.I.G.	S.P.	Civil Staff	Dy S.P.	Insp./ S.I.	A.S.I./ H.C.	Other Ranks	Supporting Staff	Total
1	2	3	4	5	6	7	8	9	10	11
1.	PTC Assam	—	1	—	2	43	37	88	11	182
2.	PTC Andhra Pradesh	—	1	—	7	13	10	—	—	31
3.	PTC Haryana	1	1	3	2	36	146	112	117	420
4.	PTC Gujarat	1	1	—	—	20	25	42	—	89
5.	PTC Karnataka	1	1	4	7	6	17	20	57	113
6.	PTC Kerala	1	1	3	—	6	18	61	—	90
7.	PTC Maharashtra	1	—	7	1	13	33	10	73	138
8.	PTC Bihar	1	1	—	1	13	30	35	2	83
9.	PTC Manipur	—	1	—	1	11	11	36	13	73
10.	PTC Nagaland	—	1	—	1	9	15	38	—	64

1	2	3	4	5	6	7	8	9	10	11
11.	PTC Orissa	1	1	3	4	49	71	118	75	322
12.	PTC Punjab	1	2	22	4	37	73	10	140	289
13.	PTC Rajasthan	—	1	1	4	12	29	44	72	163
14.	PTC Tamil Nadu	—	1	—	—	9	5	—	—	15
15.	PTC I Uttar Pradesh	1	1	3	26	9	38	—	42	120
16.	PTC West Bengal	1	—	—	1	63	75	89	5	234
17.	PIS Delhi	—	1	—	2	24	49	75	6	157
18.	CTC I CRPF Neemuch	—	1	—	5	23	115	123	76	355

Staffing Pattern of Police Training Schools/Centres

The staffing pattern of 15 police training schools/centres has been given in the table below :

S. No.	Trg. School/Centre & State	D.I.G.	S.P./ A.S.P.	Civil Staff	Dy. S.P.	Insp./ S.I.	A.S.I./ H.C.	Other Ranks	Suppor- ting Staff	Total
1	2	3	4	5	6	7	8	9	10	11
1.	RTS Dargaon, Assam	—	1	—	1	22	28	43	—	95
2.	EMP Patna, Bihar	—	1	—	5	37	111	65	29	248
3.	RTS Chowkey	—	1	—	1	13	13	49	37	114
4.	RTS Baroda, Gujarat	—	1	—	1	47	69	—	114	232
5.	PTS Rajnandgaon, Madhya Pradesh	—	1	1	2	20	34	—	44	102
6.	RTS Akola, Maharashtra	—	1	8	1	11	23	14	56	114
7.	PTS Shillong, Meghalaya	—	1	—	1	4	4	10	—	19
8.	RTC Bahadurgarh	—	—	—	1	9	31	—	16	57
9.	NAPTC Nagaland	—	—	—	2	11	16	61	—	91

1	2	3	4	5	6	7	8	9	10	11
10.	P.T.C. Nayagarh, Orissa	—	1	—	1	11	13	22	30	77
11.	P.R.T.C. Jahankalan, Punjab	—	—	—	1	19	79	39	63	202
12.	P.T.S. Kishangarh, Rajasthan	—	1	1	—	9	30	17	1	59
13.	A.T.C. Sitapur, Uttar Pradesh	—	1	6	4	9	16	45	—	81
14.	R.T.C. II C.R.P.F, Avadi	—	2	—	6	45	115	203	99	470
15.	R.T.C, Delhi	—	1	—	1	32	52	30	—	116

(Haryana) and C.T.C. I C.R.P.F., Neemuch are having a good proportion of various ranks in the staff. Inclusion of civil staff in training institutions of the police shows that certain non-police subjects like sociology, criminology and behavioural sciences have been introduced in training programmes. This also indicates shift from outdoor training to in-door training. More posts in higher gazetted ranks indicate that there is intensive supervision of training by higher ranking officers.

Table at page no. 128 shows that campared to training colleges, police recruit training centres do not have that intensive supervision by the higher ranking officers. The analysis of staffing pattern indicates that out of the 15 police training schools/recruit training centres, 12 institutions are commanded by officers of the rank of S.P. Civil Staff as lecturers are sanctioned in only four institutions. More or less, a similar pattern of staffing is visible in the various training institutions with minor variations according to the requirements of various states. Eight institutions have a good number of followers/class IV staff who form the supporting staff for the institutions. Strength wise, R.T.C. II C.R.P.F, Avadi has the maximum sanctioned strength in all the police recruit training centres surveyed.

The overall picture of police training institutions that has emerged from the present research study indicates that there are three kinds of training institutions in the states engaged in task of training of the police personnel :

(*i*) State police training colleges for the training of Dy. Supdts. of Police, Inspectors and Sub-Inspectors of the state ;

(*ii*) Police training schools for the training of head constables and constables ;

(*iii*) Armed police training centres for the training of the junior members cf the armed police battalions.

This organisational pattern is somewhat uniform in the big states like Uttar Pradesh, Rajasthan, Assam, Bihar and Karnataka. In Uttar Pradehs, Maharashtra, Gujarat and Punjab, the police training colleges are headed by Dy. I.G.P. while in most of the other states, officers of the rank of S.P, are functioning as heads of the police training institutions. The strength of rank-wise staff also varies from institutions to institutions. For smaller states and union territories like Manipur, Nagaland, Tripura, Arunachal Pradesh and Mizoram, the etsablishment of police training colleges is unviable and hence the North-East Police Academy, Barapani, Shillong has been established to fill the void. Most of the police training institutions are not located in or near big cities with the seats of universities. This presents a handicap in utilising the availability of scholars and guest teachers for imparting instructions in some of the areas in social and behavioural sciences and current affairs. The police officers are also unwilling to be posted as trainees to small places because educational facilities for higher studies of their children are not available. Because of these distant and inaccessible locations, the present training institutions are not coveted places for postings. The police officers are unenthusiastic for posting to these training institutions. The survey of most of the training institutions conducted for the present study reveals that most of these training centres have been accommodated in an ad hoc fashion in buildings constructed for altogether different purposes such as old forts or temporary line. The lay out and design of most of the buildings do not make adequate provision for administrative offices, class rooms lining space and residential accommodation. The staff pattern continues to be irrational and unsatisfactory for instructional purposes. Experienced, competent and senior officers are not available as trainers. Most of the respondents of the sample felt that there was an urgent need for the upgradation of the staffing pattern of police training colleges and schools all over the country. More officers of the rank of Dy. Ss.P., inspectors and sub-inspectors need to be posted and authorised in these police training institutions. As a general norm, an indoor class should not consist of more than 30 trainees in the case of lecture method and fifteen trainees in the case of syndicate and tutorials. For outdoor training, there should be one instructor for a aquad of 15 to 20 trainees for drill and musketry and one for every 30 to 40 in physical training.[17] Madhya Pradesh Police Commission recommended one instructor for 15 trainees as good ratio for outdoor training. During the course of visits to training institutions, it was pointed out that a large number of vacancies were lying unfilled for a very long time and this has resulted in the neglect of the training enterprise. In one police training college, the Police officers who were posted there had not joined their assignments and were extending their leave periods again and again and were making simultaneous efforts to get posted out. In some of the training institutions, the authorisation system was found inadequate and the system of attachment of additional staff was also not working as desired. The data collected from the field reveal that many police training institutions do not have separate departments of legal studies, Police science and social sciences. Expertise of the trainers in the subjects remained undeveloped. There was no earmarking of staff to impart necessary training in the field. There was no departmental organisation to ensure constant inter-communication within the staff alongwith a pooling of feed-back from the trainees. Department-wise libraries were scarce and case studies programmes were unheard of. During the course of the present study, it was found that indoor classes had too many students. Due to the shortage of staff and too many existing vacancies being the order of the day, even indoor classes were found to have 60 to 100 trainees in some of the training institutions. In one training college, 120 S.I. cadets were found listening to the instructor in a small dingy class room which was actually meant for 30 trainees. Due to vacancies on the staff, several batches of trainees were combined to constitute one class. The faculty of police training colleges need support from guest lecturers and professional experts from the department but many heads of the police training colleges are not empowered in this regard.

The rates of honoraria also vary from institution to institution and in most of the places these are too meagre to attract the competent faculty. The data of the present study discover that the outdoor staff in most of the training institutions of the country was not properly trained. The rules prescribe that the outdoor instructors should not be below the rank of a senior head constable but those working in police training colleges can be of the rank of a sub-inspector or inspector. The study indicates that with the expansion of police force in the country, the work-load on police training institutions has become very heavy. The existing facilities have to be expanded and the staff in practically all the states police training institutions has to be increased. With the changing times, it will be necessary to reorient the present faculty in the newer challenges and increasing responsibilities of the police force. This will bring greater need for more in-service and specialised refresher courses for senior policemen. The institutionalised refresher training for all will enhance work-load on police training institutions of future. Augmentation of staff will become imperative. Placement policies will need streamlining and more qualified and better motivated staff will be to required undertake the responsibilities of training.

At present, the institutionalised training of armed police in the states leaves much to be desired. There is need for establishing minimum one police training centre in every state to cater to the training needs of the armed police personnel. The present system of armed police training at the battalion level does not introduce uniformity in the training venture. The staffing pattern of police training institution in most of the states needs improvement. Separation of staff for training and administration in training institutions can help in achieving effective training. The training faculty may also be divided into outdoor and indoor training staff. Besides being different, both of them should be selected from qualified personnel disposed to academics. Ad hocism in staffing pattern of police institutions needs to be minimised. It should be replaced by the prescribed pattern of organisational structure and personnel. The services of eminent academicians as guest faculty to lecture to the trainees is a change in the desired direction. These eminent scholars and social scientists should be encouraged to undertake police research. The trainers should be well epuipped to meet the academic requirement of the training institutions. A periodical review of these needs has to be carried out by the police headquarters in consultation with the Directorate of police training. Structural relationship between training institutions needs to be demarcated so that each part of the staff can be related to the other part and to the whole in a systematic manner. The organisational pattern of training institutions must respond satisfactorily to size up responsibilities and needs of the police organisation and should be capable of coping with training requirements. There is also need for standardizing academic and professional qualifications for the training officers, instructors and even heads of the training institutions.[19] Police training has to be occupationally oriented. The experience and academic requirements to instruct in a law enforcement curriculum differ from those in traditional academic field. A considerable amount of actual police experience is a necessity and possession of the doctorate degree is not essential in an occupationally oriented curricula such as law inforcement.[20]

The organisation of police training has to be built on scientific lines so that proper training environment could be evolved for a truly professional approach. There is also need to reorganise and reutilise training potentials and resources available in training institutions. The expansion and re-organisation should take place in a rational, scientific and logical manner.[21] Periodical reviews of the organisation of police training by high powered committees consisting of representatives of training division, department of personnel, training division of Bureau of Police Research and Development and Inspectors-General of Police of the states should be statutorily prescribed to plug the operational loopholes in time and amend the system of administration of police training in the light of experience attained.

Conclusion

In India, organisation of police training is in the hands of the governmental agencies. Ministry of Home Affairs, Government of India has played an important role by establishing a number of national level institutions for imparting specialised and advanced training. The Bureau of Police Research and Development provides advice in initiating and conducting research and developmental work and also co-ordinates training efforts of various states. Induction of civil staff indicates that there is shift from outdoor training to indoor training and non-police subjects like criminology, sociology and behavioural sciences have been introduced in the training curriculum.

REFERENCES

1. See : Arul, F.V., "*Police Training*", Indian Police Journal (July, 1958) p. 40

   Gammage, Allen Z., "*Police Training in United States,*" (Charles, C. Thomas, Springfield, 1963)

   National Police Agency "*Training of Police*", 1974, Tokyo, Japan.
2. Article 246 of Schedule VII of the Constitution.
3. The Organisation of the Government of India—The Indian Institute of Public Administration, (Somaiya Publications Ltd., Bombay, 1971) pp. 120-121.
4. For details see Iyenger, N.K.' "*Growth and Development of Forensic Science in India*", Indian Police Journal, Delhi (Indian Police Centenary issue 1961), pp. 145-51
5. C.D.T. Schools can presently train 180 S. Is/Inspectors annually. See Report of the Committee on Police Training, M.H.A., G of I, New Delhi, 1974, pp. 77.
6. For details, See Institute ot Criminology and Forensic Science, New Delhi, printed at C.R.P.F. Press, New Delhi, pp. 1-16.
7. For details, see Tondon Shrawan—"*Importance of Research & Development in Modernising Police Force*", Police Research and Development Quarterly Journal (Quarter IV, 1977) pp. 1-2.
8. For details of proposed staff, see B.P.R.&D., M.H.A., New Delhi, "*Strategy for Police Research, Development and Training in India*" (Ed.); Tondon, S. Prasad K.N., and Iyer T.G.L., 1979, pp. 55-58.
9. Articles 353, 355 of Indian Constitution. Commentary—Lal, Jagdish, 1980, Delhi Law House, Delhi, pp. 159-61.
10. See Mathur, K.M., "*Internal Security and Some Reflections*", the Crapler Vol. VI, No. 1, Aug. 31, 1977.
11. Report of the Administration of Police for the year 1978. Punjab Govt. (cyclostyled report) p. 32. P.T.C. has earned a very good name for its high standard of training.
12. *Hindustan Times*, Delhi, 4th May, 1981.
13. For details, see A Syndicate Study on post N.P.A, Practical Training for Probationers of I.P.S.,—Senior officers course XXXVI S.V.P, N.P.A. Hyderabad.
14. For more details, see D.P. Khola Committee Report on Central Police Training College, Mt. Abu (1966) & Appendix XVII of Gore Committee on police training, p. 217.
15. Committee on Police Training (Chairman Gore) *op. cit.*, pp. 42-43.,
16. See Appx. XXV, Practical Training of S.Is.—Civil Police (12 months) Committee Report on Police Training, p. 255.

17. For similar views, see Committee Report on Police Training, M.H.A. Government of India, 1974, p. 73.
18. Similar views have been held by Catheryn Seckler Hudson, see *Organisation & Management : Theory and Practice*, Washington, D.C., the American University Press, 1977, pp. 126-31.
19. Letter from C. Donglas Gournley—Head of Police Science and Administration, Los Angeles State College, Los Angeles, California, April 27, 1961 quoted by Ganmage Allen Z. "*Police Training in the United States*", Charles C. Thomas Springfield, 1963, p. 133.
20. Cf. See Misra, S.C. : "*Police Administration in India*", A Publication of National Police Academy, Mount Abu, p. 176.

CHAPTER SIX

POLICE TRAINING PROGRAMMES IN INDIA

POLICE in India are characterised by a formal hierarchical structure in which people and activities are arranged in a pyramidal form. All ranks of police, upto the level of Dy. Supdt. of Police are borne on the state cadre and the state governments are responsible for their training. The higher ranks belong to Indian Police Service and are allotted to various states cadres and their basic refresher training is carried out in central training institutions. The training in the states is normally divided into three levels based on ranks i.e. other ranks, subordinate officers and gazetted officers. This applies to both specialised and non-specialised training. Basic training is imparted at direct entry levels which are usually constables, sub-inspectors and Dy Supdt. of Police in most of the states. Refresher training is imparted to reorient the serving personnel after periodic intervals with a view to provide an opportunity for study, reflection and a readjustment of values and attitudes which is facilitated by stay in an institution because it breaks the routine. Gore Committee on police training recommended a series of refresher specialist and promotion courses for all ranks with a view to bring in an attitudinal transformation in the police force.[1] The United Nations have held that the desirable standard is to earmark ten per cent of the working career of 30 years for training.[2] The present study has formulated the hypothesis that the police training institutions in India are concentrating more on basic training programmes rather than on refresher training courses for various ranks. For purpose of this study, refresher training will include all courses whether specialised, advanced or promotional which are organised for serving police personnel excluding basic training programme. Basic training will include initial training imparted in the institutions alongwith follow-up practical training at various levels. This, for the purpose of this study, all training programmes will fall in either of the two categories.

In India, the total strength of civil police as on 31 December, 1976 consisted of 5,90,337 policemen, out of which 1,467 were I.P.S. officers, 2,723 were Dy. Ss. P., 42,997 were S.Is. and Inspectors and 5,43,150 were officers below the rank of S.Is.[3] Percentage-wise I.P.S. officers constitute 0.24 per cent, Dy. Ss.P. 0.46 per cent inspectors and S.Is. 7.28 per cent and officers below the rank of S.Is. constitute 92 per cent of the total force.

Training of Indian Police Service Officers

The sanctioned strength of officers of the rank of Inspectors-General of Police, D.Is. G.P. and Ss.P. was 1,184. Besides there were 238 junior posts of I.P.S. Thus, the total strength of I.P.S. for purpose of analysis can be taken to 1,422 officers.[4] On appointment to Indian Police Service through the Union Police Service Commission, the probationers are required to undergo a four months' foundational course at Lal Bahadur Shastri National Academy of Administration at Mussorie followed by a 15 days' course at the National Civil Defence College, Nagpur and a five days' course in the detection and handling of explosives in the Chief Directorate of Explosives at Nagpur. Thereafter, they undergo one year's professional police training at S.V.P.N.P.A. Hyderabad followed by a fortnight's attachment with Army units. Thereafter, they are imparted one years' practical training in the states in which they work in various capacities in district and state police headquarters. On completion of this practical training in the states, they attend the Basic Trg. Terminal Course of one month's duration at S.V.P. N.P.A. Hyderabad. This entire period constitutes the basic training. However, certain states prescribe different period for practical training in the states varying from 11 months to 13 months.

TABLE 6.1
Showing details of number of I.P.S. Officers who attended Basic and Refresher courses

Year	Basic Trg.	Senior Offrs, Course	Course at I.S.A. Mt. Abu	Course at I.C.P.S.	Remarks
1	2	3	4	5	6
1971	50	31	—	NA	
1972	49	18	—	71	
1973	64	48	—	148	
1974	84	43	—	86	
1975	84	43	—	118	
1976	66	62	—	160	
1977	95	66	23	140	
1978	109	50	88	186	All these courses
1979	49	54	69	127	are complementary
1980	50	41	41	155	to each other
Total	702	456	221	1191	

Thereafter, these probationers are required to undergo following courses as a part of career planning :

(*a*) A fleet management course of 12 days' duration at the Central School of Motor Transport (Sagar) M.P.

(*b*) Weapons and Tactics course at Central School of Weapons and Tactics at Indore.

(*c*) 10 days' course on Wireless at Central Police Radio Training Institute, New Delhi.

(*d*) A ten days' Internal Security Course at Internal Security Academy, Mt. Abu.

(*e*) 10 days' course on Police-community relations at Institute of Criminology and Forensic Science, New Delhi.

(*f*) A four weeks' Advance Course in Criminology at the Institute of Criminology and Forensic Science, New Delhi.

(*g*) Senior Officers' Course after five to eight years of service at S.V.P. N.P.A., Hyderabad.

Besides these career courses, senior police officers undergo a number of other courses at the Indian Institute of Public Administration, New Delhi, Institute of Secretariat Training and Management, New Delhi, L.B.S. National Academy of Administration, Mussorie and Indian Institute of Management, Calcutta, Bombay, Ahmedabad. Table showing courses for I.P.S. officers in the Institute of Criminology and Forensic Science during the last three years is given at page no. 141 and table indicating courses for senior police officers at the I.C.P.S. during the last three years is also available at page no. 162. Table at page no. 141 shows that a large number of trainees drop out from the course and many course capacities are not fully utilised, yet a large number of senior level police officers have done refresher courses. Thus, in respect of senior level police officers, the hypothesis that there is greater emphasis on basic training than on refresher training, is not validated. The study clearly indicates that senior level police officers are giving due emphasis to refresher courses during the last ten years. It is mostly true that some officer may have done a number of these courses as those are not exclusive.

However, the trend indicated in the table is clearly visible and it is established that refresher courses are getting due emphasis so far as I.P.S. officers are concerned. Table at page no. 139 shows that 1868 officers attended refresher training during

TABLE 6.2

Showing Courses for I.P.S. Officers in the Institute of Criminology and Forensic Science during The Last Three Years :

Name of Course	Year	Duration (days)	Course S. No.	Capacity	Nomination	Actual attendance	Drop out of Cance-llation	Level of trainees
1	2	3	4	5	6	7	8	9
1. Orientation	1979	10	7	6	—	6	—	D.I.G.
Course on	1980	10	8	6	—	6	—	D.I.G.
Research								
Methodology	1981	10	9	6	8	7	1	D.I.G.
2. Advanced	1979	24	29	25	—	21	—	S.P.
Course In	1980	24	28	25	—	34	—	S.P.
Criminology		24	29	24	—	19	—	S.P.
		24	30	25	—	26	—	S.P.

1	2	3	4	5	6	7	8	9
		24	31	25	—	22	—	S.P.
	1981	24	32	25	24	21	3	S.P.
		24	33	25	29	24	5	S.P.
		24	34	25	28	24	4	S.P.
		24	35	25	36	24	2	S.P.

TABLE 6.3

Showing Courses for Senior Police Officers at I.C.P.S. During Last Three Years

Name of Course	Year	Duration (days)	Course Sr. No.	Capacity	Nomination	Actual attendance	Drop out/ cancel-lation	Level of Trainees
1	2	3	4	5	6	7	8	9
1. Police	1979	10	34	30	—	13	—	S.P.
Community		10	35	30	—	11	—	S.P.
Relations		10	36	30	—	15	—	S.P.
	1980	10	37	30	—	9	—	S.P.
		10	38	30	—	12	—	S.P.
		10	39	30	—	10	—	S.P.
	1981	10	40	30	14	14	—	S.P.
		10	41	30	21	17	4	S.P.
		10	42	30	14	9	5	S.P.

1	2	3	4	5	6	7	8	9
2. Research	1980	36	10	8	—	8	—	S.P.
Methodology		36	11	8	—	9	—	S.P.
	1981	36	12	8	9	7	2	S.P.
		36	13	8	7	6	1	S.P.

last ten years while the total strength of I.P.S. was 1422. Even assuming that some officers may have attended all the three different types of courses at three different institutions, it can be easily accepted that over 90 per cent of the officers have done refresher training during the last ten years. Senior officers course alone has been attended by 32 per cent of the officers. Internal security courses have been done by 15.54 per cent of the total I.P.S. officers. 83.7 per cent of the total I.P.S. officers have attended refresher courses at the Institute of Criminology and Forensic Science.

Training of Deputy Superintendents of Police

On 31st December, 1976 there were 2,850 officers of the rank of Asst. Superintendents of Police and Deputy Supdts. of Police out of which 238 posts were of junior I.P.S. cadre. Thus, only 2,615 posts of Dy. Ss. P. were sanctioned on 31 December, 1976.

TABLE 6.4

Showing strength of Asst. Supdts. of Police/ Dy. Supdts. of Police As on 30.12.1976 and imparted Basic Training

S. No.	State/U.T.	Number of A.Ss.P./ Dy. Ss.P.	Number undergone basic Trg. during last the years
1	2	3	4
1.	Andhra Pradesh	147	35
2.	Assam	114	52
3.	Bihar	214	NA
4.	Gujarat	85	23
5.	Haryana	76	NA
6.	Himachal Pradesh	23	NA
7.	Jammu & Kashmir	27	NA
8.	Karnataka	120	49
9.	Kerala	88	8

1	2	3	4
10.	Madhya Pradesh	175	NA
11.	Maharashtra	224	44
12.	Manipur	32	NA
13.	Meghalaya	14	NA
14.	Nagaland	13	NA
15.	Orissa	137	28
16.	Punjab	92	129
17.	Rajasthan	226	142
18.	Sikkim	14	NA
19.	Tamil Nadu	182	24
20.	Tripura	19	NA
21.	Uttar Pradesh	617	165
22.	West Bengal	211	62
	Total	2850	761
	U.Ts.		
23.	A.&.N. Islands	8	NA
24.	Arunachal Pradesh	1	NA
25.	Chandigarh	2	NA
26.	D.&.N. Haveli	1	NA
27.	Delhi	70	NA
28.	Goa. Daman & Diu	7	NA
29.	Lakshadweep	—	NA
30.	Mizoram	16	NA
31.	Pondicherry	6	NA
	Total	111	Nil
	Grand Total	2961	761

I.P.S. Juniors—238

Posts of Dy. S.P. 2723

TABLE 6.5

Showing State-wise number of Dy. Ss. P. who were imparted Basic Trg. during Last Decade

S. No.	State/U.T.	Duration	1971	1972	1973	1974	1975	1976	1977	1978	1979	1980	Total
1	2	3	4	5	6	7	8	9	10	11	12	13	14
1.	Andhra Pradesh	one yr.	—	—	—	—	—	—	7	17	2	9	35
2.	Assam	—do—	—	—	—	—	—	20	9	10	4	9	52
3.	Gujarat	—do—	5	7	—	—	1	—	3	1	5	1	23
4.	Karnataka	—do—	5	1	1	—	7	7	7	7	7	7	49
5.	Kerala	—do—	—	2	—	—	—	3	2	—	—	1	8
6.	Maharashtra	—do—	—	6	2	3	4	4	6	1	13	5	44
7.	Orissa	—do—	6	5	7	3	2	3	—	—	1	1	28
8.	Punjab	—do—	8	23	19	12	19	8	5	18	6	11	129
9.	Tamil Nadu	—do—	—	8	—	4	2	3	3	—	2	2	24
10.	Uttar Pradesh	12 ms	—	28	13	6	—	9	21	26	31	31	165
11.	Rajasthan	10 ms		year-wise		details		not	given				142
12.	West Bengal	14 ms	8	2	4	6	6	10	4	8	9	5	62
	Total		32	82	46	34	41	67	67	88	80	82	761

Basic training of Dy. Supdts. of Police is generally conducted in the state police training colleges except in states of Nagaland, Mizoram, Arunachal Pradesh, Himachal Pradesh, Jammu & Kashmir, Sikkim and Meghalaya as these states send their officers to National Police Academy or the police training colleges of neighbouring states. Police Academy or the police training colleges of neighbouring states extend the training facilities. Police Training College Phillaur, Punjab, P.T.C. Moradabad, P.T.C. Dargaon and North-Eastern Police Academy, Barapani, Shillong are some of the police colleges where Dy. Ss.P. of other states are also getting training alongwith their own state cadre officers.

TABLE 6.6

Showing names of states where refreshers course are held/ are not held for the officers of the rank of Dy. Superintendents of Police

S. No.	State/U.T.	Whether Ref. Courses are held or not	Remarks
1	2	3	4
1.	Andhra Pradesh	No	
2.	Assam	No	
3.	Gujarat	No	
4.	Haryana	Yes	6 Offrs. undergone
5.	Karnataka	No	
6.	Kerala	No	
7.	Manipur	No	
8.	Negaland	No	Reorientation Course started w.e.f. Jan. 1981.

1	2	3	4
9.	Orissa	No	
10.	Punjab	Yes	
11.	Tamil Nadu	No	
12.	Uttar Pradesh	Yes	
13.	Delhi	No	
14.	Rajasthan	Yes	64 Offrs. trained so far.
	26.65%	Yes	
	73.33%	No.	

Internal Security Academy is conducting courses of 18 days' duration for Dy. Ss.P. Number of trainees who have attended this course is as under :

Year	No. of officers attended
1977	14
1978	91
1979	115
1980	111
1981	85
Total	416

Tables at pages 149 and 150 show that during the last four years approximately 18 percent of the total Dy. Ss. P. of India have been trained by the I.S,A. and I.C.F.S. which comes to 45 percent in ten years. Similarly, during the last three years 13.5 percent of the total Dy. Ss. P. of India have been trained by I.C.F.S. New Delhi. Table below shows that between last 10 years, I.C.F.S. imparted refresher training to 34.27 percent of officers. Even if it be accepted that some officers attended

TABLE 6.7

Institute of Criminology and Forensic Science is conducting a number of courses for Dy. Ss. P. and course-wise details are shown below :

S. No.	Name of the course	Year	S. No.	Capacity	Nomination	Actual attendance	Drop out/ Cancel-lation
1	2	3	4	5	6	7	8
1.	Behavioural Orientation Course 10 days	1979	7	20	—	16	—
			8	20	—	19	—
			9	20	—	17	—
			10	20	—	11	—
			11	20	—	15	—
		1980	12	20	—	14	—
2.	Methodology of Behaviour Modification 24 days	1981	6	12	18	13	5
3.	Role of Police in dealing with juvenile delinquency (Senior) 18 days	1979	23	20	—	10	—
		1980	25	20	—	13	—
		1981	27	20	22	16	6

1	2	3	4	5	6	7	8
4.	Orientation for Forensic Science 12 days	1979	37	20	—	15	—
			38	20	—	16	—
			39	20	—	20	—
			40	20	—	9	—
			41	20	—	25	—
		1980	42	20	—	21	—
			43	20	—	12	—
			44	20	—	16	—
			45	20	—	22	—
		1981	46	20	12	10	2
			47	20	18	10	8
			48	20	19	13	6
			49	20	28	21	7
						354	

The Table indicates that capacity of all courses remains mostly underutilized.

courses both at I.S.A., Mount Abu and I.C.F.S., New Delhi still the figures of Dy. Ss. P. who attended some refresher during last ten years can not be less than 45 percent and maximum could be much more. This is in spite of the fact that refresher courses for Dy. Ss. P. mostly under-utilised.

TABLE 6.8

Showing number of Dy. Ss. P. who attended courses at I.C.F.S., Delhi

Year	No. of Dy.Ss.P. attended course
1972	38
1973	123
1974	71
1975	.84
1976	105
1977	164
1978	143
1979	86
1980	98
1981	103
Total	1015

According to the study 761 Dy. Ss. P. got basic training whereas 1501 trainees attended refresher courses. Thus, the hypothesis that police training institutions are concentrating more on basic training than on refresher training stands disproved in respect of training of Dy Supdts. of Police.

Training of Subordinate Officers

In India, the total strength of subordinate officers (inspectors and sub-inspectors) as on 31st December, 1976 wes 42,997. The table at page nos. 153 and 154 shows the number of officers of the rank of S.Is. and inspectors who received basic and refresher training. Table at page no. 155 shows state-wise split of trainees who attended basic course of S.Is. in state police training colleges. Table at page no. 157 shows number of states where refresher course is conducted for S.Is. and total number of officers who attended such course. Table at page 158 indicates figures of inspectors who attended refresher training in states in P.T.Cs. Table at page no. 159 shows total number of subordinate officers who received refresher training and the percentage of S.Os. who received refresher training out of total strength of various states. At page 160 the table indicates total number of officers who attended various refresher courses at the I.C.F.S., New Delhi.

TABLE 6.9

Showing number of officers given Basic & Refresher Training in India

S. No.	State/U.T.	Total strength of Insps./S.I. as on 31.12.1976	Total nos. imparted basic trg. during last decade	Total nos. of imparted refresher trg. during last 10 years
1	2	3	4	5
1.	Andhra Pradesh	2343	443	114
2.	Assam	1691	764	50
3.	Bihar	3137	NA	NA
4.	Gujarat	1738	860	NA
5.	Haryana	438	27	229
6.	Himachal Pradesh	200	NA	NA
7.	Jammu & Kashmir	233	NA	NA
8.	Karnataka	1707	732	NA
9.	Kerala	955	383	NA
10.	Madhya Pradesh	2577	NA	NA

1	2	3	4	5
11.	Maharashtra	4302	1871	401
12.	Manipur	266	NA	17
13.	Meghalaya	230	NA	NA
14.	Nagaland	133	NA	NA
15.	Orissa	1984	1087	217
16.	Punjab	890	689	NA
17.	Rajasthan	1747	644	1637
18.	Sikkim	58	NA	NA
19.	Tamil Nadu	2754	860	129
20.	Tripura	468	NA	NA
21.	Uttar Pradesh	6942	5277	409
22.	West Bengal	6068	1161	NA
	Total	40861	14738	3203
U.Ts.				
23.	A. & N. Islands	45	NA	43
24.	Arunachal Pradesh	58	NA	NA
25.	Chandigarh	40	NA	NA
26.	D. & N. Haveli	4	NA	NA
27.	Delhi	1720	419	NA
28.	Goa, Daman & Diu	62	NA	NA
29.	Lakshadweep	15	NA	NA
30.	Mizoram	134	NA	NA
31.	Pondicherry	58	NA	NA
	Total	2136	419	43
	Grand Total	42997	15217	3246

TABLE 6.10

Showing number of S.Is./A.S.Is. imparted Basic Training

S.No.	State/U.T.	Duration	1971	1972	1973	1974	1975	1976	1977	1978	1979	1980	Total
1	2	3	4	5	6	7	8	9	10	11	12	13	14
1.	Andhra Pradesh	One yr.	—	—	—	—	—	—	291	152	—	—	443
2.	Assam	—dc—	133	199	107	60	—	197	1	34	3	30	764
3.	Gujarat	—do—	—	48	54	56	119	110	101	135	237	—	860
4.	Haryana	—do—	—	—	—	—	—	—	—	21	—	6	27
5.	Karnataka	—do—	79	71	57	72	—	92	—	202	—	159	732
6.	Kerala	—do—	47	—	—	191	4	127	4	10	—	—	383
7.	Maharashtra	—do—	250	113	168	183	175	207	208	192	174	201	1871
8.	C.T.C. 2 C.R.P.F. Avadi	40 Wks.	12	74	26	6	13	4	8	3	—	—	146
9.	Orissa	One yr.	127	132	72	88	57	17	133	69	171	221	1087
10.	Punjab	—do—	85	43	28	19	48	353	36	13	17	47	689

1	2	3	4	5	6	7	8	9	10	11	21	13	14
11.	Tamil Nadu	—do—	—	113	—	185	—	—	275	—	—	287	860
12.	Uttar Pradesh	—do—	—	394	—	733	—	706	—	606	1990	848	5277
13.	Rajasthan	—do—			year-wise		details	not		given			644
14.	West Bengal	—do—	31	76	90	163	176	85	90	173	141	136	1161
15.	Delhi	—do—	—	—	66	32	—	73	—	101	82	65	419
	Total		764	1263	668	1788	592	1971	1147	1711	2815	2000	15363

TABLE 6.11

Showing states where Refresher Training is given to Sub-Inspectors or otherwise

S.No.	State/U.T.	Whether Ref. Trg. given or not	Total trained in the years
1	2	3	4
1.	Andhra Pradesh	Yes	85
2.	Assam	Yes	50
3.	Gujarat	No	NA
4.	Haryana	Yes	218
5.	Karnataka	Yes	—
6.	Kerala	No	—
7.	Maharashtra	Yes	163
8.	Manipur	Yes	17
9.	Orissa	Yes	217
10.	Tamil Nadu	Yes	129
11.	Uttar Pradesh	Yes	409
12.	West Bengal	No	—
13.	Delhi	No	—
14.	Rajasthan	Yes	1502
15.	Punjab	Yes	103
16.	A. & N. Islands	Yes	29

TABLE 6.12

Showing names of States where Refresher Course for Inspectors are held or otherwise

S.No.	State/U.T.	Whether Ref. Course held or not	Total trained in ten years
1	2	3	4
1.	Gujarat	No	—
2.	Haryana	Yes	11
3.	Andhra Pradesh	Yes	29
4.	Karnataka	Yes	—
5.	Kerala	No	—
6.	Maharashtra	Yes	238
7.	Manipur	No	—
8.	Nagaland	No	—
9.	Orissa	Yes	—
10.	Tamil Nadu	Yes	—
11.	West Bengal	No	—
12.	Delhi	No	—
13.	Rajasthan	Yes	135
14.	Punjab	Yes	71
15.	A. & N. Islands	Yes	4
16.	Uttar Pradesh	Yes	—

TABLE 6.13

Showing percentage of Inspectors and Sub-Inspectors who were imparted Refresher Training during the last ten years

S.No.	State/U.T.	Sanctioned strength of Insp./SIs.	Total Insp/S.Is. trained	Percentage
1	2	3	4	5
1.	Andhra Pradesh	2343	144	4.86
2.	Assam	1691	50	2.95
3.	Gujarat	1738	—	—
4.	Haryana	438	229	52.28
5.	Karnataka	1707	—	—
6.	Maharashtra	4302	401	9.32
7.	Manipur	266	17	6.39
8.	Orissa	1984	217	10.93
9.	Punjab	890	174	19.55
10.	Rajasthan	1747	1637	93.70
11.	Tamil Nadu	2754	129	4.68
12.	Uttar Pradesh	6942	409	5.89
13.	West Bengal	6068	—	—
14.	A. & N. Islands	45	43	95.55
15.	Delhi	1720	—	—
16.	Kerala	—	—	—

Institute of Criminology and Forensic Science is conducting courses on orientation to criminology and forensic science, Role of police in dealing with juvenile delinquency and police photography for inspectors and sub-inspectors and the numbers of officers trained during the last few years are as under :

TABLE 6.14

Year	Inspectors	Sub-Inspectors	Total
1	2	3	4
1972	17	18	35
1973	20	27	47
1974	13	25	38
1975	12	35	47
1976	18	27	45
1977	14	23	37
1978	11	17	28
1979	15	12	27
1980	—	29	29
Total	120	213	333

while 15, 217 inspectors and S.Is. attended basic training 3,246 subordinate officers received refresher training during last ten years in state training colleges. The data collected from 16 states indicate that 75 percent state institutions are conducting refresher training for S.Is. and 62 percent institutions are conducting refresher courses for inspectors. Table at page 159 shows that in some states during last ten years 93 percent of the total strength of subordinate officers attended refresher courses. During last ten years I.C.P.S. imparted refresher training to 120 Inspectors and 213 S.Is. Central Detective Training Schools of Calcutta, Hyderabad and Chandigarh are also imparting refresher training to S.Is. and Inspectors. Closer analysis of table at page 159 indicates that Haryana gave refresher training to 52 per cent of Inspectors and S.Is., Rajasthan 93.70 per cent and A.&N. Islands 95.5 per cent of strength. Thus, it is established from the research data that though percentage of Inspectors and S.Is who attended refresher courses in state training colleges varies, the overall picture which emerges shows that refresher training is organised in majority (68 per cent) of the state training institutions are conducting refresher courses and thus the hypothesis stands disproved as far as sub-inspectors/ inspectors are concerned.

Training of Officers Below the Rank of Sub-Inspectors

The officers below the rank of S.Is comprise of Asst. Sub-Inspectors, havildars and constables. In some states and in para-military organisations, Lance Naiks and Naiks are two ranks in between constables and havildars. Tables at page no. 162 and 163 show total sanctioned strength of all ranks below the rank of Sub-Inspectors and number of trainees who attended refreshers training in the states. Table at page no. 165 shows number of havildars who received basic training in state training institutions. At page no. 166 is the table that indicates the states where refresher training is imparted to head constables/havildars and total number trained during last ten years.

Refresher training of constables and head constables/ havildars in 60 per cent of the states is conducted in the district police lines under the supervision of the District police lines staff. This practice is in vogue in Uttar Pradesh, Rajasthan, Madhya Pradesh, Bihar, Punjab and other states. Training allowances are given to police constables, head constables, sub-inspectors and reserve inspectors in all districts for training constables and recruits.[5]

TABLE 6.15

Showing Total Sanctioned Strength of all Ranks Below Sub-Inspector and Ref. Trg. Imparted to Them

S. No.	State/U.T.	Total no. officers below rank of S.Is.	Ref. Trg. given to Const.	Ref. Trg. given to H.Cs.	Total trained in ten years	Per-centage
1	2	3	4	5	6	7
1.	Andhra Pradesh	33354	327	310	637	1.90
2.	Assam	10036	—	—	—	—
3.	Bihar	38089	—	—	—	—
4.	Gujarat	35129	—	2070	2070	5.89
5.	Haryana	10681	4866	614	5480	51.30
6.	Himachal Pradesh	5195	—	—	—	—
7.	Jammu & Kashmir	6154	—	—	—	—
8.	Karnataka	29659	—	—	—	—
9.	Kerala	16935	—	—	—	—
10.	Madhya Pradesh	32967	—	—	—	—

11.	Maharashtra	69133	—	124	124	0.17
12.	Manipur	2613	615	264	879	33.63
13.	Meghalaya	2760	—	—	—	—
14.	Nagaland	3390	—	—	—	—
15.	Orissa	17639	—	—	—	—
16.	Punjab	20150	2694	3194	4886	24.25
17.	Rajasthan	31690	423	320	734	2.34
18.	Sikkim	665	—	—	—	—
19.	Tamil Nadu	36027	—	453	453	1.25
20.	Tripura	2038	—	—	—	—
21.	Uttar Pradesh	74920	—	—	—	—
22.	West Bengal	44168	—	—	—	—
	Total	523392	8925	6349	15274	
	Union Territories					
23.	A. & N. Islands	1209	721	—	721	—
24.	Arunachal Pradesh	581	—	—	—	—

1	2	3	4	5	6	7
25.	Chandigarh	1048	—	—	—	—
26.	D. & N. Haveli	68	—	—	—	—
27.	Goa, Daman & Diu	1373	—	—	—	—
28.	Lakshadweep	285	—	—	—	—
29.	Delhi	13351	—	668	668	0.50
30.	Mizoram	11109	—	—	—	—
31.	Pondicherry	594	—	—	—	—
	Total	19758	721	668	1389	—
	Grand total	543150	9646	7017	16663	

TABLE 6.16

Showing Number of Head Constables Imparted Basic Training

S. No.	States/U.T.	1971	1972	1973	1974	1975	1976	1977	1978	1979	1980	Total
1	2	3	4	5	6	7	8	9	10	11	12	13
1.	Andhra Pradesh	—	—	—	—	—	—	170	170	—	14	354
2.	Gujarat	—	194	199	215	215	406	427	140	274	—	2070
3.	Orissa	—	—	—	—	—	—	—	—	—	232	232
4.	Rajasthan	—	—	—	—	—	—	161	464	469	304	1398
5.	Uttar Pradesh	—	—	—	—	405	249	250	256	567	268	1995
6.	Delhi	228	75	420	228	75	199	198	201	198	199	2021
7.	C.T.C. II C.R.P.F. Avadi	23	56	51	18	4	3	13	4	—	—	172
	Total	251	325	670	461	699	857	1219	1235	1508	1017	8242

TABLE 6.17

Showing States where Refresher Training is Given to Head Constables or Otherwise

S.No.	State/U.T.	Ref. Trg. given or not	Total trained in ten years
1	2	3	4
1.	Andhra Pradesh	Yes	310
2.	Gujarat	Yes	2070
3.	Haryana	Yes	614
4.	Karnataka	Yes	—
5.	Kerala	No	—
6.	Maharashtra	Yes	124
7.	Manipur	Yes	264
8.	Orissa	No	—
9.	Punjab	Yes	2194
10.	Delhi	Yes	668
11.	Rajasthan	Yes	320
12.	Tamil Nadu	Yes	453
13.	A. & N. Islands	Yes	15
14.	West Bengal	Yes	—

Basic training of constables in more than 70 per cent states is done both in training institutions and in district police lines. The basic training imparted to constables in the district police lines in sometimes followed by training in training institutions also. However, for the purpose of present research study, basic training of constables carried out in police training centres and schools only have been taken into consideration. The number of constables who got basic training in various police training institutions in 14 states and Union Territories is given in the table at page no. 167.

TABLE 6.18

Showing Number of Constables Imparted Basic Training

S. No.	State/U.T.	1971	1972	1973	1974	1975	1976	1977	1978	1979	1980	Total
1	2	3	4	5	6	7	8	9	10	11	12	13
1.	Andhra Pradesh	—	—	—	—	—	—	200	556	303	78	1137
2.	Assam	—	—	—	—	330	264	372	593	1280	288	3127
3.	Gujarat	1238	1820	1339	1236	1027	1591	1468	699	1637	1580	13635
4.	Haryana	—	—	—	—	—	997	1204	335	981	1110	4627
5.	Kerala	1141	1253	1014	874	161	931	332	431	514	5	6656
6.	Manipur	—	—	—	45	314	253	174	163	335	315	1599
7.	Nagaland	194	315	153	229	115	268	116	102	223	—	1716
8.	Orissa	118	148	317	478	257	220	417	351	450	586	3342
9.	Punjab	946	1288	917	2343	1415	1836	1284	648	750	1621	13048
10.	Rajasthan	—	—	—	—	—	126	645	269	215	75	1330
11.	Tamil Nadu	—	—	—	—	—	—	—	—	1444	1341	2785
12.	West Bengal	882	1233	1113	958	686	851	1789	1602	1265	820	11199
13.	Mizoram	—	—	99	414	44	37	20	92	176	84	966
14.	Delhi	521	600	912	412	1245	1075	1166	1263	620	856	8670
	Total	5040	6657	5864	6989	5595	8449	9187	7104	10193	8759	73837

Table given at page no. 168 shows the states where refresher training for constables is held or otherwise. This table also indicates the number of constables so trained in refresher courses during the last ten years.

TABLE 6.19
Showing States where Refresher Training for Constables is Held or Otherwise

S. No.	State/U.T.	Whether Ref. Trg. held or not	Total trained
1	2	3	4
1.	Andhra Pradesh	Yes	327
2.	Assam	Yes	Course started w.e.f. Oct. 1981.
3.	Gujarat	No	--
4.	Haryana	Yes	4866
5.	Kerala	No	—
6.	Manipur	Yes	615
7.	Orissa	Nil	—
8.	Punjab	Yes	2694
9.	Rajasthan	Yes	423
10.	West Bengal	Yes	—
11.	Mizoram	Yes	—
12.	Delhi	No	—
13.	A. & N. Islands	Yes	721
14.	Maharashtra	No	—

Diagram number-3 given on page-169 shows the percentage of training institutions where refresher training for various ranks is conducted in India. The diagram depicts that for all ranks the percentage of refresher training is above 60 per cent.

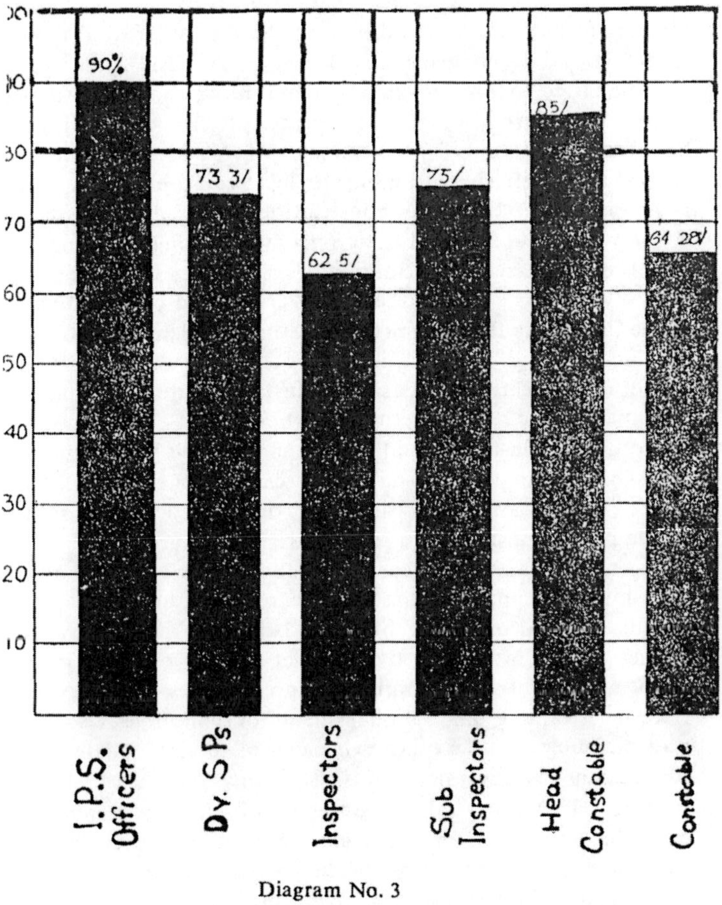

Diagram No. 3

Diagram showing percentage of states conducting Refresher Training for various ranks in training institutions

A close study of the table at page no. 162 shows that out of all the states, only three states namely, Haryana, Manipur and Punjab have given refresher training to more than 24 per cent of their sanctioned strength during the last ten years. All other states have not been able to impart training to more than even 6 per cent of the other ranks. As shown in tables at page nos. 165 and 167, basic training has been imparted to 73,837 constables and 8,242 head constables respectively during the last ten years. Refresher training has been imparted to only 16,663 number of head constables and constables. Refresher training to head constables is imparted in 85 per cent of the training institutions of India. Thus, it can be conveniently accepted that refresher training is getting due attention. The refresher training of constables is carried out annually or in a few states in every second year in District police lines. As the magnitude of the problem of refresher training is very large, it is not possible for existing training institutions to carry it out as these institutes are even unable to impart basic training to the new entrants. The in-take of police training institutions all over the country being limited, refresher training of constables is carried out at the district level. There is a tactical reason for this practice because by keeping the constables in the districts, they are available for emergencies also. In the present study, no data regarding refreshing training of constables carried out at district police lines have been collected, the task being too vast. However, during interviews with the district police officers, it was confirmed by them that district police lines do carry out refresher training and annual firing of constables as far as possible subject to the other exigencies of service. State Police Regulations lay down detailed instructions for such refresher courses. Therefore, in the absence of data, percentage of constables trained in any particular year can not be ascertained. The research data show that 64.28 per cent of the states are organising refresher training for constables even in training institutions. Thus, the hypothesis stands disproved in respect of constables and head constables also. The present research carried out a study of opinions of various ranks about the hypothesis which is tabulated below at page no. 171.

TABLE 6.20

Showing Opinion of Officers about the Hypothesis that Training Institutions are More Concerned with Basic Training than with Refresher Training

Rank	Agree	Partly agree	Disagree	Total
1	2	3	4	5
Is.G.P./D.Is.G.P.	16	2	2	20
Ss.P.	22	12	6	40
Dy. Ss. P.	20	16	4	40
Inspectors	23	15	2	40
Sub-Inspectors	25	3	2	30
Constabulary	41	8	1	50
Total	147	56	17	210
Percentage	66.81	25.45	7.72	

The opinion clearly indicates that there is a general belief among serving officers that training institutions are concentrating more on basic training course than on refresher training. This wrong notion has come to their mind because of lack of proper understanding of the refresher training system which continues throughout the year and is attended by eight to ten per cent of the constabulary. Thus, it can be contended that to say that training institutions are more concerned with basic training courses than with refresher training is not based on facts and the hypothesis stands disproved.

Police training of I.P.S. officers is generally conducted by the police training institutions of the Central Government whereas the training of Dy. Supdts. of Police and all other ranks is normally conducted in the state police, training institutions. Course contents of basic training courses as well as refresher courses are generally more or less uniform in India and are based on the syllabus laid down by the Report of the Committee on Police Training. The duration of various courses differ from state to state. Training programmes are generally conducted by the police trainers posted in the training institutions with the help and collaboration of quest speakers.

In-service Training for Police in India

In-service training means only that part of training which is imparted to employees after they have completed their basic training. Staff development is a perpetual process and there is no point at which a person stops getting education. The aim of in-service training is the infusion of the whole organisation with a common spirit, a common understanding of the purposes and objectives of the organisation and the relation of the individual assignments to these purposes and objectives. In-service training is a vital factor in increasing organisation fitness to carry out its mission effectively. In-service training in police has acquired a special significance in the recent years. While induction of basic training prepares policemen to acquire skills, techniques, attitudes and knowledge needed to perform their duties at the time of entry into the police force, in-service training prepares policemen, who are already in service, to meet the new challenges in a fast changing socio-economic and political environments of a developing polity. Training is a life-long process and the concept of training as being a one-shot affair, to be provided at the entry point in service, is no longer valid. The in-service training is needed for police officers to meet the following challenges to the police service :

(1) Political pressures and directions ;

(2) The impact of technological changes and new scientific advance ;

(3) Unionisation of the public service ;

(4) Increased citizen involvement and rising expectations of the public ;

(5) National policies and programmes for upliftment of the weaker sections of the society and commitment to the socialistic pattern of society ;

(6) Changing pattern of crime and violence ;

(7) Invention of new armaments and equipment.

In-service training ensures a constant input of fresher knowledge, newer skills and better attitudinal and behavioural patterns and thus prepares a police officer to face the rapidly changing technological and administrative environment in a better manner. Administrative environment has four dimensions :

(*i*) political (*ii*) social

(*iii*) economic (*iv*) managerial

In-service training is expected to accelerate maturing process by enabling police officers to have a chance to look at themselves and their work in an objective and detached manner. In-service training is now-a-days recognised as part of the warp and woof of administrative dynamics. The police in India have a difficult role and this requires the development of proper attitudes and the ability to anticipate, analyse and take decisions to meet the most difficult and challenging situations. In-service training programmes have to provide special emphasis to the deep social awareness for comprehending and reacting to complex situations arising out of development process including conflicts, social disorganisation, scarcity and controls, regional imbalances and conflicts arising out of religious, political, economic and ethnic causes. In-service training of senior police officer assumes great significance in the context of increasing responsiveness towards the legitimate demands and difficulties of the citizens. In-service training to senior police officers can provide them structured opportunities of exposure to other disciplines and organisations in order to acquaint them with the latest concepts of administration, management, secularism and to promote a better understanding of the police in the community and police-public relations. In-service training is basically an educational process utilising a systematic and organised procedure by which police personnel learn conceptual and theoretical knowledge, acquire skills and techniques and develop attitudes and behaviour patterns. In-service training is today supported by a vast amount of empirical findings and modern concepts. Some of these important concepts are as under :

(*i*) There is no time limit for learning and it can continue throughout a man's professional career.

(*ii*) There always exists some gap between actual performance and optimum capacity and in-service can increase the effectiveness and performance of the individuals.

(*iii*) In-service training can increase the effectiveness of an individual by narrowing down "the unknown areas" of one's knowledge.

(*iv*) In-service training helps in the development of coherent thinking, problems solving ability, depth of insight, human technical and conceptual skills, and thus over-all development of personality.

(*v*) In-service training helps in bringing change in the individuals in crucial areas of following output variables and thus ultimately bring changes in organisational effectiveness :

(*a*) knowledge change (*b*) Attitude change

(*c*) Behaviour change (*d*) Performance change

(*e*) End-operational change

(*vi*) William James of Harvard University estimated that employees could retain their jobs at a mere 20-30 per cent of their potential. His research led him to believe that if the same employees were given in-service training and motivation, they could work at 80-90 per cent of their capacities.

(*vii*) There is need for in-service training at all levels in the public services for enhancing performance levels and providing constant input to their knowledge, skills and capabilities.

(*viii*) Welfare state committed to the ideals of socialism and secularism needs motivated and committed public servants. In-service training programmes develop an awareness of social responsibility in public servants.

The Police Commission of 1902-1903 (Sir Fraser as President) appointed by Lord Curzon recommended that knowledge of members of the police force in India should be kept up by periodical training at headquarters or by regular drill and target practice at the police stations. This concept gave birth to the concept of in-service training to the Indian police. In 1905, Provincial Training Schools for police in each district were established for providing basic and in-service training to police officers of the country. Thus, India is the pioneer in starting in-service training in the world. In-service training in the police was started in the U.S.A. in 1908 by August Vollmer at Burkeley. In recent years, great emphasis is being given to in-service training. Eighty-nineth Report of the Estimates Committee of the Lok Sabha on Cabinet Secretariat (Department of Personnel and Administrative Reforms) 1975-76 made specific recommendations concerning in-service training. Administrative Reforms Commission (Report on Personnel Administration) Government of India 1969 made specific recommendations that systematic efforts to provide mid-term career management training should be provided to public servants. Committee on Police Training (Gore Commission) 1974 had also recommended refresher courses and other in-service programmes for various levels of police officers of the country. The proposal was made in 1953 for starting a special refresher course for I.P.S. officers but it was ultimately started in June 1960 and was later named advanced course. This course was redesignated as senior officers course in 1969. Top management course for the officers of the level of Deputy Inspectors-General of Police was started in February, 1979. At present, I.P.S. officers after completion of their basic induction course at S.V.P., N.P.A., Hyderabad and other places have to attend the following courses as a part of career planning :

(1) Fleet management course at Sagar, Madhya Pradesh.

(2) Weapons and Tactics course at Central School of Weapons and Tactics at Indore.

(3) Wireléss course at Central Police Radio Training Institute, New Delhi.

(4) Internal Security Training Courses at Internal Security Academy, Mount Abu (Rajasthan).

(5) Police Community Relations Course at Institute of Criminology and Forensic science, New Delhi.

(6) Advanced Course in Criminology at the Institute of Criminology and Forensic science, New Delhi.

(7) Senior Officers Course at S.V.P., National Police Academy Hyderabad, Andhra Pradesh.

(8) Executive Development Programme at some institute or centre.

National Police Commission in its sixth report (March 1981) has recommended Junior Management Course for Superintendents of Police, Senior Management Course for Deputy Inspectors-General of Police and Top Management Course for Inspectors-General of Police. For officers who are promoted into the I.P.S., Commission has suggested a special six month course. The author has surveyed the data about in-service training imparted to the I.P.S. officers. According to the data, in-service training course attended by I.P.S. officers at various training institutions during 1971 to 1980 are shown below :—

In-service Training for Dy. Ss.P.

In-service course for Deputy Superintendents of Police is at present organised at Internal Security Academy, Mount Abu, Rajasthan; Detective Training Schools, Institute of Criminology and Forensic Science and State Police Training Institutions. Research study carried out by the author indicates that there are no in-service training programmes organised for the rank of Dy.Ss. P., in Andhra Pradesh, Assam, Gujarat, Karnataka, Kerala, Manipur, Nagaland, Orissa, Tamil Nadu and in-service training courses are organised in police training institutions in

TABLE 6.21

Year	Senior Officers Course	Course at I.S.A. Mount Abu (Raj)	Course at I.C.F.S.	Remarks
1	2	3	4	5
1971	31	—	NA	I.P.S. Officers
1972	18	—	71	constitute less
1973	48	—	148	than 4 per cent
1974	43	—	86	of the entire
1975	43	—	118	police force.
1976	62	—	160	
1977	66	23	140	
1978	50	88	186	
1979	54	69	127	
1980	41	41	155	
Total	456	221	1191	

the state of Haryana, Punjab, Uttar Pradesh and Rajasthan. The following table shows inservice training courses attended by officers of the rank of Dy. Ss.P. from all over India at I.C.F.S., New Delhi and Internal Security Academy, Mount Abu are as under :

TABLE 6.22

I.C.F.S. New Delhi			I.S.A. Mount Abu		
1972	—	38	1977	—	14
1973	—	123	1978	—	91
1974	—	71	1979	—	115
1975	—	84	1980	—	111
1976	—	105	1981	—	85
1977	—	164			
1978	—	143	Total		416
1979	—	86			
1980	—	98			
1981	—	103			
Total		1015			

In-service Training for Subordinate Officers

The research data indicate that during the last 10 years, more refresher training was organised in the state of Bihar, Gujarat, Himachal Pradesh, Jammu & Kashmir, Karnataka, Kerala, Madhya Pradesh, Nagaland, Punjab, Sikkim and Tripura. No. of subordinate officers who attended various in-service courses during the last 10 years of some states are given below :

TABLE 6.23

S. No.	State/UT	Total Nos. imparted basic trg. during last decade	Total No. of imparted refresher trg. during last 10 year
1	2	3	4
1.	Andhra Pradesh	443	114
2.	Assam	746	50
3.	Gujarat	860	NA
4.	Haryana	27	229
5.	Karnataka	732	NA
6.	Kerala	383	NA
7.	Maharashtra	1871	401
8.	Manipur	NA	17
9.	Punjab	689	NA
10.	Orissa	1087	217
11.	Rajasthan	664	1637
12.	Tamil Nadu	860	129
13.	Uttar Pradesh	5277	409
14.	West Bengal	1161	NA
	Total	14738	3203

1	2	3	4
	Union Territories		
15.	A. & N. Islands	NA	43
16.	Delhi	419	NA
	Total	419	43
	Grand Total	15217	3246

Percentage of subordinate officers who are imparted refresher training during the last 10 years is given below :

TABLE 6.24

S. No.	State/UT	Sanctioned strength	Total Insps. S.Is. trained	Percentage
1	2	3	4	5
1.	Andhra Pradesh	2343	114	4.86
2.	Assam	1691	50	2.95
3.	Gujarat	1738	—	—
4.	Haryana	430	229	52.28
5.	Karnataka	1707	—	—
6.	Maharashtra	4302	401	9.32
7.	Manipur	266	17	6.39
8.	Orissa	1984	217	10.93
9.	Punjab	890	174	19.55
10.	Rajasthan	1747	1647	93.70
11.	Tamil Nadu	2754	129	4.68
12.	Uttar Pradesh	6942	409	5.89
13.	West Bengal	6068	—	—
14.	A. & N. Islands	45	43	95.55

In-service Training for all Ranks below the Rank of Sub-Inspectors

Percentage of other ranks (below S.Is.) who have been given in-service training during the last 10 years is indicated below :

TABLE 6.25

S. No.	State/UT	Total Strength	Total trained in 10 years	Percentage
1	2	3	4	5
1.	Andhra Pradesh	33354	637	1.90
2.	Gujarat	35129	2070	5.89
3.	Haryana	10681	5480	51.30
4.	Maharashtra	69133	124	0.17
5.	Manipur	2613	879	33.63
6.	Punjab	20150	4888	24.25
7.	Rajasthan	31690	734	2.34
8.	Tamil Nadu	36027	453	1.25
9.	A. & N. Islands	1209	721	—
10.	Delhi	13351	688	0.50

Police personnel below the rank of sub-inspectors constitute approximately 90 per cent of the police force and their institutionalised in-service training is in great neglect at present. In the state of Bihar, Assam, Karnataka, Mizoram, Orissa, Sikkim, Tripura, U.P. and West Bengal no institutional refresher training was organised for other ranks. However, these figures are misleading as generally in-service training for officers below the rank of sub-inspectors is organised at the Distt. police headquarters and sub-divisional police headquarters and the figures are not available.

Table given below indicates whether institutionalised in-service training for constables is held in various states or not.

TABLE 6.26

S. No.	State/UT	Whether refresher trg. held or not	Total trained
1	2	3	4
1.	Andhra Pradesh	Yes	327
2.	Assam	Yes	Course started w.e.f. Oct. 1981
3.	Gujarat	No	—
4.	Haryana	Yes	4856
5.	Kerala	No	—
6.	Manipur	Yes	615
7.	Orissa	Nil	—
8.	Punjab	Yes	2594
9.	Rajasthan	Yes	423
10.	West Bengal	Yes	—
11.	Mizoram	Yes	—
12.	Delhi	No	—
13.	A. & N. Islands	Yes	721
14.	Maharashtra	No	—

The above data indicate that in-service training programmes are not being organised at proper times in police training institutions. Due to their large number, it is not possible to give them adequate in-service training.

Types of In-service Training for Police

In-service police training consists of the following types of courses :

(*a*) Courses for police specialists like drivers, mechanics, radio operators and radio fitters, intelligence and map reading course.

(*b*) Annual refresher courses including annual training in musketry and firing with authorised weapons.

(*c*) Courses for special areas like police-public relations, investigation of cases, finger-prints training, weapons, field craft, tactics.

(*d*) General short training courses such as crime prevention course, behavioural orientation course, internal security course.

(*e*) Management courses for supervisory staff like executive development course, management development course and top management course.

(*f*) Promotional courses primarily meant to prepare police officers to take jobs of higher responsibility of senior ranks.

(*g*) Advanced courses like drill instructor course, P.T. instructor course, unarmed combat course, tear smoke course and civil defence course.

In-service training for constables, head constables, sub-inspectors, inspectors and Deputy Superintendents of Police is generally organised in state police training institutions. In-service training in police needs to be organised more methodically, scientifically and realistically so that it may not lose its vibracy and degenerate into ritualism. While dealing with the problems of in-service training for the police force, one is overwhelmed by the magnitude and dimensions of the problem. With our limited resources and limited capacity to provide in-service training in training institutions, it becomes necessary to give due attention to non-institutional methods of in-service training. In-service training through correspondence courses can be a useful method which has not yet been tried in India. The present in-service training arrangements in the different states are unsatisfactory qualitatively as well as quantitatively because of the lack of a genuine conviction about the value of training. Most of the in-service training programmes have not been linked with the channels of promotion to the various levels of higher responsibility to ensure better motivation and greater effectiveness in the field. In-service training programmes do not bring the required impact on the organisation because there is absence of a proper environment in the organisation. Motivation, morale in the organisation, opportunities for growth, fulfilment of aspiration, recognition of merit are some of the factors which directly impinge on the effectiveness of the in-service training programmes. Since there is an element of compulsion and discipline, there is very high percentage of attendance in in-service training programmes of subordinates and other ranks. But in respect of senior ranks, the percentage is varying from forty to sixty per cent in various courses depending on other factors like season, location of the training institutions and the other conveniences of the trainees. However, young senior officers are increasingly seeing the utility and relevance of in-service training courses to their job needs. This trend, very encouraging to senior officers at times, is not spared for in-service training programmes due to non-availability of training reserves and other operational commitments. Non-Governmental training institutions like Administrative Staff College and Indian Institute of Public Administration are doing useful work in providing in-service training to police and other administrative officers. Most of the participants to senior level in-service courses are receptive and have open mind but there is generally an apathy on the part of the participants to prepare good cases/project reports based on their real life experiences. For in-service training programmes only those officers who are not wanted by the states are generally shunted out to attend all sorts of training programmes without observing any roster for training in many of the states. Many officers are not relieved from their places of postings due to paucity of training reserves and operational commitments.

In-service police training programmes have the difficulty of getting a correct mix of academicians and senior members of the services on the faculty. Availability of retired police personnel and university professions depends on a number of factors and there is always a certain amount of uncertainty which causes frequent changes in the training schedule. The selection of training faculty depends upon the commitment of the programme organiser and availability of required resources. In most of the in-service training programmes organised by the state police training institutions police trainers conduct in-service training as these institutions have very meagre resources to invite outside speakers and experts. Serving senior police officers are also generally reluctant to visit training institutions to deliver talks on their subjects of specialisation. Selection of competent trainers for in-service courses is generally not done properly at least for junior and middle level courses. Police institutions generally do not provide sufficient incentives and a pleasant environment to work and therefore competent and qualified trainers are not attracted or retained in these institutions.

Training techniques and methods used for in-service training need to provide more participation from the participants but most of the training institutions continue to adopt old and traditional methods of instructions. The training material including books, documents, reports, extracts from magazines and journals, specially prepared papers and case studies, is generally not adequate and up-to-date for most of the in-service police training programmes. Libraries of most of the police training institutions in India are inadequately equipped and there is no constant flow of latest books, journals and training monographs. Very few case studies prepared in the Indian context are available for utilisation and in-service courses continue to utilise case studies and training films prepared in the Western countries. Workshops, seminars, penal discussions, brain storming session, buzz sessions, syndicate reports, role playing and other such new training techniques are hardly used in the in-service training courses organised for various ranks at state police training institutions. National level institutions like I.I.P.A., New Delhi, S.V.P., N.P.A Hyderabad, I.S.A. Mount Abu and Institute of Forensic Science and Criminology are to some extent utilizing these training methods and strategies in in-service courses organised for the seminar level police officers. However there is more overlap in the contents of various courses than should be necessary. Executive development programmes and management development programmes cover more or less similar ground and course contents to a large extent and most of the training material is still foreign. There has to be more effort in the direction of developing training materials locally.

Evaluation of In-service Training

Evaluation of in-service training programmes is an important area which needs immediate attention of all concerned. When large sums of money are being spent on training, it is important to know how far the results are commensurate with the investments. The methodologies of evaluation are still not very clear and foolproof. Evaluation of in-service training programmes can be divided into the following four logical steps :

Step 1 — *Reaction* — how the trainees expressed their reaction to the training effort ?

Step 2 — *Learning* — what principles, facts, techniques and skills were learnt by the trainees ?

Step 3 — *Behaviour* — what behavioural changes were noticed in the trainees after the training programme.

Step 4 — *Results/outcome* — what will be the immediate outcome, intermediate outcome and ultimate outcome of training in terms of improved quality of performance of the trainees and their overall impact on organisational effectiveness.

A scientific and systematic evaluation of an in-service training course will also include contextual evaluation, in put evaluation, output evaluation, process evaluation and cost evaluation. Thus, evaluation is a very complex, time consuming, continuous and tedious job and is likely to be biased and subjective if not carried out on scientific lines by experts. So far any proper evaluation of in-service training programmes has not been attempted in India. A systematic evaluation of the overall training programmes has not been done so far, even in the federal public service of the U.S.A (Bob. L. Wynia—"Executive Development in the Federal Government" Public Administrative Review—July-August 1972, pp. 312-313). The systematic evaluation of police in-service training programmes in India therefore needs to be carried out immediately. Bias in evaluation can be minimised by getting the assessment both by a member of the training faculty and by the outside experts. Systematic evaluation should become a normal administrative practice in all police training institutions and the evaluation must reveal broadly the extent of usefulness of these programmes as perceived by their trainees and their sponsoring organisations. Evaluation must indicate (*a*) whether the job efficiency of the trainees has improved as a result of training (*b*) whether their attitudes and behaviour have changed and whether they are more receptive to the public (*c*) whether the course objectives with which the programme was started have been achieved. The task of undertaking evaluation work is really a very challenging and difficult job. But the challenge could be met by setting up an evaluation unit in each training institution. A proper machinery equipped with qualified and trained persons, devoted and committed to training evaluation, will go a long way in ultimately improving the quality of in-service training. In India, at present, only trainees' reaction is taken at the end of the in-service courses and it is generally considered at the evaluation and feed back of the course. No scientific evaluation has been made about learning, behaviour and final outcome of the course.

Systems Concept of In-service Training

A meaningful approach for a proper understanding of the in-service training efforts as a system concept consists not in regarding the conduct of training programme as the sole process involved but in viewing the in-service training programme as a link in the chain of professional development of the employee in a given environment. The principal subsystems of a system concept of training are :

(*i*) Identification of training needs ;

(*ii*) Formulation of objectives for in-service training ;

(*iii*) Design of training programmes ;

(*iv*) Implementation of training programmes ;

(*v*) Evaluation and feedback of training ;

Identification of Training Needs

Identification of training needs of police organisation for in-service programmes can be broadly divided into three categories :

(*a*) organisational needs ; (*b*) individual needs ;

(*c*) group needs.

Needs can be career related or job related or developmental in nature and have to be analysed properly for designing suitable in-service training programmes for police officers of various ranks and categories analysis of employee and the organisation and analysis of organisational tasks, duties and role expectations can help in proper identification of training needs. The needs for in-service training can be broadly classified as (*i*) standing needs ; (*ii*) emergent needs and ; (*iii*) future needs and in-service training programmes have to design the programmes to fulfil these needs.

Objectives of In-service Training

In-service training programmes have to achieve the following objectives :

(*a*) To maintain the present standards of efficiency, effectiveness and performance ;

(*b*) To improve the present standards of performance and organisational effectiveness ;

(*c*) To provide the police officers new skills, techniques and knowledge to meet the changing job requirements and role expectations ;

(*d*) To prepare the employees to perform jobs at higher levels and accept bigger responsibilities ;

(*e*) To broaden the mental horizon of the police officers to enable them to successfully meet the developing new challenges of the administrative environment ;

(*f*) To narrow the gap between theory and practical experience and to evolve theories relevant to the actual field work ;

(*g*) To learn and improve new skills and techniques to handle latest equipment ;

(*h*) To enable the police officers to exchange ideas and to keep abreast of up-to-date trends in organisation, methods and procedures.

The ultimate objective of all in-service training programmes is to improve organisational effectiveness, prepare individual for present and future jobs and bring required attitudinal and behavioural modification in the trainees and to usher in organisational development. In-service training is a suitable intervention in the organisational development process. Organisational development is the process of developing and organisational climate and culture by coping with inadequacies of interpersonal and inter-group behaviour so that individual goals can be made to conform to organisational goals to bring out fulfilment of the needs of dignity, growth and satisfaction of the human resources in an organisation.

General Observations about In-service Training

The researcher has come to the conclusion that inadequacies of in-service training programmes are mainly imbalances of curriculum, poor instructors, insufficient training material, lack of motivation in participants and lack of proper learning climate in training institutions. The author during interview with a trainee was told that in-service courses provide little additional learning or knowledge and training is a necessary evil and empty ritual. The lack of imagination, the excessive use of authoritarianism, and de-intellectualisation have made in-service training programmes uninteresting and dull. In-service training programmes do not inspire trainess to take up their role hopefully and identify themselves with the organisational goals. In-service training programmes do not provide the required socio-emotional and inter-personal relationship between the trainees and the trainers due to lack of proper training environment in the institutions. In-service training programmes cannot succeed in a cold, depressive and stress conditions and the police organisation must strive to create a nurturant atmosphere for an effective in-service training. During in-service training programmes "defreezing of attitudes" should be taken up systematically since unlearning is not easy. In-service police training should try to eliminate completely or reduce the prevailing role ambiguity of the police in the context of present socio-political environment. The success of any in-service training programme is dependent on the attitudes of employees and their desire to learn. Trainees have to actively participate in the training process to make in-service training really meaningful to the organisation.

In-service training should aim at assisting the police functionaries to resolve their inner conflicts and assist them in grasping the real life situations in a professional manner. In-service training programmes should aim to "imprint" organisational goals upon the trainees. The training strategy should include the ways and means as to how "imprinting" can be done effectively and what psychological "reinforcers" are to be used. In-service training has to be alive to the individual trainee's differences, environmental factors and organisational's role expectations. In-service training need not be restricted to training institutions, it can be organised at sub-divisional or district headquarters in the shape of films, slides, guest lectures, demonstrations, panel discussions and seminars. Correspondence courses can also form an important part of in-service training. These new vistas of in-service training are yet to be visualised by the organisation. The budgetary, professional and psychological hurdles to in-service training can be removed by dynamic leadership and concerted organisational efforts. In-service training cannot be a substitute for on the job training and work experience. The cadre management committee of the police should ensure that well-considered on the job training programmes are also drawn for various categories of police personnel. Police organisation and top management should provide every encouragement and facility for self development of the police personnel. This can include :

(*a*) Permission for appearing in academic examinations and reimbursement of expenditure on books ;

(*b*) Liberal grant of leave for study ;

(*b*) Encouragement of original work ;

(*d*) Facilities for attending seminars and conferences as part of duty.

REFERENCES

1. Report of the Committee of Police Training (Gore—Chairman) M.H.A., Govt. of India, New Delhi, 1974, pp. 39-68.
2. United Nations, Hand book of Training in the Public Services, quoted by conference on Training—Report of the Proceedings Feb. 24-25, 1969. Sponsored by Training Division, M.H.A. at Indian Institute of Public Administration, New Delhi, pp. 67-68.
3. *Crime in India*, 1976—B.P.R. & D., M.H.A., Govt. of India, 1980, pp. 99.
4. The Civil List of Indian Police Service, issued by the Govt. of India, M.H.A., New Delhi, 1976, p. 79.
5. Report of the Uttar Pradesh Police Commission 1960-61. Allahabad ; Superintendent, Printing and Stationery, U.P., 1962, p. 107.

CHAPTER SEVEN

THE ENVIRONS OF POLICE TRAINING IN INDIA

EFFECTIVE police training can only be the final outcome of a desirable series of inter-actions between the police trainee, the trainer and the training environment which includes the institution, its faculty, its leader and his policies.[1] The concept of training environment is much wider than given above and includes many more things. The "environs" of training are the complex sets of variables involving the trainers, the trainees, campus environment, the physical facilities, training techniques and the inter-relationship between various environmental factors. The environs of training institutions over a period of time exert considerable influence over the individuals who inhabit that environment.[2] "Environs" of police training are those physical and non-physical constituents which facilitate and influence training activity. This training environment becomes the learning climate when viewed through the trainees' eyes. Broadly, environs of training may be divided as under :

Tangible Constituents	**Intangible Constituents**
1. Physical facilities	1. Time constituent duration and season of course
2. Trainers, head of Trg. institution, incentives and facilities to trainers	2. Location of trg. institutions

3. Administrative and supporting staff	3. Institutional sub-culture and Org. norms, value system, discipline, turn-out, punctuality
4. Organisational and Administrative set-up.	4. Psychology of Administrative authorities
5. Trainees—type and level	5. Psychology of sponsoring authorities
6. Trg. techniques and methods	6. Psychology of trainers
7. Planning and supervision of Trg.	7. Psychology of trainees
8. Trg. contents, programmes and objectives	8. Motivation for learning and self-development
9. Financial allocation and expenditure	9. Inter-personal, Inter-group relationships
	10. Organisational climate and health.

The intangible constituents require psychological study and social survey. Therefore, they have been omitted from the present research. The various tangible constituents also are too wide in scope and therefore, only physical facilities and a few other factors have been dealt with in the present study. The physical facilities include parade ground, P.T. ground, firing range, accommodation for trainers and trainees, residential quarters for the staff, library and reading room, class rooms, auditorium, hospital, model police station and other sand models etc. Physical facilities contribute considerably to the rate of absorption by the trainees, whole-hearted concentration on the job of training and better rapport between trainers and trainees. The type and the quantum of these facilities will vary according to the total requirements which will depend upon the location, time, number of courses to be conducted, number of trainees at any time on the campus, strength of the staff and the type and level of training to be imparted in the institution and other socio-economic-cultural factors.

Environs have both direct and indirect impact on learning process and the total personality of the trainees. Social campus atmosphere can be conducive for all round development of trainees. Training facilities and healthy training environment can promote integrated training of the policeman as a "whole-man". Training institutions can help develop "total personality" of the trainees by organising a large number of clubs and associations such as the literary professional and current affairs study circle, cultural and fine-arts association, reporters and journalists club, social service league, recreation club, swimming and boating club, camera club, radio club and the like. Such organisations can help in training the police officers along the lines of the "whole-man" concept. A training institution will not be successful in achieving the training objectives of imparting skills, knowledge, attitudes and behaviour to the trainees unless the training environment and the social dimensions of the trainees are in harmony. The trainees when assembled in a training institution become a group with their built-in closeness of learning as well as living. Trainees develop inter-action between themselves. Police trainees coalesce into an effective group as they share common objectives and develop common tasks and are influenced by the environment of the training institutions. The environment is a live model of organisational standards such as the police trainers' hope will shape their work back in the field. Environment of training institutions provides the setting that keeps on motivating trainees to learn more and improve their performance. Police trainees generally expect consistency in four facets of the training environment :

(*a*) Between a trainer's statement and his behaviour ;

(*b*) Between different trainers in the same programme ;

(*c*) Between training objectives and the physical environment ;

(*d*) Between training objectives and institutional arrangements.

Training environment influences the total personality of the trainees as well as trainers. It builds up a police sub-culture which trainees imbibe and get internalised during the training period. Environment affects working and living conditions of trainees and affects motivation to learn. Environment have both direct and indirect impact on trainees—physical facilities give direct impact while the learning climate provides indirect influence. The power of hearing, seeing and other sensuary powers are indirectly effected by the environment. Trainees get infected from the organisational health of the training institutions and draw various lessons by noticing the administrative standards of the training institutions. The learning climate is ruled by the trainees perception of trainers' behaviour and trust-worthiness.[3] The head of the training institution, the quality of trainers and faculty members and their inter-relationship with trainees produce the learning climate.

In this chapter the researcher has formulated the following hypotheses for test :

1. "The police training institutions in India are in a general state of neglect and more so in respect of physical facilities obtained on their campuses." Report of the Committee on Police Training found the over all picture "very disappointing". Heads of the police training institutions in their symposis have found physical facilities in an unsatisfactory state. The hypothesis has been formulated to find out the present position of physical facilities existing in the training institutions.

2. "Training tools and equipment for police training are out-dated in most of the training institutions of police. Very little innovative efforts have been made to render them functional." The Report of Committee on Police Training found that the most common method of instruction being followed in training institutions was the lecture method supplemented by demonstrations and written or verbal instructions. This method was not achieving the desired results. The hypothesis has been formulated to find out the present position of

utilisation of various instructional methods and aids recommended by the Gore Committee.

3. "The expenditure incurred on police training in various states of India is percentage-wise low in proportion to the total costs of police budgets of the state." The hypothesis has been formulated on the basis of the Report of the Committee on police training which examined total expenditure of 21 states on police and percentage of expenditure incurred on police training for 1969-70 and 1970-71 and found that the expenditure which the states incur on police training is very small. The hypothesis has examined the expenditure of the last ten years to examine the present position.

4. "The police training institutions in India are inadequately staffed for purpose of administration of the training of police force of the country". There is a general belief among police officers that the training institutions have inadequacy of staff. The hypothesis has been formulated to test this general belief.

Physical Facilities

The researcher visited a number of training institutions of the country to have first hand information about the physical facilities available to the training institutions. The physical facilities surveyed in the present study include living accommodation for trainees, instructors, common-room, furniture in class-rooms, training ground for parade, P.T. & games, auditorium, hospital, model police station, traffic point sand model, firing range, availability of separate demonstration squad, adequacy of residential accommodation for trainers. A study of 25 training institutions has been carried out by the researcher through the help of mailed questionnaire. The study found that 60 per cent of the training institutions in the country do not have adequate living accommodation for trainees (for details, see table at page no. 196 and 197). Due to increase in the number of trainees in the last few years, the available living accommodation falls short of the requirements. In P.T.C. 1 and P.T.C. 2, Moradabad, very large batches of Sub-Inspectors were

TABLE 7.1

Showing Physical Facilities Available in Training Institutions

A=Adequate
I=Inadequate

S. No.	Trg. Institution	Living Accomm. Trainees A/I	Instrs. common room avail-able or not	Furni-ture in class rooms A/I	Trg. ground A/I	Acomm. for Lib/R. Room A/I	Hospi-tal avail-able or not	Audi-torium avail-able or not	Model P.S. avail-able or not	Traffic point H. Room avail-able or not	Control Room M. Room avail-able or not	Model Room V.I.P. available or not	
1	2	3	4	5	6	7	8	9	10	11	12	13	14
1.	P.T.C., Dargaon	A	Yes	A	A	A	Yes	No	No	No	No	No	Yes
2.	P.T.C., Dargaon	A	No	I	I	A	No	No	No	No	No	No	No
3.	A.P.T., Dargaon	I	Yes	I	A	I	Yes	No	No	No	No	No	Yes
4.	P.T.C., Anantpur	I	No	I	A	I	Yes	No	Yes	No	No	No	No
5.	P.T.S., Delhi	I	No	A	I	I	No	No	No	No	No	No	No
6.	P.T.C., Junagarh	I	Yes	A	A	A	Yes	No	Yes	No	No	No	Yes
7.	P.T.S., Baroda	I	Yes	A	A	I	Yes	No	Yes	No	No	No	Yes
8.	P.T.C., Madhuban	I	No	I	A	A	No	No	No	No	No	No	No
9.	P.T.C., Mysore	I	Yes	A	A	I	No	Yes	Yes	No	No	No	No

1	2	3	4	5	6	7	8	9	10	11	12	13	14
10.	P.T.C., Nasik	I	Yes	A	A	A	Yes	No	Yes	Yes	No	No	No
11.	R.P.T.S., Akola	I	No	A	I	I	No	No	Yes	No	No	No	No
12.	M.P.T.C., Pangei	A	Yes	I	A	A	No	No	No	Yes	No	No	Yes
13.	P.T.S., Nagaland	A	No	A	A	A	Yes	Yes	No	No	No	No	Yes
14.	N.A.P.T.C., Nagaland	A	No	A	A	A	Yes	No	No	No	No	No	Yes
15.	P.T.C., Angul	I	No	A	A	I	Yes	Yes	Yes	No	No	No	Yes
16.	P.T.S., Nayagarh	I	No	A	I	I	No	No	No	No	No	No	Yes
17.	P.T.C., Phillaur	A	Yes	A	A	A	Yes	No	Yes	No	No	No	Yes
18.	R.P.A., Jaipur	A	Yes	A	A	A	Yes	No	Yes	No	No	No	No
19.	P.T.C., Madras	A	Yes	A	A	A	Yes	No	No	No	No	No	No
20.	P.T.C., I, Moradabad	I	Yes	A	A	I	Yes	Yes	No	No	No	No	No
21.	P.T.C,, Moradabad	A	Yes	A	A	I	Yes	No	No	No	No	No	Yes
22.	P.T.C., Barrackpore	I	No	A	A	I	Yes	Yes	No	No	No	No	No
23.	C.T.C., II C.R.P.F., Avadi	I	No	I	A	I	Yes	No	No	No	No	No	No
24.	I.S.A., Mt. Abu	I	No	A	I	I	Yes	No	No	No	No	No	No
25.	S.V.P., N.P.A, Hyderabad	A	Yes	A	I	A	Yes	Yes	Yes	No	Yes	No	No

undergoing training at the time when the researcher visited the colleges. Their living accommodation was found unsatisfactory. Insufficient living accommodation badly affects training as trainees are unable to study at leisure time in congested living conditions. On interview with trainees, it was learnt that many trainees go out to parks and other near about places where they could get some peaceful and quiet atmosphere for study. One trainee S.I. said, "Probably prisoners in open jails live better than we are living here". Some police trainees realised the difficulties of the training staff and said "Our living conditions are preparing us for the difficult and challenging life ahead." Regarding availability of training grounds, the study found that 80 per cent institutions have required ground and only 20 per cent institutions reported inadequacy of parade and P.T. grounds. It was discovered that some 52 per cent of the training institutions had the availability of separate instructors' room while 48 per cent institutions suffered from non-availability of the facility. Regarding availability of desks and chairs in the class-rooms for trainees, 76 per cent institutions reported availability and 24 per cent reported inadequacy. 52 per cent of the training institutions reported non-availability of required accommodation for library and reading room. The study indicated that 76 per cent of the training-institutions have no auditorium to conduct joint sittings of all trainees. Auditoriums can be used for cultural entertainment programmes of trainees as well as for inaugural and closing sessions of seminars and other training functions. About residential accommodation of the members of faculty, the study has found that 64 per cent training institutions have not been able to provide residential accommodation to the members of the instructional staff. Non-availability of residential accommodation is a great hurdle in getting suitable persons on the staff. Many of the training institutions have reported non-availability of residential accommodation for their staff and a clear picture emerges if table given at p. no. 199 is seen. 18 institutions were found to have hospitals and only seven institutions did not have their own hospitals. Thus, 72 per cent training institutions have hospital facilities available. 60 per cent of the police training institutions were

TABLE 7.2

Showing Shortage of Rankwise Residential Accommodation for Police Training Faculty

S.No.	Trg. Institution	S.P.	DyS.P.	No	Insp.	SI/ASI	Hd.Ct.	Ct.	Min & Others	Total	Remarks
1	2	3	4	5	6	7	8	9	10	11	12
1.	P.T.C., Anantpur	1	2	—	3	7	—	—	1	14	
2.	P.T.C., Dargaon	—	—	—	—	25% of the subordinate ranks i.e. SI downwards					
3.	A.P.T.C., Dargaon	—	—	—	—	—	3	—	3	6	
4.	P.T.C., Junagarh	1	—	—	16	27	—	42	8	94	
5.	P.T.C., Madhuban	—	—	—	1	33	62	74	81	251	
6.	P.T.C., Mysore	—	—	1	—	4	6	—	7	18	
7.	P.T.C., Trivandrum	—	1	—	2	3	16	—	—	22	
8.	P.T.C., Nasik	—	3	—	4	17	—	—	8	32	
9.	R.P.T.S., Akola	—	1	—	8	4	—	14	56	83	
10.	M.P.T.C., Pangei	1	1	—	—	—	5	32	—	39	
11.	P.T.C. Angul	1	4	—	11	4	45	7	76	148	
12.	P.T.C., Phillaur	—	2	1	15	29	—	75	124	246	

1	2	3	4	5	6	7	8	9	10	11	12
13.	P.T.C., Madras	1	—	—	4	—	—	—	—	5	
14.	P.T.C., II Moradabad	1	14	—	2	—	23	—	42	82	
15.	P.T.C., Barrackpore	—	—	—	4	27	32	43	2	108	
16.	P.T.C., Delhi	—	—	—	1	9	27	4	54	95	
17.	P.T.C., 1 Barwaha (C.R.P.P.)	—	—	—	7	18	66	151	48	290	
18.	C.T.C., II C.R.P.F. Avadi	—	—	—	50% of the actual posted strength						
19.	P:T.S., Rajnandgaon	—	2	—	10	5	33	40	25	115	
20.	P.T.C., II C.R.P.F. Avadi	—	—	—	—	—	—	7	21	28	

found not to have model police station where trainees can be shown police station records and could be given training in police station work. For teaching trainees about police station, availability of model police station is necessary. 92 per cent of the training institutions do not have model control rooms and traffic point sand models. Pistol, Musketry, Rifle firing is an important part of training. A separate firing range was required for carrying out firing practice with short and long range weapons. 56 per cent of the institutions did not have attached firing range and have to depend on army or other authorities for utilising the range.

The physical facilities in training institutions according to this study can be evaluated as "inadequate". During the last ten years, number of trainees has increased while the physical facilities could not be increased in the same proportion. The police training institutions do not have required number of class-rooms and in door classes and are generally taken under the shades of trees in open. The sample study of 25 training institutions gives a picture of this inadequacy of physical facilities. The present study points out that no training institution has model for crowd control at V.I.P. meeting place and 92 per cent institutions not having model control rooms and traffic point models for imparting training. Training institutions do not have regular class-room facilities for conducting indoor training. The living facilities for the trainees are woefully inadequate in a majority of training institutions. During the visit of the researcher to the training centres, he found some trainees accommodated in tents, some were in Nissen huts with no ceiling whatsoever to protect them from the rains and sweltering heat of the summer. In many training centres recruit constables were required to sleep on the floor provided with barely 3′ × 6′ = 18 sq. ft. of space. Glaring inadequacies were found even in other essentials like toilets, dinning-rooms, messes and bath rooms. Even supply of adequate water was reported to be a problem in some training institutions. The maintenance of existing buildings in many institutions left much room for improvement. About 60 per cent of the institutions have been accommodated in an ad hoc basis in buildings constructed for altogether different purposes. The working group of Annual Conference of the central training institutions in April, 1977 has suggested certain minimum physical facilities for training institutions.[4] If the yardstick laid down in the monograph is applied to police training institutions, it becomes clear that physical facilities are inadequate in more than 70 per cent of the police training institutions of the country. The hypothesis of the present study that the police training institutions in India are in a general state of neglect and more so in respect of physical facilities obtained on their campuses stands proved and validated as given vividly in table at p. no. 203 and diagram No. 4 given at page number 203A.

The location of 64 per cent of the training institutions surveyed was found unsuitable. In places like Barwaha, Mount Abu, Junagarh, Phillaur, Rajnandgaon, Hayagarh police officers particularly at higher levels are not interested due to lack of proper educational facilities for their children. Police training colleges should be located in or near suitable academic centres so that they are able to draw upon the teaching talent available in universities and colleges.[5]

Training Techniques and Methods

A pilot study of 20 training institutions was carried out for the present study with the help of a questionnaire. The questionnaire listed some 26 training techniques and methods and the tabulated percentage depicting use of techniques and methods is presented in diagram No. 5 given on page No. 203A and in the table below.

Table given above indicates that lecture method, demonstration method, exercise (drill) and use of black-boards, sand models and graphs are used in all the 20 training institutions surveyed. These methods, however, are not outdated and continue to be very popular but useful. The newly suggested methods require innovative skills of trainers and availability of equipment/structured training material and are being used only in a few training institutions.

The effective use of suitable training techniques for a training programme generally depends on a number of factors, such as, training objectives and the expectations of the training

TABLE 7.3
Showing Physical Facilities Available in 25 Training Institutions

S. No.	Item	No. of institutions having facilities	No. of institutions having no facilities	Percentage of institutions having no facilities
1	2	3	4	5
1.	Adequate living accommodation	10	15	60
2.	Instructors' common-room	13	12	48
3.	Furniture in class-rooms	19	6	24
4.	Trg. ground for P.T./Prade/Sports	20	5	20
5.	Adequate accommodation for Lib. & Reading-room	12	13	52
6.	Auditorium	6	19	76
7.	Hospital	18	7	28
8.	Model Police Station	10	15	60
9.	Model Control Room	1	24	96
10.	Traffic point S. Model	—	25	100
11.	V.I.P. Meeting/Crowd Control Send Model	—	25	100
12.	Firing Range	11	14	56
13.	Demonstration squad	5	20	80
14.	Adequacy of Instructional staff	7	18	72
15.	Adequacy of residential accommodation for Instructional staff	9	16	64

TABLE 7.4

S. No.	Training techniques/methods	Percentage
1	2	3
1.	Lecture method	100
2.	Demonstrations	100
3.	Practical Trg./Practice/Exercise (drill)	100
4.	Use of Black-boards, Plannel Boards, Sand Model and Graphs	100
5.	Observation method or Field Trips	55
6.	Group discussion	50
7.	Case study	35
8.	Role Playing	25
9.	T Group sensitivity	15
10.	Syndicate method	25
11.	In-basket method	30
12.	Incident method	25
13.	Projects/Problems	30
14.	Panel discussions	25
15.	Seminar method	25
16.	Workshops	20
17.	Brain-storming	15
18.	Management Games	35
19.	Tutorials/Guide system	50
20.	Individual preparation of papers on assigned problems	50
21.	Conference/Symposium	15
22.	Use of close-circuit TV and Video-Tape	15
23.	Use of Training films	50
24.	Use of film strips, slides & other audio-visual aids	45
25.	Use of Tape-recorders	50
26.	Other techniques/methods like :	
	(*a*) Buzz session	10
	(*b*) Micro-lecture	10
	(*c*) Delphi method	10

institutions, expectations of the trainees sponsoring department, the expectations of the participating trainees, the availability of time and resources, the skill and capacity of the police trainers, the level and experience of the participants and police, the overall training environment of police training and the institution's interest and motivation of the police trainer in his training assignment. In choosing training methodologies, the police trainers have to keep into consideration the needs of the target training group including its characteristics sq., size, age, experience, background, expectations and level of motivation. The three-fold process of (*a*) adoptation, (*b*) adaptation and (*c*) rejection is an important responsibility of a trainer in choosing training methodologies. Political framework, economic framework, social framework, management concepts and techniques are some of the subjects on which adequate material for teaching purpose was not easily available. Even case studies were not available for use by trainers. National Police Academy, Hyderabad and Internal Security Academy, Mount Abu had prepared some case studies on police subjects and problems relating to internal security. Police Training College, Trivandrum had also brought out an anthrology of short cases involving dilemmas faced by the police and case materials for developing an appropriate police attitude in public relation at the cutting edge level.[6] Training material in India was quite inadequate. Training materials in scientific investigations, interrogation, law and order situations, political agitations need to be prepared. Trainers face problems without adequate available background material for training. Though various training techniques and methods are in vogue in varying degrees in police training colleges, extensive and effective use of these methods was not being done mainly due to the disinterest of the trainers. Even many police trainers do not know these training techniques and methods which are generally popular in the West.[7] Most of the trainers in police training institutions particularly at Inspector and below levels were found not very conversant with the various modern training techniques and, therefore, very generally adopt age-old traditional methods of lecture with use of board and chalk. Police training colleges of some of the bigger states had gradually started spending funds for purchasing training aids like tape-recorders, training films and 16 mm projectors out of the modernisation grants. Even close-circuit television and video-tape have been purchased by the N.P.A. Generally, overhead projectors, training film and other expensive training aids were seen lying unutilised in several police training colleges and the trainers were not making use of these equipments. Syndicate method has been a very popular method for advanced training used at S.V.P., N.P.A., Hyderabad and I.S.A, Mt. Abu. Seminar method is also a useful training method for senior officers.

The research survey carried out by the researcher to know whether latest techniques and methods of training were not being used in police training institutions in India and given in the tabulated form below :

TABLE 7.5

S. No.	Respondents	Agree	Partly agree	Disagree	Total
1	2	3	4	5	6
1.	Is.G.P./D.Is.G.P.	9	8	3	20
2.	Ss.P.	23	14	3	40
3.	Dy. Ss.P.	21	14	5	40
4.	Inspectors	34	5	1	40
5.	Sub-Insps.	16	6	8	30
6.	Constabulary	25	22	3	50
	Total	128	69	23	220
	Percentage	58.18	31.36	10.45	—

The analysis of the data indicates that 58.18 per cent agreed to the statement and 31.36 per cent partly agreed to the statement. This validates the hypothesis of the researcher that latest training tools and equipments for police training are not being fully used in police training institutions and very little innovative efforts have gone to render them functional. There are a number of reasons for this state of affairs. Firstly, many police trainers in India were not conversant with their proper use. Secondly, as most of the police trainers were not interested in staying in training institutions, they did not exert themselves and exhibit required interest. Thirdly, there was no separate training for police trainers in the use of training techniques. Fourthly, due to large number of trainees and shortage of instructional staff, police trainers were over-worked and did not get proper time to prepare their lessons with the help of latest training techniques. Fifthly, except in case of I.P.S. officers and Dy. Ss.P., the level of trainees was so low that they could not participate actively in class-room discussions. Training Institutions did not have adequate supporting staff for use of over-head projectors and 16 mm projectors. Training films having Western orientation and background with difficult pronunciation were not useful for trainees of the level of Inspectors and below. The general environment of the training institutions was also not conducive for the use of latest training techniques. Lastly, so far suitable training material for training, utilising these techniques had not been made available and innovations were not expected from trainers who were themselves not highly educated. Even there was no encouragement from Principals and other senior officers to other trainers for utilising these training techniques and aids.[6] The study found that "one training institution had three overhead projectors but two were out of working order and the third was received three months back but not yet unpacked". Thus, it can be concluded that due to various organisational and motivational factors, very little innovative efforts have been put to use these latest training techniques. Thus the hypothesis stands only partly proved and partly disproved.

Financial Expenditure

The Study postulates a hypothesis that the expenditure incurred on police training in India is rather low and as compared to the total costs of police budget of the states, it is disproportionate. In its publication, 'Training in the Public Service', the United

Nations have recommended that in service of 30 years, all the civil servants must get three years of training including basic training and have also recommended one per cent of the total wage bill as optimum expenditure on training. This yardstick is logical because every employee is to spend one tenth of his service period on training, taking an overall view every year, ten per cent of the total number of employees would be undertraining. Because, approximately one trainer is required for ten trainees, the total number of trainers required will be one tenth of ten per cent, that is one per cent of the total number of employees will be required for training. Thus, one per cent of the total expenditure of training enterprise can be considered as yard-stick for the present study. In some of the more advanced countries also a notional one per cent of the wage bill is considered as a reasonable figure to be expended for training.[9] The first conference on training sponsored by the Training Division in 1969 recommended : earmarking of one per cent of the wage bill for training purposes in various organisations. This is accepted as an ideal and sufficient provision for training in the budget of the various government organisations on this basis.[10] Second Conference of state training institutions held in January, 1973 at Mysore recommended that as a matter of policy, the Government should provide one per cent of the personnel budget for training.[11] State-wise expenditure incurred on police training has been tabulated year-wise and given in percentage form at page no. 209. This table indicates that during 1977-78, out of 18 states, nine states spent less than optimal expenditure. It can be said that fifty per cent states have spent more than required one per cent. During 1978-79, 50 per cent states have spent more than optimal expenditure. Thus, it is proved that fifty per cent of the institutions have spent more than one per cent on training. A review of expenditure on training over a decade shows that eight states have spent less than one per cent continuously. The hypothesis that the expenditure incurred on training is inadequate in most of the states is partly proved since during 1980-81, about fifty per cent of the states spent more than the standard yardstick. Thus, the hypothesis that the expenditure

TABLE 7.6

Showing Percentage of Police Training Expenditure in Police Budget of States

(figures are given in percentage)

S. No.	State/U.T.	1971-72	1972-73	1973-74	1974-75	1975-76
1	2	3	4	5	6	7
1.	Andhra Pradesh	0.47	0.52	0.64	0.48	0.38
2.	Assam	0.86	0.74	1.23	3.03	1.30
3.	Bihar	0.66	0.67	0.56	0.62	0.54
4.	Gujarat	1.23	1.32	1.25	1.24	1.18
5.	Haryana	—	—	—	—	0.95
6.	Jammu & Kashmir	0.98	2.23	2.01	1.61	1.85
7.	Karnataka	0.56	0.58	0.60	0.55	0.72
8.	Kerala	0.88	0.73	0.65	0.83	0.92
9.	Madhya Pradesh	0.79	0.73	0.74	0.71	0.62
10.	Maharashtra	0.54	0.56	0.54	0.54	0.53

1	2	3	4	5	6	7
11.	Orissa	0.89	0.95	1.02	0.89	0.81
12.	Punjab	1.64	1.38	2.49	2.57	2.21
13.	Tamil Nadu	0.38	0.94	0.74	0.69	1.07
14.	Tripura	—	—	—	1.03	1.54
15.	Uttar Pradesh	0.79	0.70	0.63	0.83	0.78
16.	Goa	—	0.80	0.64	0.67	0.91
17.	A. & N. Islands	—	—	—	—	—
18.	Delhi	—	—	—	—	—

(figures are given in percentage)

S. No.	State/U.T.	1976-77	1977-78	1978-79	1979-80	1980-81
		8	9	10	11	12
1.	Andhra Pradesh	0.35	0.36	0.37	0.39	0.42
2.	Assam	1.48	1.48	1.56	1.56	1.75
3.	Bihar	0.53	0.34	0.76	0.74	0.66
4.	Gujarat	1.26	1.38	1.48	1.55	1.27
5.	Haryana	0.94	1.68	2.10	2.30	2.04
6.	Jammu & Kashmir	1.64	1.70	1.72	1.79	1.42
7.	Karnataka	0.61	0.67	0.75	0.75	0.70
8.	Kerala	0.78	0.78	0.76	1.15	1.11
9.	Madhya Pradesh	0.64	0.66	0.69	0.70	0.62
10.	Maharashtra	0.63	0.63	0.59	0.61	0.56

		8	9	10	11	12
11.	Orissa	0.96	1.13	1.09	1.05	1.18
12.	Punjab	2.18	2.73	2.63	2.54	2.28
13.	Tamil Nadu	0.68	0.66	0.84	0.87	0.87
14.	Tripura	1.72	1.48	1.18	1.24	0.43
15.	Uttar Pradesh	1.35	1.15	1.02	1.08	0.76
16.	Goa	0.95	0.84	0.76	0.88	—
17.	A. & N. Islands	—	0.23	0.13	0.17	0.23
18.	Delhi	4.4	4.08	3.80	3.55	3.75

incurred on police training in various states of India is percentage-wise low in proportion to the total costs of police budgets of the states is partly proved.

TABLE 7.7

Showing Response of Police Officers that the Expenditure Incurred on Police training Institutions in India is very low as Compared to total Police Budget

Respondents	Agree	Partly agree	Disagree	Total
1	2	3	4	5
Is.G.P./D.Is.G.P.	15	3	2	20
Ss. P.	23	13	5	40
Dy. Ss.P.	32	5	3	40
Inspectors	37	3	—	40
Sub-Inspectors	22	5	3	30
Constabulary	30	16	4	50
Total	158	45	17	220
Percentage	71.81	20.45	7.72	—

The data presented above indicate that 71.81 per cent of the respondents agreed to the statement. The analysis of the percentage of expenditure of states shows that the common belief shared by the serving officers is partly true. Opinions were also obtained on the statement that police training in India is not getting required attention and financial support from the state governments. The tabulated data are presented below :

The percentage of opinion survey indicates that 53.63 per cent agreed to the view while 34.09 per cent partly agreed. Proposals for sanction of research cells in training institutions, sanction of civil posts of social scientists and management

TABLE 7.8

Police Training in India is not getting the Required Attention and Financial Support from the State Governments

Respondents	Agree	Partly agree	Somewhat disagree	Total disagree	Total
1	2	3	4	5	6
Is.G.P./D.Is.G.P.	11	5	2	2	20
Ss.P.	20	14	3	3	40
Dy. Ss. P.	23	14	2	1	40
Inspectors	23	13	3	1	40
S.Is.	19	5	2	4	30
Constabulary	22	24	—	4	50
Total	118	75	12	15	220
Percentage	53.63	34.09	5.45	6.18	—

specialists, increase in authorisation of transport, funds for construction of quarters for the staff are some of the common items which have been pending with 80 per cent of the state governments for consideration. The Centre has asked state governments to run crash courses for officers and ranks as also develop additional refresher courses for various ranks.[12] Research survey of 25 institutions by the present study shows that 72 per cent of the training institutions have inadequate staff. There were many factors for inadequacy of staff. In ninety per cent cases, the training institutions were started on ad hoc basis and later economy cuts were exercised when sanctions for training institutions were conveyed by the Government. Inadequacy of staff were also felt when the capacity of the courses were increased at later stages without proportionate increase in staff. The trainees in refresher courses are not motivated and this causes frustration to the trainer to enumerating such dificiencies which are beyond his

TABLE 7.9

Showing Staffing Pattern—Trainee Trainer Ratio and Percentage of Budget

S. No.	State	P.T.S. Total Staff	Outdoor	Indoor	Percentage
1	2	3	4	5	6
1.	Andhra Pradesh	31	1:25	1:25	0.42
2.	Assam	182	1:40	1:40	1.75
3.	Bihar	83	NA	NA	0.66
4.	Gujarat	89	1:25	1:40	1.27
5.	Haryana	420	1:12	1:35	2.04
6.	Jammu & Kashmir	NA	NA	NA	1.42
7.	Karnataka	113	1:25	1:20	0.70
8.	Kerala	90	1:18	1:33	1.11
9.	Madhya Pradesh	NA	1:8	1:40	0.62
10.	Maharashtra	138	1:20	1.30	0.56
11.	Orissa	322	1:20	1:37	1.18
12.	Punjab	289	1:25	1:40	2.28

1	2	3	4	5	6
13.	Tamil Nadu	15	1:25	1:25	0.87
14.	Tripura	NA	NA	NA	0.43
15.	Uttar Pradesh	120	1:20	1:40	0.76
16.	Goa	NA	NA	NA	NA
17.	A. & N. Islands	NA	NA	NA	0.23
18.	Delhi	157	1:25	1:30	3.75

The figures given above indicate that states where the percentage of expenditure is more than one per cent, the staff is reasonably adequate. Some interesting co-relation could be worked out if total strength of the trainers of the state is made available and compared with percentage of expenditure. This aspect is beyond the scope of the present research and can be taken up by some other researcher in future.

control. These deficiencies may be real or imaginary. It ultimately results in transferance of guilt of trainers to the inadequacy of the trainers. 70 per cent of the trainers posted in training institutions have no specialised training in the instructional job.

Educational background of trainers of one training school of Rajasthan showed that 10 per cent instructors teaching law were L.LB. degree holders; 10 per cent were graduates, 12 per cent were middle pass and 68 per cent were matriculates. In India, no minimum training requirements or educational qualifications have been laid down for police instructors. There were no attractive monetary incentives for instructors. Many training institutions did not provide rent free accommodation to instructors in both state and central govt. training institutions. A sample study of the special pays being presently given to the instructional faculty in various police training institutions indicates a wide variance from state to state (Table at p. no. 218). The monetary incentives show again some variance in various states. Some states are giving rent-free accommodation to the instructors of all ranks while others do not. In 75 per cent of the training institutions all the energy of police trainers and administrators goes into current operational and administrators goes into current operational and maintenance of training activity. The Principal stated that he can not get additional financing and staff for the planning, research and innovations that institutional development calls for. The consensus among Principals was that "the D.I.G. to whom they have to report does not approve innovation and that they are powerless to act".[13]

State-wise ratio of trainer to trainees has also been worked out by the researcher and is given at page no. 220.

The yard-stick for adequacy or inadequacy has been laid down by the Madhya Pradesh Police Commission 1965-66 when it recommended that there should not be more than 15 trainees for outdoor classes and not more than 30 in indoor classes under one instructor and in sanctioning the staff we recommend this yard-stick be adopted.[14]

TABLE 7.10

Showing Rates of Special Pay to Training Faculty

S. No.	Trg. Institution	Principal	V. Principal	Chief Instr.	Dy. S.P. Instr.	Drill Instr.	Insptr.	S.I.	H.C. Instr.
1	2	3	4	5	6	7	8	9	10
1.	P.T.C., Dargaon	200	100	100	50	50	—	30	20
2.	P.T.C., Mysore	200	—	—	—	25	25	10	5
3.	P.T.C., Agartala	200	75	—	—	—	—	25	—
4.	P.T.C., Delhi	—	75	75	—	50	50	40	15
5.	P.T.C., Anantapur	150	150	—	—	25	25	10	5
6.	R.P.A., Jaipur	150	—	—	—	—	—	—	—
7.	A.T.C., Sitapur	100	—	—	75	—	—	—	—
8.	P.T.C., Sagar	*	75	—	—	—	60	50	15
9.	B.S.F., Tekanpur	*	—	—	—	—	40	38	25
10.	P.T.C., Hazaribagh	*	150	—	75	—	50	40	15
11.	P.T.C., Madhuban	*	100	100	100	40	40	30	30

1	2	3	4	5	6	7	8	9	10
12.	P.T.C., Nasik	150	75	—	65	50	50	30	10
13.	P.T.C., Angul	100	75	75	75	50	30	20	15
14.	P.T.C., Barrackpore	*	150	75	75	50	40	25	7
15.	P.T.C., Junagarh	No special pay at all							
16.	C.R.P.F., Neemuch	—	—	—	75	—	40	30	20
17.	P.T.C., Moradabad	*	150	—	50	40	40	25	10
18.	P.T.C., Phillaur	*	50	—	50	40	40	30	30

* D.I.G.P.

TABLE 7.11

Showing Statewise Ratio of Trainees to Trainer

S. No.	State		Outdoor	Indoor
1	2		3	4
1.	Andhra Pradesh		1:25	1:25
2.	Assam		1:40	1:40
3.	Delhi		1:25	1:30
4.	Gujarat	P.T.C.	1:20	1:30
		R.T.C.	1:25	1:40
5.	Haryana		1:12	1:35
6.	Kerala		1:18	1:33
7.	Karnataka		1:25	1:20
8.	Maharashtra	P.T.C.	1:20	NA
		P.T.S.	1:20	1:30
9.	Madhya Pradesh		1:18	1:40
10.	Manipur		1:12	1:30
11.	Nagaland		1:6	1:30
12.	Orissa		1:20	1:37
13.	Punjab		1:20	1:40
14.	Tamil Nadu		1:25	1:25
15.	Uttar Pradesh	P.T.	1:40	1:40
		I. T.	1:20	1:40
16.	West Bengal		1:15	1:25

The Table shows that 75 per cent of the institutions have inadequate outdoor staff as the ratio of trainer to trainees is more than one to fifteen. 50 per cent of the training institutions have one to thirty ratio for indoor training. Thus, the overall view which emerges is that over-all staff in training institutions is inadequate. The survey study of 25 institutions shows that 72 per cent of the training institutions are having inadequate staff. The researcher has also collected opinions of serving officers regarding the adequacy of staff. The responses of the respondents are tabulated and given below :

TABLE 7.12

Showing Opinions that most of the Training Institutions in India are having Staff for Administration of Training which is...

S. No.	Respondents	Most Inadequate	Somewhat Inadequate	Adequate	Surplus to the requirements	Total
1	2	3	4	5	6	7
1.	Is.G.P./D.Is.G.P.	9	7	4	—	20
2.	Ss. P.	5	31	4	—	40
3.	Dy. Ss. P.	15	17	8	—	40
4.	Inspectors	13	19	6	2	40
5.	Sub-Insps.	9	8	9	4	30
6.	Constabulary	10	18	21	1	50
	Total	61	100	52	7	220
	Percentage	27.72	45.45	23.63	3.18	—

The opinion study indicates that 27.72 per cent of the respondents felt that the staff in training institutions was most inadequate while 45.45 per cent held that staff is somewhat inadequate. The survey of police training institutions of India reveals that out of 25 training institutions, 20 do not have any demonstration squads. Thus, 80 per cent of the institutions do not have demonstration squads which are necessary for arranging various demonstrations. Riot control demonstration, role play, route lining, guard of honour etc. are some of the aspects of training which require separate squads/staff for proper conduct of training. The present study also compiled the views of the officers on that statement that police trainers in most of the training institutions are not qualified, motivated and competent to teach. The reply of the respondents is given below in the tabulated form :

TABLE 7.13

Showing that Police Trainers in most of the Training Institutions in India are not Qualified, Motivated and Competent to Train/Teach

Respondents	Agree	Partly agree	Disagree	Total
1	2	3	4	5
Is.G.P./D.Is.G.P.	7	11	2	20
Ss. P.	19	18	3	40
Dy. Ss. P.	20	17	3	40
Inspectors	23	13	4	40
Sub-Insps.	13	7	10	30
Constabulary	19	21	10	50
Total	101	87	32	220
Percentage	45.90	39.54	14.54	—

The present study shows that 45.90 per cent of the police officers agreed to the view and 39.54 per cent partly agreed to the view. A number of vacancies remain unfilled in training institutions for long periods. Police officers posted to training institutions were generally unwanted elsewhere. Police training institutions are the dumping grounds for unwanted, inconvenient, disgruntled and undesirable elements of the organisation.[15] The training institutions got many instructions to improve training to face various types of situations from the Centre, the Prime Minister and others but normally good trainers are not available at P.T.Cs. to carry out these responsibilities.[16] One D.I.G. held that Is.G.P. should take more interest as they are at their own level, can do a great deal in matters of postings of staff to training institutions. In a few cases of P.T.Cs., the researcher visited, he found that a large percentage of officers posted there were not happy. Selection of the staff for P.T.Cs. often continues to be done on considerations other than merit and suitability.[17] It is held that in many instances officers of the rank of Ss.P. do not suggest proper names of officers to fit for P.T.Cs. Even Ss.P. are equally responsible as they are very reluctant to go themselves to P.T.Cs. The researcher has reached the conclusion that a vicious circle has gradually been built up and it is the responsibility of all ranks to see that good officers get posted to the P.T.Cs. The study has revealed that in Kerala, option is normally taken before a person is posted to a training institution and, as such, it is very difficult to get proper persons as they generally do not give their willingness for posting to training institutions. A number of training institutions have to manage with more than 20 per cent vacancies in the staff. Officers posted to training institutions proceed on leave or do not join as early as they can. Thus, the hypothesis that the police training institutions in India are inadequately staffed for the administration of police training of the country is proved.

Police Trainees

Police trainees who are detailed for refresher and other in-service courses are generally very much reluctant to attend such courses, even in the case of senior officers because they find training redundant. An impression has gained over the years in police ranks that only inconvenient, easily dispensable and indisciplined officers are sent for training.[18] Possibility of a transfer from place of posting and inadequate allowances by many states constitute two major causes of reluctance on the part of the officers to go out on training.[19]

Power for Nominating Officers for Police Training within the Country

Analysis of data collected by the present study reveals that some of the state Is.G.P. moved their state government to delegate powers to nominate officers for training within the country. The position of the states is as under :

TABLE 7.14
Showing Powers of Is.G.P. of States for Nominating Officers for Training

S. No.	State	Whether power delegated	To what extent and remarks
1	2	3	4
1.	Andhra Pradesh	Yes	Upto 30 days
2.	Assam	No information	—
3.	Arunachal Pradesh	Yes	No limits
4.	Bihar	Delegation refused	
5.	Gujarat	Under consideration	
6.	Haryana	Delegation refused	
7.	Maharashtra	Yes	15 days
8.	Kerala	Under consideration	
9.	Karnataka	Yes Not for Offrs.	Only for N.G.Os. upto 12 days
10.	Maghalaya	Yes	Only for N.G.Os.
11.	Manipur	Yes	for N.G.Os. upto 12 months
12.	Sikkim	Yes	No limit
13.	Madhya Pradesh	Under consideration	
14.	Rajasthan	Yes	30 days
15.	Jammu and Kashmir	Yes	90 days
16.	Himachal Pradesh	Yes	80 days

Many states are not able to send their trainees for various courses because the nomination power does not lie with the respective Inspectors-General of Police and State Government takes time in clearing the proposals.

Categories of Trainers and Their Duties

Training in police organisations is concerned with the acquisition or development of those skills, techniques, knowledges, attitudes and experiences which enable an individual to make his most effective contribution to the community as a law-enforcing officer. Those who are entrusted with the task of training others, are generally called "instructors" or trainers. Trainers can be of any rank but for purpose of broad classification, police trainers can be divided into five categories :

(*a*) Head of training institutions.

(*b*) Trainers of gazetted rank.

(*c*) Trainers of subordinate rank.

(*d*) Trainers of A.S.I. and below ranks.

(*e*) Trainers who are civilians and on deputation from other fields.

By analysing the major duties and responsibilities of trainers in police training institutions, it has been found that the main duties of police trainers are as under :

(*a*) Teach training classes as scheduled in weekly training programmes.

(*b*) Evaluate performance of trainees.

(*c*) Keep training records on trainees trained.

(*d*) Develop training material, including overhead transparencies, flip charts and training manuals.

(*e*) Develop training objectives and programmes as directed by the senior training officers and heads of the institutions.

(*f*) Assist in the evaluation of current training programmes.

(*g*) Act as guides to trainees in developing social qualities.

(*h*) Handle other projects as assigned by the senior training officers.

(*i*) Motivate the trainees to learn. The selection and development of a competent instructional staff is a major responsibility of the heads of the police training institutions.

(*j*) Act as facilitative trainers whose role is of coaching supporting, monitoring and preparing the learning environment for effective adult learning.

Training Directors and heads of the police training institutions have the following main duties and responsibilities as a training officer :

(*a*) Enlist support from all concerned and particularly from the chief of the organisation.

(*b*) Develop, in conjunction with top management, a training policy for the organisation.

(*c*) Identify training needs of the organisation.

(*d*) Evaluate training courses periodically.

(*e*) Develop and apply methods for checking the effectiveness of the training programmes.

(*f*) Design training programmes.

(*g*) Select trainers and other staff for the training purpose.

(*h*) Make training material available.

(*i*) Procure training aids, equipment and other requirements.

(*j*) Administer training by carrying out duties of planning, organising, staffing, directing, coordinating, reporting and budgeting of training.

(*k*) Administer the training institutions and make physical facilities available to the trainees and trainers.

(*l*) Act as advisers to the organisation on training matters.

General Problems of Trainers

Problems of different categories of trainers are somewhat common though there are certain specific problems with each category of trainers. In India, most of the state police training colleges which cater for the training of Deputy Superintendents of Police, inspectors, sub-inspectors and head constables, heads of the institutions are of the rank of Deputy Inspector-General of Police or Superintendents of Police. State police training schools which mainly cater for training of constables are headed by officers of the rank of Superintendent of Police and in few cases by Deputy Superintendents of Police. The problems of heads of the police training colleges and schools are generally common to all the states. As trainers, these heads of the police training institutions have four main functions of planning, organising, leading and controlling. The author has carried out detailed research on the various problem of trainers of police training institutions in India. Some of the main problems of trainers identified by the author are enumerated below :

(*a*) *Inadequate staff and additional work-load* : The author after a survey of 25 police training institutions of the country, has found that in most of the training institutions, sanctioned staff is never hundred percent posted and there are large number of vacancies in various ranks of trainers. To cope with the training requirements, most of the trainers get additional work-load which at times does not get proper attention.

(*b*) *Social stigma for posting to training institutions* : The training institutions are generally considered dumping ground for posting of unwanted, inconvenient and disgruntled police officers and gradually posting to a training institution carries a social stigma. Thus, even willing and competent trainers do not get due social recognition in the organisation.

(*c*) *Paucity of books and training material* : A survey of available books and training material indicates that for training of constables, head constables and subordinate officers, trainers face the problem of paucity of books and training material. Particularly in regional languages, adequate training material is not available.

(*d*) *Lack of training in the art of instruction* : Eightyfive percent to ninetyfive percent of the trainers posted in training institutions are themselves not trained in the art of instructions. They are not trained in the use of various instructional methods and aids. Training of trainers course for Dy.S.P. and Superintendents of Police have been recently started by the S.V.P. National Police Academy, Hyderabad, but it has not yet made any impact in the training institutions. Most of the trainers in various training institutions are not trained as trainers.

(*e*) *Lack of physical facilities* : Training institutions are not getting adequate funds and there is shortage of living accommodation in many training institutions for the trainers.

(*f*) *Lack of incentives to trainers* : Adequate incentives to compensate the field posting are lacking in training institutions. Adequate incentives in the form of rent free accommodation, special pay or rank promotion, schooling facilities for children, special recognition by way of subsequent promotion or good postings are not available in many training institutions. Present incentives are not adequate and do not attract good and qualified staff to training institutions.

(*g*) *Lack of proper system of scientific evaluation of training* : At present no scientific evaluation of training is carried out. Trainers do not get proper feed-back about training conducted by them.

(*h*) *Lack of support from organisation* : Police training is not getting adequate support from the organisation and training arrangements are unsatisfactory qualitatively as well as quantitatively. The most important reason for this situation is lack of a genuine conviction about the value of training in the police organisations.

(*i*) *Lack of interest by trainees* : Trainees find a big gap between realities of a police life and the training imparted to them and subsequently trainees do not exhibit adequate interest in training. Trainees find training as a ritual where unwilling and ill-equipped instructors perform the necessary rites of drilling and lecturing.

(*j*) *Input over-load* : Trainers feel that many subjects are required to be taught in limited time and therefore they have to rush through the syllabus. This input over-load in training puts a very heavy burden on the trainers. Input over-load is particularly more in indoor subjects like law.

(*k*) *The problem of understanding the psychology of adult learning* : Police trainers have to impart training to adults who have their own speed of perception, assimilation and retention. Past experience and motivation i.e. experience and interest provide the necessary stimulus for continued adult learning. "The theory of use or disuse" as originally propounded by Lamarck is useful in the context of adult learning. Since police trainees are all adults, police trainers have the problem of understanding the psychology of adult learning. Adults have generally resistance to change due to their desire to retain the status-quo and inability to see the need for the change. Their attitudes become too rigid and efforts for attitudinal changes are generally resisted. Trainers have to understand and apply the following simple rules of adult learning :

(*i*) Adult learning is aided by active practice rather than passive reception.

(*ii*) Adult learning is easy if the message draws on prior experience of adults.

(*iii*) Motivation, stimulus, response and reinforcement and participation and practice are important factors of adult learning.

Due to limited educational background, it is difficult for the trainers of the rank of subordinate officers and other ranks to understand the various complicated problems associated with the psychology of adult education.

(*l*) *Long working hours and inadequate time for preparation* : In most of the training institutions, there are long working hours for trainers and they do not get adequate time for preparation.

(*m*) *Training assignment with administrative duties* : In most of the training institutions, trainers are also given a number of administrative duties and thus limit their free time for preparation. Trainers do not get adequate time to prepare lesson plans for the next day.

(*n*) *Large number of trainees in proportion to trainers* : Ordinarily an indoor class should not consist of more than 30 to 40 trainess and outdoor class should not consist more than 20 trainees for one instructor. But in most of the training institutions the number of trainees is too large in proportion to the trainers.

(*o*) *Problem of close social interaction with trainers* : Trainers are not able to come into close contact with the trainees as the number of trainees is generally very large. Thus the individual qualities of the trainees are not properly identified. Trainers do not get any entertainment allowance or hospitality allowance and therefore they do not encourage social interaction with the trainees. Personal and social qualities of the trainees cannot be evaluated when the interaction is not close and continuous.

(*p*) *Rank consciousness of trainees* : Trainers, particularly of subordinate and lower ranks find trainees having rank consciousness with the result that a correct trainer-trainees relationship is generally not developed in most of the training colleges. During his interview, the author learnt that many trainers complain about the indifference of trainees if they were of senior rank. For a healthy trainer-trainee relationship, the barrier of rank should not arise but unfortunately in a hierachical organisation the realities are otherwise.

(q) *Loss of status and social recognition* : Police Officers particularly of the rank of Sub-Inspectors and above, carry a certain status in society but once they are posted in training institutions, they feel loss of status and social recognition.

(r) *Lack of adequate motivation and job satisfaction* : In police training institutions police officers do not find adequate job satisfaction and motivation to work as trainers.

(s) *Lack of proper research facilities* : To keep training institutions intellectually vibrant and up-to-date in their knowledge of police problems, research has to be one of the basic functions of the training institutions. But unfortunately very few training institutions have research cells with qualified staff. There is lack of proper research facilities in training institutions and necessary infrastructure has not yet been built up in training institutions.

(t) *Lack of specialised knowledge and expertise* : Gore Committee on police training has recommended a number of subjects like behavioural science, management, for which specialised knowledge is required. In India, most of the training institutions have not been able to get qualified trainers who are specialised in the given field. As a result, the present trainers who have not been given any training or specialised knowledge of these subjects are required to take such topics. In the absence of any specialised training, trainers feel great problems in satisfying the trainees on these subjects. Police trainers in most of the training institutions take subjects in which they have not been able to acquire experience. There are no provisions for getting guest speakers in many police training institutions.

(u) *Inadequate training aids* : Training films, film strips slides, tape recorders and other modern training aids are not available in many of the training institutions.

(*v*) *Lack of adequate resources for training* : Due to inadequate resources, trainers feel great difficulty in imparting good training. Due to lack of adequate resources many police training institutions do not possess a well-equipped library with a documentation cell and microfiling facilities. Libraries do not contribute to books and latest journals. Even transport is not sufficient in many training institutions.

(*w*) *No fixed tenure of trainers* : At present, there is no fixed tenure of trainers and those officers who are posted in training institutions continue to try their efforts to get out of the training assignments as the posts of trainers' are not having any attraction. There is no planned turnover of the staff and no constant infusion of new blood. Many trainers leave training assignments on promotions if their promotions accrue in the meantime and are not allowed their full term.

(*x*) *No interaction with trainers of other states/institutions* : So far there is hardly any interaction in the form of visits to other training institutions by the trainers. This interchange of instructors can promote better understanding and advancement of knowledge and skills by interaction with colleagues of other training institutions. Present rules of state police do not cater for such exchange and interchange.

(*y*) *No system of evaluation of trainers* : At present, in most of the police training institutions, trainers do not get any evaluation about their training capabilities and thus do not get adequate feed-back to improve their instructional abilities.

(*z*) *Lack of encouragement and support from heads of the training institutions* : In most of the states, heads of police training institutions are not interested in training assignments. Such heads of the police training institutions display indifference to the problems of trainers and do not encourage innovations by subordinates. The heads of the police training institutions generally do not properly evaluate the effectiveness of their trainers, nor evaluate the system of training in their training institutions. Even motivated, enthusiastic and well trained trainers do not get proper encouragement and support for their work from their heads of the institutions.

Though the general problems of various police trainers of India are mentioned above, there are numerous special problems related to various police institutions. Some of the problems mentioned can be easily resolved if the state governments accept the broad recommendations of the Gore Committee on police training and various other recommendations which are made from time to time by the symposium of heads of the police training institutions of the country.

Inter-relationship between Trainers and Trainees

The study seeks to analyse relationship of trainers with trainees in police training institutions of India. It was observed that in most of the training institutions, trainers maintained distance from trainees and a close or intimate rapport was not allowed to be established between them. Due to rank hierarchy and rigid discipline, the trainees were not frank and free with their trainers. There is a sort of authoritarian, discipline-oriented stress in the training system of 90 per cent of the training institutions. In India, we have authoritarian stress training with a rigorous militaristic frame-work with strict and harsh discipline with punitive physical training for mistakes. The police training in India is stress training with high ambiguity and low clarity of requirements. Police training brings with it "depersonalisation" in the trainees.[20] Trainees are considered stereotyped, they are preceived as devoid of human character and relationship is based on respective statuses instead of individual merits. Depersonalisation implies an insensitivity to and intolerance for the attitudes and behaviours that differ from ones own and is the tendency to dichotemize people' ideas and things without proper regard or appreciation for their nuances. The police training in India seems to institutionalise role distance by reinforcing and sanctioning the police trainees belief that his training is irrelevant to police work and is a waste of time. The atmosphere of training institutions is one of strict militaristic discipline frequently recognising the inferior status and shortcomings of trainees and superior-inferior relationship between trainers and trainees.

The data indicate that police training institutions in India were in a general state of neglect particularly in respect of physical facilities. This proposition has been proved by the data collected and analysed for the study. The opinion sutdy of 220 serving officers of various ranks and the opinion given by these ranks of serving police officers reinforces this conclusion. The results of the opinion poll is tabulated below :

TABLE

Showing that Police Training Institutions in India are in a General State of Neglect Particularly in Respect of Physical Facilities

	Agree	Partly agree	Disagree	Total
1	2	3	4	5
Is.G.P./D.Is.G.P.	16	3	1	20
Ss.P.	18	17	5	40
Dy.Ss.P.	16	15	9	40
Inspectors	24	8	8	40
Sub-Insps.	15	7	8	30
Constabulary	28	16	6	50
Total	117	66	37	220
Percentage	53.18	30.00	16.81	

Thus, in the study 53.18 per cent of the respondents agreed to the opinion while 30 per cent partly agreed. The study also discovered that police training in 65 percent of the states was in a general state of neglect as a whole.[71]

In police organisation, training is a peripheral activity rather than a central one and training performs the role of the "family-priest" who gives pious advice, often to be merely heard and not necessarily acted upon. The personnel connected with police training have a low self-image and are generally people who either do not make the grade in field or are inconvenient to the superiors. Police organisation in India do not treat training as professional skills and in many cases training centres are considered dumping ground for inefficient and/or inconvenient persons. What kind of training in the general professional subjects and particularly, in developing right attitudes can be expected from such persons who are themselves unhappy, disgruntled, have been battered by service storms. Generally, they talk lightly, irresponsibly about the service and service conditions and rarely bring out good aspects of the service.[22]

Training Programmes

In most of the training programmes, there is an input overload with the result that trainees are not able to grasp the subjects properly and trainers have to rush through the subjects to cover the syllabi. They are not able to discuss the subject in depth with the result that trainees do not get adequately thorough knowledge of the subject. Input over-load is particularly more in indoor subjects like law and investigation of crime. Police training in India do not have realistic goals and objectives of various courses are most unrealistic. There is a great gap between what is done in the field and what is taught in police training centres.[23] In police training colleges, subordinate officers are preached high ideals but in the field low practices are tolerated and encouraged. While in training, they are taught to register all cognisable offences as soon as they are reported but in the field they are asked to make a preliminary enquiry first and then record the F.I.R. while in theory they are taught to be free and unmindful of crime figures, in practice they have to ensure that crime figures do not increase disproportionately to the last year's figures. They are taught use of scientific methods of investigation but in field use of third degree is encouraged and connived for quick results. In training, they are taught not to make bogus records but in field they are required to make bogus cases u/s 109 for good statististical purpose. While honesty, integrity and high code of conduct is taught in training centres, they are encouraged in field to get hold of so-called witnesses who in reality were nowhere near the scene of the crime. In field, they were told how to tutor up false witnesses and how to get cases convicted by courts. They were told to observe dignity of individual in training but in field they are encouraged in the art of staging bogus encounters in dacoity infested areas and in Naxalite areas.

In police training in India, broadly there are four imbalances in training programmes—input over-load, unrealistic goals, alienation and linkage failure.[24] Input over-load brings a feeling of discouragement and inadequate internalisation of learning. Unrealistic goals result in excesive expectations followed by failure and ultimately cause doubts about relevance of whole training. Alienation of participants causes distrust and violation of participants. Linkage failure makes trainees unprepared for role conflicts, work pressures and vested interests which they face in real life situations. The alienation and gap is particularly noticeable in police training in the realm of attitudes and values. There is tremendous variation in the contents of training from state to state and even within the states in different training centres. The technique of instructions are outdated and there is no useful training material available for training. There is considerable room for improvement in the standard of instruction. Most of the states are almost without training manuals and pamphlets.[25] Police training college I Moradabad, Directorate General, C.R.P.F., N.P.A., Hyderabad and I.S.A. Mount Abu have done some commendable work in the field of preparation of training material for various ranks. However, not much training material has so far been published for training for lower and subordinate ranks. An analysis of various police training programmes for police conducted at various training institutions indicate that although apparently there seems to be diversification of themes in the training courses, yet on close scrutiny, it is found that an embarrasingly wide components of themes figure in most of the courses and sometimes the same speakers come in various institutions to deliver the same talks.

Many of the police training programmes do not deal with the live problems and issues currently faced by the police officers in the field. Most of the courses have greater input of theory and idealism. There appears to be a big hiatus between training as an operative preposition and the prevalent politico-administrative grim realities of life. Police training courses are likely to be dysfunctional if its contents are not realistically filled up and communicated. While most of the present available training courses are aimed at middle and junior levels, the rub lies with the junior and lowest parts of the police organisation. The police at constable and head constable level need more training because citizens generally come in contact with this level in most of cases. It is observed that the participants from police organisations are generally chosen on the basis of sheer availability not in terms of those who ought to be or need to be trained. Some officers are sent for one course after another because they are considered easily separable by their organisations. In most of the state police organisations, there is absence of a regular follow-up of the trainees. Training institutions do not maintain any further connection with the trainees. When a course is over, trainees disperse apparently never to be heard of again, with no formal contact with the training institutions. The concept of personnel development and career planning has not yet been developed in police organisations in the country.

The Concept of Evaluation of Training

Evaluation of training is a systematic assessment of training so as to study the effectiveness of training and to measure the actual results. A continuous qualitative assessment of training programmes is necessary for making them effective and useful.

"Evaluation of training" in its broadest sense can be defined as "a sub-system which determines the effectiveness of a training system and includes full range of value judgements about training, from what trainees think of the programme, of improved quality, efficiency, effectiveness, and change in attitudes and behaviour pattern of the trainees and ultimately in the organization as a whole". Evaluation can be of trainees, trainers, institutional methods, instructional material, instructional environment and short term or long term change in attitudes and behaviour pattern of the organization. Evaluation is an essential phase of the instructional process.

The nature, level and contents of the courses, the methods of instructions, the quality and quantum of instructional staff, training environment, relevance of course to the role expectations all need periodical evaluation and review with the object of constantly making the training meaningful and relevant to the police work. An objective and systematic evaluation can serve as the basis for further improvement in teaching as well as learning. Evaluation is generally used in its broadest sense to include the full range of value judgements about all aspects of training to determine the effectiveness of a training programme. Evaluation is an attempt to find out what changes in people, things, employees, procedures and situations have been accomplished through training programmes and what was actually hoped to be accomplished.

The Need for Evaluation

A system of evaluation is necessary :

(*a*) To find out whether the goals and contents of training programmes are compatible with the mission and current needs of the police organization ;

(*b*) To find out whether the goals and objectives of training are being reached in the most effective manner so that any necessary modification may be made ;

(*c*) To provide a feed-back to the management about the utilization of training resources and utility of training programmes ;

(*d*) To plan and revise training by adopting better techniques and designs by identifying the shortfalls and gaps in training programmes ;

(*e*) To justify the cost of expenditure incurred on training resources ;

(*f*) To carry out the diagnosis of the trainee's strength and weaknesses, designing and providing remedial instruction and assessing the individual's capabilities ;

(*g*) To identify, measure and record evaluation of trainers in objective terms by pointing out their strong and weak points as trainers and giving constructive counsel to them concerning their shortcomings. "The trainer must evolve a method of receiving feed-back from his trainees and wherever possible as assessment from his colleagues."

(Gore Committee on Police Training—p. 96)

(*h*) To assess the effectiveness of training methods, techniques and aids in isolation from the training courses.

The Scope of Evaluation

The scope of evaluation according to an expert committee should extend to the following :

(*a*) That the objectives of the training programme are clearly defined and are couched in concrete terms ;

(*b*) That the training content is prepared, keeping fully in view the precise requirements of the field ;

(*c*) That the training programme is conducted efficiently and effectively ;

(*d*) That the trainers are fully equipped not only with the specialised knowledge of their subjects but also with the techniques of training ; and

(*e*) The trainees acquire not only the job skills but also the correct approach and attitude to their work."[26]

The nature, level and content of the training programmes, the method and techniques of instructions and the quality and quantum of the training staff of institutions—all need a systematic periodical review and evaluation with the objective of constantly improving the training programmes. The impact and effectiveness of the training programmes upon the trainees and ultimately upon the organization has to be judged and evaluated through field experience, observation, opinion surveys, and feed-back from various clusters of the poilce organization. Training programmes which include attitudinal development, need more comprehensive planning, adequate resources, sufficient time and intensive effort both by the instructors and the students in order to achieve a positive and lasting effect for the effectiveness of any training programme. Organizational climate, institutional environment and the training system are also important factors in determining the effectiveness of training. For scientific evaluation of training programmes in police, all aspects of the training system are required to be appraised and evaluated for validity. Criteria tests need to be administered to evaluate training objectives, individual lessons course material, course duration, course programme, instructional techniques and the quality of instructional staff for a proper evaluation of training programme. However, the need for sound objectives arises again in the area of evaluation. Mager says when clearly defined goals are lacking, it is impossible to evaluate a course or programme efficiently. (Mager Robert F.—Preparing Instructional objectives—California, p. 3). There is a need for devising a suitable training strategy of State police training institutions on the basis of which the training programmes for various subordinate and lower ranks, both in methodology and contents, may be reviewed and updated periodically.

Various Steps in Evaluation

Evaluation of training can be divided by breaking it down into the following four logical steps :[27]

Step— 1 *Reaction* — How well did the trainees like the course ?

Step— 2 *Learning* — What principles facts, techniques and skills were learned ?

Step— 3 *Behaviour* — What changes in job behaviour resulted from the programme ?

Step— 4 *Results* — What were the tangible results of the training in terms of reduced cost, improved quality, improved quantity etc ?

With the help of these four logical steps, evaluation changes from a complicated elusive generality into clear and achievable goals.

Step-1 Reaction

To evaluate effectively, training directors have to measure reactions and feelings of the trainees in such a form that the reactions can be tabulated and quantified. The reactions can be obtained by making the forms anonymous so that trainees may give their honest, object, frank and critical views, feelings and opinions on various aspects of training. Reaction of trainees is very easy to measure and almost in all police institutions some reactions of police trainees are recorded at the end of the course. Opinions about trainers particularly of outside resource personnel are also obtained from trainees. Generally, reaction from is so designed that the reactions can be tabulated and quantified for a meaningful rating and evaluation. The first essential step in the evaluation process is to measure the reactions of the trainees about the subject-matter, overall rating of training programme and additional suggestions for further improvements.

Step-2 Learning

Learning evaluation is simply an attempt to assess the amount and quality of learning which has taken place in the trainees in terms of knowledge, skills and experience. Class-room activities such as individual class performance, participation in discussions, interest exhibited during training sessions can be used as learning evaluation techniques. Paper and pencil tests, oral tests, essay tests, multiple choice tests, ture/false tests, matching tests, short answers and competition tests, training assignments, individual on group projects are some of the techniques used for evaluation of learning. Measuring of learning is very difficult to measure and a great deal of work is required in planning and execution of evaluation procedure, in analysing the data that is obtained and in interpreting the results. In all police training institutions in India, tests and examinations are being conducted particularly in basic courses to measure the learning of trainees and some kind of training reports are generally sent to the organization about the trainees. These reports are generally called as trainees performance reports and contain a pen-picture of the trainees alongwith details of marks obtained in the examination. A systematic evaluation of trainees should be continuous, comprehensive and related to the objectives which the training programme is designed to achieve. The system of evaluation in force, at present, consists mainly of written examinations ,in theoretical subjects and practical tests in outdoor work. This formal evaluation is accompanied by a continuous and informal evaluation through group discussions, role playing tutorials and other problem oriented exercises. Trainees are also watched for assessment of attitudes and evaluation of personal and social qualities in informal manner by the trainers and other members of the training institution. For the assessment of attitudes, seperate file is maintained for each trainee in which all relevant incidents relating to the trainee's day to day behaviour in the class room and outside are recorded. Heads of the training institutions with the help of other members of the staff on the basis of their conduct and behaviour make assessment of personal and social qualities. However, there is lot of subjective element in this type of assessment. On completion of training course, generally a course report alongwith the marks obtained in the examination and pen-picture of the trainees is sent to the organization concerned.

Step-3 Behaviour

Evaluation of training in terms of on the job behaviour is more difficult than the reaction and learning evaluations because there can be a big difference between knowing principles and techniques and using them on the ground. Following guidelines can be followed in evaluating training in terms of behavioural changes :

(*a*) A scientific and systematic appraisal should be made on the job performance on before and after basis through interview or questionnaire method.

(*b*) The evaluation of behaviour should be done by the following :

(*i*) the trainee ;

(*ii*) the trainer including training director ;

(*iii*) trainee's boss ;

(*iv*) trainee's peer group ;

(*v*) trainee's subordinates.

(*c*) A comprehensive statistical analysis should be made to compare before and after performance and identify behavioural changes brought by training programme.

(*d*) A control group (not receiving the training) should be used.

(*e*) Periodical post-training appraisals at specified intervals should be made so that trainees have an opportunity to put into practice what they have learnt to add a scientific validity of the study.

The author during his research on administration of police training in India, has come to the conclusion that in India, no police training institution has so far carried out any systematic evaluation of behavioural changes brought in the trainees by training programmes. Measuring changes are very time consuming and complicated procedure and unfortunately very few training officers have the specialised background, skill, training and time to engage in extensive evaluations.

Step 4 Results

The evaluation of training in terms of results is extremely difficult because there are so many complicating factors which have to be taken into consideration. "The separation of other variables" makes it very difficult to measure results that can be attributed directly to a specific training programme. Improved efficiency, reduction in grievances improved efficiency, reduction in grievances improved morale, reduced costs, improved turnover, increase in quality and quantity of productivity and effectiveness, improved decision-making, better police community relations are some of the results that are aimed at by the specific training programmes. At present, our research techniques of evaluation are not adequate in this field. In India, so far no police training institution has carried out any evaluation of results related to any training programme. The nature, level and contents of the courses, the method of instructions and the quality and quantity of instructional staff will all need highly scientific evaluation if the long term and short term results of training to the police organisation are to be worked out in terms of improved efficiency, better decision-making and high morale.

Types of Training Evaluation

There are following types of training evaluation :

(*a*) *Context evaluation*—current operational context, individual difficulties, organizational differences.

(*b*) *Input evaluation*—Determining facts and opinion about the available human and material, training resources, evaluation of trainers.

(*c*) *Process evaluation*—monitoring the training as it is in progress—continuous examination of administration arrangements and feed-back—evaluation of training sessions and training infrastracture.

(*d*) *Outcome evaluation*—(*i*) Immediate outcome.
(*ii*) Intermediate outcome.
(*iii*) Long term outcome.

(*e*) *Cost Evaluation*—*Per trainee cost and per course cost.*

Context evaluation is primarily a question of assessing training needs and evaluating training in relation to actual job needs. Input evaluation is related to gaining information about what human and material resources are available both inside and outside the organization and assessing the resources put by the training organization in terms of personnel, material, facilities, training methodology, training tools, literature and other inputs for organizing the training. Process evaluation refers to the monitoring of training as it is in progress and implies continuous examination of administrative arrangements session assessmnet and feed-back from the trainees. Outcome evaluation measures the consequences of training in the form of actual change in trainees knowledge, skills, and attitudes which can be identified as immediate, intermediate or long term outcomes of training. Outcome evaluation is a very difficult and complicated process which has to be carried out on a continuous basis. Evaluation is ultimately an ongoing process geared to the improvement of training. Evaluation of training needs co-operation and involvement of superiors who supervise the subordinates trained. There is a need for developing more scientific evaluation instruments in order to step up self correcting training systems. Training evaluation instruments have to devise strategy to correctly measure trainees, reactions, learning achieved, attitudinal and behavioural changes brought in the trainees and results in the organizational context in the form of efficiency, morale and organizational health. Evaluation of training has to be supplemented by follow-up training by developing regular evaluation of an instructor or trainer should take into account the following main factors :

(*i*) Knowledge of the subject-matter and communication style.

(*ii*) Use of a lesson plan and utilization of time.

(*iii*) Participation of class and his control over group and environment.

(*iv*) Use of instructional aids and tools.

(*v*) Clarity of speech and expression.

(*vi*) Relation with trainees.

(*vii*) Ability to answer questions of trainees.

(*viii*) Overall impact and impression of the instructor and interest/motivation he has created in trainee to study the subject.

Outcome evaluation can be stated in terms of results such as improved efficiency, improved morale, reduced costs, reduction in grievances and improvement in police-public-relations.

Main Research Conclusions on Evaluation of Police Training in India

(*a*) There is a great gap between what is done in the field and what is taught in police training institutions.

(*b*) In most of the training programmes, there is an input overload with the result that trainees do not grasp the various subjects thoroughly and trainers have to rush through the subjects to cover the syllabi.

(*c*) Input overload is particularly more in indoor subjects like law and investigation of crime.

(*d*) In police training institutions there is alienation of participants which causes distrust and violation of participants.

(*e*) Linkage failure makes trainees unprepared for role conflicts, work pressures and vested interests which they face in real life situations.

(*f*) There is tremendous variation in the contents of training from state to state and even within the states in different training centres.

(*g*) Training programmes present unrealistic goals before trainees and there is a noticeable gap in the realm of attitudes and values between what they are taught and what trainees find in the field.

(*h*) The techniques of training are outdated and not much training material has so far been published for training of lower and subordinate ranks.

(*i*) Most of the training programmes do not deal with the live problems and issues currently faced by the police officers in the field.

(*j*) There appears to be a big hiatus between training as an operative preposition and the prevalent politico-administrative grim realities of life.

(*k*) Training institutions do not maintain any further communication with the trainees after their completion of the course.

(*l*) The concept of personnel development and career planning has not yet been developed in police training institutions.

(*m*) No systematic evaluation of training programmes in terms of context evaluation input evaluation and process evaluation has been carried out in any police training institution of the country.

(*n*) No outside agency or organization has carried out any systematic outcome evaluation in terms of long term results to the organization.

(*o*) The present system of getting evaluation of the training programmes from the trainees does not provide any objective or considered evaluation of programmes as trainees are reluctant to come out with frank views.

(*p*) Evaluation of trainees carried out by the trainees on the basis of class performance, written examination and tests is not very scientific and objective.

(*q*) Police training programmes in India are stress training programmes with high ambiguity and low clarity of requirements at lower and junior levels. We have an authoritarian stress training with a rigorous militaristic frame-work with strict and harsh discipline with punitive physical training for mistakes.

(*r*) Police training brings with it "depersonalisation" in the trainees. Depersonalization brings a sense of self estrangement to a person who experiences a part of the self as something alien to him. Trainees are considered stereotyped, they are perceived as devoid of human character and relationship is based on respective statuses instead of individual merits.

(*s*) The police training in India seems to institutionalise role distance by re-enforcing and sanctioning the police trainee belief that his training is irrelevant to police work.

(*t*) Police training programmes are evaluated in terms of reactions of trainees only in police institutions.

Outcome evaluation of training programmes has not been attempted so far in India.

(*u*) Evaluation of trainees who attend police training programmes is done on the basis of tests, written examinations and class-room performance, but evaluation of personal and social qualities with a rating scale as suggested in appendix-XVIII of the report of the Committee on Police Training M.H.A. (Gore Committee) is not carried out.

Difficulties in Getting Proper Scientific Evaluation of Training

A speaker at the 1968 conference of the American Society for Training and Development said that on the basis of a very recent survey of the literature for the past ten years, it appears that about 100 articles or reports for this ten year period have dealt with evaluation of training of which eleven appeared to be respectable evaluations. The question of evaluation of effectiveness of training progrommes is indeed difficult.

Major difficulties encountered in securing reliable evaluations are as follow :

(*a*) Evaluation is made generally from a personal rather than objective view point.

(*b*) Failure to recognise the difference between ability and performance of trainers and trainees or in other words what a man could do and what he actually does.

(*c*) Whenever training comes under criticism, like the proverbial doctors, training directors bury their mistakes under the hundreds of corporate variables that affect training outcome. Training directors blame the quality of trainees, the heavy workload, the supervision that follows thinking and operational environment of the field.

(*d*) Evaluation requires people with time to dig out the facts, people with sophisticated measuring devices and evaluation instruments and people who have courage to admit that training programme was not wholly successful. Shifting through training records, interviewing all trainees, playing with the mean, median and mode like statistical tools and carrying out a comprehensive objective evaluation are not particularly glamorous training activities and generally dedicated people are not available for such jobs.

(*e*) Due to organizational culture of strict discipline, fear of victimisation and lack of moral courage, trainees are reluctant to give their frank and free reactions in writing. Thus, reactions evaluation does not bring out any useful criticism or gaps in training administration.

(*f*) Over-generalization in concept, superficial indication of "happiness data" (saying pleasant things), justification of expenditure for training by inviting supportive response are some of the problems of evaluation.

(*g*) Maintaining the annoymity of the respondents does not assure either accurate or useful responses from trainees.

(*h*) One of the problems of evaluation is the failure to differentiate between research and evaluation through currents methods of evaluation are emerging from those developed in behavioural and social science research, but the aim of evaluation is administrative and limited. Evaluation has a limited purpose of decision making and its scope is to be confined to its limited objects while the research has a much wider scope.

(*i*) Informal evaluation can be based on field trips or discussions and even written evaluation questionnaires if trainers go out to the field and carry out informal discussions with various people. But this practice is not in vogue in India.

(*j*) Evaluation of training becomes difficult when objectives of training are not identified in quantifiable terms.

It is commonly accepted by the heads of the police training institutions in India that much remains to be done in developing training evaluation methods. Length of the training programme, the adequacy of instructions, the course content, training objectives and final outcome of training in terms of organizational improvement are some of the aspects which need effective evaluation effort. Training Division of Bureau of Police Research & Development, Training Directors of the police organizations of the states and the head of the police training institutions must pool their expertise and available resources to carry out evaluation of various training programmes. Research centres of Police Headquarters with the help of training staff of police training institutions specially of research cells have to carry out evaluation of various training programmes with the help of trainees who can be motivated to give their reactions, opinions and even contructive criticism of the training programmes attended by them. It cannot, however, be denied that quantitative evaluation of training programme is a very difficult matter. In a bibliography of "Selected Readings on Police" prepared by Bureau of Police Research and Development, New Delhi in 1978, out of 131 recommended readings on Recruitment and Training, there is only one article directly dealing with evaluation of a training programme for police. This indicates that the area is still unexplored and much remains to be done.

(*k*) Evaluation of training can not be done in isolation as it is ultimately linked with other facets of training, namely-identification of training needs, formulation of training objectives, design and implementation of training and formulation of training policy. To sum up, evaluation can be explained with the help of the various words which form it, as given below :

E—Evaluation is a systematic assessment of training with a view to analyse the effectiveness of training.

V—Valid criteria for measuring training effectiveness must be used.

A—A realistic approach to evaluation is specific information about particular programmes for purpose of making changes to achieve their improvement.

L—Learning evaluation is an attempt to assess the amount and quality of learning (in terms of knowledge and skills).

U—Utilize reactions of trainees about course contents, course duration and other information in a tabulated quantified manner as are relevant for evaluation.

A—Arrange behavioural evaluation before and after training the help of trainees, trainers, trainee's boss, trainee's peers and trainee's subordinates.

T—Try to find out training results by separating other variable.

I—Input evaluation will give assessment of instructors, instructional material, instructional techniques and other inputs of the training programmes.

O—Obtain feed-back from trainees, trainees' bosses, trainees subordinates in both formal and informal manner through personal contacts.

N—Need for a continuous qualitative evaluation of training programmes for maintaining effectiveness and follow-up action.

Conclusion

The VII Finance Commission grant for upgradation and the modernisation grant for police given by the Government of India can go a long way in solving some of the problems of the police training as it has now become possible to expand the staffing pattern of the training institutions as well as for equipping the training institutions with modern training aids and equipments. However, these grants can not be spent on residential or non-residential buildings for training institutions. Physical facilities in institutions such as administrative buildings, parade grounds, playgrounds, hostels for trainees, residential accommodation for trainees continue to be inadequate. However, distinction has to be made between "lavish facilities" and the "essential facilities" necessary for effective training. Reasonably furnished administrative offices : spacious class-rooms with lightings and proper furniture, library with latest books and reading material with qualified library staff, storerooms; model police station, wireless station and model police control rooms, lecture halls, demonstration rooms, adequate motor transport fleet with MT section and garage ; trained horses and riding section with stables, hospital with X-ray, dental care and surgical facilities; cook-houses and messes with furniture for different ranks of trainees and trainers; extensive parade grounds and play grounds; firing range; auditorium with sound system and a stage; training films and 16 m m projector with other training aids and trained personnel to handle the concerned are some of the most essential facilities which should be provided in all the police training centres in India. Available resources of state and central governments should be made available to provide such facilities in all training institutions and a more conducive training environment should be built up in all training centres so that effective training may be imparted. It is highly imperative that a climate be created to raise the dignity and status of police training institutions so that an all round good training environment may be created in the country. Police training colleges and schools should be staffed with hardworking, dedicated, experienced and successful field officers who have the capacity and desire to train the "new breed" of police officers with an eye towards "professionalism" in police work[28]. To attract these types of trainers, all training institutions should provide 100 percent family accommodation to the staff with other incentives and special pay. The accommodation so provided should be rent-free with free electricity and water. Training institutions should provide sumptuary allowance to all ranks of instructional staff to enable them to meet the trainees frequently at their residence. The instructional staff should have free exchange visits with other training institutions of India and abroad. Training centres should be located at better places and school for children be started in training centres. Report of Sub-Committee to recommend incentives to police trainers headed by Sri A.A. Ali should be implemented along with the Gore Committee report on police training so that environs of police training may improve. To achieve all these facilities from

Inspectors-General of Police down to Sub-Inspectors, every body will have to make a concerned effort in this direction and like the military training centre, instructional work has to be given a place of pride and prestige in the police sub-culture. Trainees have to be provided better allowance during training period and training courses have to be linked up with career planning. A healthy and conducive training environment with good inter-personal relationship between trainers and trainees alone will produce effective training results. The researcher has come to the conclusion that due to stress training, learning climate is not conclucive. As 80 percent of the trainers are disinterested in their job, the trainees do not get proper motivation. There is a need to develop institutional structures for a supportive climate in police training.[29] The institution building should be carried out in a systematic manner and periodical redefinition of the institution's objectives be laid out giving proper priorities. Definite criteria for selecting new trainers and setting standards of performance are pre-requisites for institution building. Regarding adequacy or inadequacy of staff, the yard-stick fixed by the Madhya Pradesh Police Commission has been accepted by the researcher. 75 percent of the institutions covered in the present study revealed to have inadequacy of staff. The hypothesis that the police training institutions are having inadequate staff has been proved by the research analysis. The expenditure on police training has been worked out as percentage of the total state police budget. One per cent of the total police budget expenditure on training is considered adequate for training institutions by the researcher. Measured by this yardstick, during last two years, 50 percent of the states studied by the researcher, spent more than the optional expenditure. Thus, the hypothesis that expenditure incurred on training in various states of India is percentage-wise low in proportion to the total costs of the police budgets of the state is partly proved. Survey study of the physical facilities existing in various training institutions proves that the hypothesis that the police training institutions in India are in a general state of neglect and more so in respect of the physical facilities obtained on their campuses. The research data has also compared the use of training techniques/methods in various training institutions. The researcher has come to the conclusion that new training tools and equipment for police training are not being used in 50 percent of the institutions in India and very little innovative efforts have ever been made to render them functional. Thus, the environs of police training in India need to be made more conducive for effective training. With a view to facilitate synchronisation of the challenges for improving the environs of police training, rigorous administrative planning at the macro-middle range and micro-levels on a continuing basis should be carried out with the fullest support of the highest levels of the police organisation.

REFERENCES

1. Diaz, S.M. "*Police Training for Modernisation*" The Indian Journal of Criminology and Criminalistics Vol. I, No 2 and 3, June-Sept. 1981, Institute of Criminology and Forensic Science, New Delhi.
2. Studies on the environments of the educational Schools have been carried out by a number of educationists and scholars—Block, B.S. "*Stability and Change in Human Characteristics*, Wiley," New York, 1964 ; Kats and Kahn "*The Social Psychology of Organisations*, Wiley, New York, 1966 ; Sareson, S.B.," *The Culture of the School and the problem of a Change*, Allyn and Bacon, Boston, 1971.
3. For Similar views, see, Dayal, Ishwar : *Management Training in Organisations* (Prentice Hall of India Ltd., New Delhi, 1970), p. 22.
4. For further details, see—"*Physical Facilities for Training Institutions*"—working group of Annual Conference of Central Training Institutions April, 1977, (ISTM Monograph No. 22).
5. Recommendations of the Seminar on the Recruitment and Training of Police Officers—P.P. Mahurkar, *Police Research and Development*, Quarter No. III & IV, Dec., 1972, p. 63.
6. See, Earayil L. Alphouse and Vadacjumchery James, "*Public Relations at the Cutting Edge level*", P.T. C. Trivandrum, Kerala, 1982.
7. For furthes details, see Wadhwani, M., Methodology of Trg., Training Monograph No. 16, Trg. Divsn., Dept. of Personnel, Cabinet Secretariat, New Delhi 1972.
8. One trainer during interview told the researcher that when he started using overhead projector for regular classes, he was told by

the Principal that bulb used in overhead projector was very costly and was not available in local market thus indirectly discouraging use of overhead projector. Another trainer pointed out that "these training aids were not meant for use but for showing to inspecting officers and to researchers like you".

9. Saxena, A.P. : *Training and Development in Govt.*" (I.I.P.A. New Delhi, 1974), p. 68.
10. Conference on Training (Feb. 24-25 1969) Proceedings, I.I.P.A., New Delhi, 1969, p. 40.
11. Second Conference of State Training Institutions January, 1973—Training Division, DP & AR, Cabinet Secretariat, New Delhi, May 1973, p. 2 (Recommendation No. 12).
12. Chawla, G.S., "*Police Forces in States*"—Centre to spend Rs. 100 Crore of Modernisation—Indian Express, Monday, July 27, 1981, p. 4.
13. One Principal of a trg. centre categorically said this statement in his interview and two other Principals agreed to the statement.
14. Report of the M.P. Police Commission 1965-66, Govt. of M.P. (Home—Police Dept.), Bhopal Government Central Press, 1967. p. 232.
15. These views were shared by 60 percent of the officers who were interviewed by the researcher. Even present heads of Police Training Centres shared the view.
16. Proceedings of the X Symposium of the Heads of Police Training Institutions in India, SVP, NPA, Hyderabad, 1981, p. 2-3.
17. These were the views expressed by one of the Spl. Is.G.P. (Trg.). For further details, see Proceedings of X Symposium of Heads of Police Trg. Institutions, op cit., p. 28.
18. See SVP, NPA Hyderabad Transaction, Vol. XXIV, Apr. 1977—XXXVII Senior Officers Course, 1977, Syndicate Study on Manpower Planning—Career Development of Constables in Police Force, p. 18.
19. See Proceedings of the X Symposium of Heads of the Police Training Institutions in India, op. cit., p. 18.
20. Depersonalisation represents both a state of mind and the basis of defining the quality of interaction between individuals and conveys a sense of self-estrangement of a person who experiences a part of the self as something alien to him. For similar views, see Harris N. Richard : *The Police Academy—An Inside View*, New York Wiley, 1973, pp. 113—163.
21. For similar views, see Udai Pareek and T.V. Rao, "*Designing and Managing Human Resources System*" (Oxford and I.B.H. Pub. Co., New Delhi, 1981), p. 138.

22. Gokhale, S.G., "*Police : Attitudes Training Institute Organisational Climate*", (NPA Magazine Vol. XXIII, Nov. 1973), p. 52.
23. For further details, see—Saksena, N.S. "*What is wrong with Police Training*", (SVP NPA Magazine Vol. XXVII, No. 1, June, 1977), pp 7-8.
24. For detailed perspective, see Mathew B. Males, "*On Temporary Systems in Mathew B. Miles (Ed). Innovation in Education*", New York, Teachers College, Columbia University, 1964), pp, 439-90.
25. Bsyley, David H, "*The Police and Political Development in India* (Princeton University Press, New Jersey, 1969), p. 95.
26. *Conference on Training*—Feb' 69, sponsored by Training Division, MHA—IIPA 1969, p. 177.
27. See—A.C. Hamblin—"*Evaluation of Training—in Industrial Training International*", Nov., 1970, pp 33-36.
28. For similar views, see Harris, Richard N., "*The Police Academy : An Inside View*" (John Willey & Sons, New York, 1973, p. 14).
29. For similar concepts, see—Harbert A, Thelen, "*Dynamics of Group at Work*" (Chicago University of Chicago Press, 1954), p. 91-2. Also Lynton, Rolf p. and Pareek Udai, "*Training for Development*" (DB Taraporevala & Sons B'Bay, 1967), pp. 332-62.

CHAPTER EIGHT

POLICE RESEARCH AND TRAINING IN INDIA

RESEARCH represents a systematic, empirical, controlled and critical investigation or enquiry of hypothetical propositions that pertain to the presumed relationships among various variables of a given phenomenon. It is a creative effort to study which helps the researcher to acquire precise knowledge of the subject under investigation. The purpose of research is to discover new facts, offer new interpretations and create new levels of knowledge. It is an essential input in the evaluation of policies and programmes undertaken to improve the existing system. Administrative research not only stimulates intellectual curiosity but motivates the researcher to enhance his understanding of the organisational and leadership behaviours of the administrative systems. Research inputs are absolute pre-requisites for the advancement of objective oriented systems. An organisation which wants to keep pace with the fast changing technological developments must constantly assess, examine and evaluate its techniques and practices. Research analysis follows studious enquiry. It incorporates new facts obtained through critical enquiry and exhaustive investigation. It is expected to give appropriate value and correct interpretation by offering practical application of the conclusions discovered for an effective solution of the problems confronting a given society. The purpose of fundamental research is to add to the sum total of human knowledge regardless of practical results while the purpose of applied research is to utilize knowledge for social or economic gains or for practical results. However, both these kinds of fundamental and applied research efforts are interdependent to one another. Administrative research has made great strides in the area of human relations. Applied research is being used in the study of training efforts and its impact on trainees' behaviour. It is being increasingly used in the study and solution of multifarious complicated problems of Human behaviour and crowd reactions during emergent situations. Conducting research on various aspects of police training or on socio-politico-economic issues relating to police and then presenting them to the academic world is likely to enhance the utility and eventually the creditability or respectability of a training institution or research centre. Until very recently the police were essentially a 'Terra incognita' to political scientists, students of public administration and the general public, though perhaps not to local politicians. College text books in political science devoted only cursory attention to police problems and the scholarly journals largely ignored them. As the focus of careful study of how police behave and why, what implications of these findings are for the distribution of power in a democracy and what changes are desirable and feasible, the police long escaped the critical attention of students of politics and administrative behaviour.[1] A well knit net-work of training, research and consultancy systems will make the contribution of a training institution more meaningful. In May 1939 the conference of Chief Ministers, Home Ministers and senior officers held at Simla recommended a scheme for the creation of a research institute with the object of conducting research and imparting training in research methodology to selected police officers but the proposal got postponed due to the out-break of World War II in the year 1939. The conference of Inspectors General of Police in 1956 again recognised its need and recommended for the establishment of research centres in the C.I.D. wings of state police organisations and a co-ordinating agency at the centre. These research wings were started in states in the C.I.D. branch and primarily dealt with crime and grave offences.

Research in police is a way of getting closer to the real world, even though there are difficulties, pragmatic as well as philosophical which stand in the research studies. In the present study, it is proposed to test the hypothesis that there is lack of co-ordination between police training and police research in India with the result the training enterprise is non-goal-oriented in terms of cost benefit.

The Police Research Advisory Board has been the appex agency for police research. The Govt. of India reconstituted the erstwhile Police Research Advisory Council into Police Research and Development Advisory Council. This Council was entrusted with the function of encouraging research on various aspects of police administration by state police research cells and other allied bodies entrusted with such work. Some of the other functions of the Council include identification of police needs and police problems in the country and rendering advice in initiating stimulations and co-ordinating police research and development work in the country.[2] In pursuance to the recommendations of Inspectors-General of Police conference, a Central Research Centre was set up in the Central Bureau of Investigation in Delhi. In 1963, a Research Division was set up, its functioning being "to assess and examine the problems of police organisation, methods, techniques and procedures and to conduct research in matters relating to crime and its prevention". A Police Research Advisory Council was also constituted, in the C.B.I. in Delhi. The functions of this body were "to consider the policy and programme of police research in India and to provide the necessary guidance to the Research Division in carrying out studies on selected projects". The Research Division has conducted some of the following studies in areas relevant to policing :

(*i*) Juvenile Delinquency—role of the police ;

(*ii*) Legal and financial implications of chit funds ;

(*iii*) Security of banks ;

(*iv*) A pilot study of urban pattern of murder ;

(*v*) Thefts by domestic servants ;
(*vi*) Thefts of cultural property ;
(*vii*) Survey of kidnapping in Delhi ;
(*viii*) Public attitude at scenes of crime.

In the year 1970, a separate organisation known as the Bureau of Police Research and Development was established under the Ministry of Home Affairs, Government of India. On its establishment it took some 14 research projects which have been pending with the Research Division of the C.B.I. including "Denotified Tribes in Transition", "Copper Wire Thefts", "Survey of White Collar Crime and Recruitment", "Training and Promotion Prospects of Sub-Inspectors of the Civil Police". Some of the states have also set up research units at police headquarters some years back. 15 states in India including Andhra Pradesh, Kerala, Madhya Pradesh had constituted these research units in their respective police headquarters.

The Bureau of Police Research and Development (B.P.R.& D)

The functions of the Research Division of B.P.R.& D are quite extensive and specialised. Its primary aim is to analyse and study crime and offer assistance in police research programmes in the states. It processes and coordinates research projects, sponsors extra-mural research, participate in social defence and crime prevention programmes. Participation in the work of the United Nations in the field of prevention of crime and treatment of offenders, maintenance of all India statistics of crime and documentation relating to police science and criminology also fall within its domain of functions. In addition, it brings out publications such as Police Research and Development Journal, the Indian Police Journal, Crime in India and other research reports.[3] Initially, the Bureau consisted two divisions viz. (i) the Research Division and (ii) the Development Division. In pursuance to the recommendations of the Committee on Police Training, a Training Division was established in July 1973 in the B.P.R.&D. Its purpose was to provide co-ordination of training at the nation level and to formulate and evolve police training polices. The research division of the B.P.R.& D has been able to complete more than 45 regular research projects since its inception in the year 1970. It publishes statistics of crime for the entire country in the form of a book entitled "Crime in India" which also includes data about accidental deaths and suicides in the country. In addition, it brings out a quarterly crime review. The development division consists of the weaponary unit and the traffic and transport units. In the field of transport, division has developed a bullet-proof one ton-vehicle. The training division of the B.P.R.&D. is mainly responsible to process and implement the recommendations by the Committee on Police Training and assist various training institutions in the country in reorganising the syllabi and curriculum of various courses on the lines of the recommendation of Gore Committee on Police Training. The B.P.R.&D. convenes the Police Science Congress, the All India Forensic Science Congress and the Conference of Directors of the Forensic Science Laboratories in India. These annual conferences provide the necessary forum for exchange of ideas among police officers and police scientists from all over India. The deliberations in these bodies provide the basis for research and development work of the Bureau. The research and development effort of the Bureau is reviewed and guided by a small council called as police research and development advisory council. It meets twice a year under the chairmanship of the Union Home Secretary. In addition, seven standing committees on different subjects have been constituted by the Government to function under the overall guidance of the Police Research and Development Advisory Council. The functions of these standing committees are as follow :

(*a*) *Standing Committee on Police Research* : It assists the Bureau in the formulation, execution and evaluation of research programme for the modernization and effective functioning of the police force.

(*b*) *Standing Committee on Police Training* : This committee examines various matters relating to police training and make suitable recommendations.

(*c*) *Standing Committee on Weaponary & Riot Control* : The functions of this committee are to keep track of developments in riot control weapons, protective equipment etc., obtain samples, make experiments, recommend measures for adoption by police forces in India and advise on indegenous manufacture of equipment, including establishment of pilot plants, where necessary.

(*d*) *Standing Committee on Police Transport* : It identifies the problems relating to police transport and advises the Bureau on matters relating to the subjects.

(*e*) *Standing Committee on Traffic Equipments* : This committee examines various matters connected with the use and development of traffic equipment to the country and makes suitable recommendations.

(*f*) *Standing Committee for Forensic Science* : It examines various matters relating to the application and development of forensic science in India and makes suitable recommendations.

(*g*) *Standing Committee on Forensic Medicine* : It is a standing committee and its objective is to examine various matters relating to the application and development of forensic medicine in India and make suitable recommendations.[4]

The Police Research and Development Advisory Council and the Standing Committees include police officers, academic experts from various fields of social, behavioural and physical sciences, management scientists, educationists and representatives from scientific and industrial organisations and laboratories and other disciplines. The Bureau, thus, helps in developing an inter-disciplinary effort for the solution of problems having a bearing on police efficiency and effectiveness. The B.P.R.&D. can offer advice about research areas and problems to universities and research institutes. It can get external research conducted by independent social scientists for an outside assessment of police problems. The organisational chart and personnel system in the Research Division of the Bureau of Police Research and Development is presented at page no. 254.[5]

The existing staff is inadequate to cope with the research requirements and proposals are lying with the Government of India for expansion of the organisation and creation of additional manpower. The B.P.R. & D. needs well-trained and qualified researchers in its Research Division. It is suggested that the B.P.R.&D. should be declared a research centre for police researchers and affiliated to Delhi University or Jawahar Lal Nehru University for the purpose of awarding M. Phil. and Ph. D. degrees to its researchers. Some research fellowships may also be sponsored by the Bureau. It should create a "data-bank" for police researchers. The research projects which have been completed so far should be published. One such survey report has been published by the C.R.P.F. Press. The Bureau has completed 47 research projects which need a wider audience.[6]

Research Centres in The States

In pursuance of the instructions given by the Government of India, some of the states have created police research units while others are awaiting their inauguration due to paucity of resources. They function in close liaison with the Bureau at the Centre. Some of the studies completed by these state research units relate to the "Impact of Democratic Decentralization and Tenancy Laws on Rural Crime", "Impact of Industrialization on Crime in Thana District (Maharashtra)", "Sociological Surveys relating to Crime in Neyveli Lignite Project Area" and "Prevention of Criminality resulting from Social Changes in certain Districts (T.N.)" Studies such as "Superstitution and Crime", "Murders in Tribal Districts" and "Student Indiscipline (M.P.)", "Problems of Ex-criminal Tribes", "Factious Crimes" and "Impact of Industrialisation on Crime (A.P.)"[7] have also been undertaken at micro and macro basis. The major functions of the state police research unit are :

(*a*) To make a continuous study of all factors having a bearing on police administration both internal and external and make concrete recommendations capable of implementation without much further processing with a view to improving police efficiency.

(*b*) To reorient the organisation, procedures and methods of police working to suit the requirements of a democratic and welfare state.

(*c*) To evaluate the effectiveness of the present organisation, procedures, methods, equipment and techniques of police working and to evolve and develop more effective organisation, equipment, method and techniques of police working.

(*d*) To stimulate thought and study of police problems at all levels of police organisation and also to locate important problems and initiate studies in respect of the same.

(*e*) To get suggestions and problems from the field and examining and devising solutions for the same and to study such other matters as may be referred by the Govt. or the I.G.P.

(*f*) To maintain contact with other research organisations or other centres of thought interested in police administration, law and criminology.

(*g*) To collect, classify and document all information and literature of police interest and to publish and disseminate the results of its studies or other useful information.

(*h*) To test the practical validity of the theories relating to crime and criminals, developed and propounded by sociologists, criminologists and other social scientists. Also to evolve and develop theories and general principles from field studies and analysis of factual information and other researches carried out.

The composition and number of the research centres, units in various states of the country are presented through the table given at p. 266. The data indicate that in most of the states of the country research centres have very small strength which can be termed as inadequate. The Andhra Pradesh Police Research Centre, notwithstanding its handicaps and deficiencies, has completed the following four major research projects :

(*i*) Faction in Rayalaseema (Kurnool), Ouddapah and Anantpur Districts ;

(*ii*) Corruption among the police officers ;

(*iii*) Implications of Panchayat Raj set-up (A.P.) ;

(*iv*) Problem of ex-criminal Tribes.

The Gujarat and Karnataka police research centres could complete 21 and 20 research projects respectively. The police research centres could complete 6 research projects in Kerala, nine in Maharashtra, six in Rajasthan, 29 in Tamil Nadu, five in Uttar Pradesh and six in Delhi. No research project has been completed so far (1982) by the police research centres functioning in Haryana, Manipur, Tripura, West Bengal, Goa Daman and Diu.[8]

The overall performance of police research centres does not seem encouraging. Most of them are not engaged in social science research in the technical sense of the term. They lack qualified and trained personnel. There are not many qualified and motivated researchers available at these research centres. The data reveal that in most of the research centres, unqualified, untrained and even rejected officers are passing their time. The quality of research projects also leaves much to be desired. It is partly because the researchers lack training in research methodology. Even the completed research projects have not been published by the research centres. The state police headquarters should be able to finance the cost of publication of these research projects. The B.P.R. & D., M.H.A. should coordinate and finance the publication of the completed research projects if these are found of good quality.

Research Cells in Training Centres

There is an apparent inadequacy of research literature on police and research facilities in state police training institutions are far from satisfactory. Actually research is not considered as a

TABLE 8.1
Showing Composition and Number of Research Centres/ Units in Various States of India

S. No.	State	I.G.P.	D.I.G.	S.P.	Addl S.P./Statistical Officer	Dy S.P.	Insp.	S.I.	A.S.I./ H.C.	Const.	Additional Assisting Staff: Peon	Steno. Typist	F.D.C./ U.D.C.	S.D.C./ L.D.C.	Typist	Total
1	2	3	4	5	6	7	8	9	10	11	12	13	14	15	16	17
1.	Andhra Pradesh	—	—	1	—	—	2	2	4	8	—	—	—	—	—	17
2.	Gujarat	—	—	—	—	1	1	1	1	—	1	—	—	—	—	5
3.	Haryana	—	—	—	—	1	1	—	—	1	—	1	—	—	—	4
4.	Karnataka	—	—	1	1	2	2	2	—	12	—	1	1	1	2	27
										Librarian-1,			Dalyath-1			
5.	Kerala	—	—	1	1	1	1	—	—	—	—	—	—	—	—	4
6.	Madhya Pradesh	—	—	—	1	1	1	1	—	2	—	—	1	1	—	9
												Librarian-1				
7.	Maharashtra	—	—	1	1	1	1	1	2	—	—	—	—	—	1	8
8.	Manipur	—	—	—	—	—	1	1	1	—	—	—	—	—	—	3
9.	Rajasthan	—	—	1	—	—	1	1	—	—	—	1	1	3	—	8

1	2	3	4	5	6	7	8	9	10	11	12	13	14	15	16	17
10.	Tamil Nadu	—	—	—	—	1	1	1	—	2	—	1	—	—	—	6
11.	Tripura	—	—	—	—	1	1	2	1	4	2	1	—	2	—	14
12.	Uttar Pradesh	—	—	1	2	1	1	—	—	—	—	—	—	—	—	5
13.	West Bengal	Spl. S.R.-1			—	—	1	1	1	—	—	—	—	—	1	5
14.	Delhi	—	—	—	1	2	2	—	1	6	—	1	—	—	2	15
15.	Goa, Daman & Diu	—	—	—	—	—	1	2	3	6	—	—	—	—	—	12
16.	Bureau of Police Research and Development	—	2(D.D.s)	5	5	2	—	—	—	—	—	—	—	—	—	14

part of training activity by police training institutions. Moreover, police training institutions have not taken up fundamental or basic police research seriously. The hiatus between theoretical knowledge of police training and practical problems of police work can be minimised if certain amount of applied police research by the instructional staff of police is carried out in the training institutions. The Gore Committee on Police Training recommended the creation of such separate research cell in every police training institution.[9] A survey of selected police training institutions for the present study revealed that most of the training institutions have not yet implemented the recommendations of the Gore Committee. National Police Academy, Hyderabad has been sanctioned one Research Officer and one stenographer for research cell but the cell has not yet started functioning as the post of research officer is yet to be filled in by the U.P.S.C. High Altitude, Defence and Survival/ I.T.B.P. Academy, Mussorie and Jagjivan Ram Railway Protection Force Training College, Lucknow have also no research cells at all. The I.G.P. Orissa sent proposal as early as 1979 to his state government for posting of extra personnel under the VII Finance Commission but the Government of India preferred to drop the scheme. The I.G.P. Tripura did not consider it even necessary to have a full-fledged research cell in his state. The instructional staff has been entrusted with the task of undertaking research on relevant issues as part of their professional duties. The I.G.P., Meghalaya did not consider the research cell idea as feasible. The I.G.P., Tamil Nadu informed the present researcher that a police research centre has been functioning at Madras with one Dy. S.P. and some junior staff under the supervision of I.G.P. (Planning and Co-ordination). In A.P., Govt. has accorded sanction for the establishment of a police research cell at P.T.C., Anantpur with nominal staff of one statistical assistant and one typist. In Indo-Tibetan Border Police, no research cell exists in its High Altitude Defence and Survival Academy, Mussoorie. The Commissioner of Police, Delhi has also sent a proposal to the Delhi Administration, who, in turn, has referred the proposal to the B.P.R.&D. for study. The IX and X Symposia of the heads of police training institutions of the country have recommended that the states must forward concrete proposals for the creation of research cells.[10] The P.TC., Nasik has a research cell comprising of one Dy. S.P., one senior public prosecutor, one public Prosecutor and one Police Inspector. This cell has carried out an elementary study on the use of guide scheme to its trainees. In Uttar Pradesh, P.T.C.,s. there are no research cells. Similarly, there are no research cells in M.P. P.T.C., Sagar, J.R./ R.P.F. Training College, Lucknow, and P.T.C., Junagarh.

The B.P.R. & D. has recommended the following organisational structure of research cells to be constituted in a Police Training Institution :

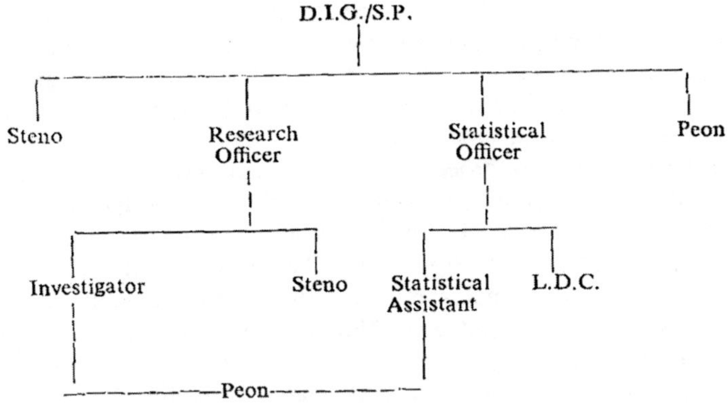

The organisational pattern of staff for research cells will cost approximately 32 lakhs per annum. The Govt. of India must finance these research agencies at least for next five years. If activised, they can play a very useful and constructive role in revising, reorganising and reinforcing the police training programmes. In the initial stages, they may confine themselves to some of the vital areas of police training such as the identification of training needs, the proportion between theoretical and practical periods of instruction in a training programme ; determining the suitability of various training methods for different instructional purposes and development of training material for various courses. To carry out meaningful research, it is desirable that these research cells are provided with a suitable infrastructure and environment for analytical study of the problems that confront the programmes of police Training at each level. Research cells in training institutions have been handicapped with the paucity of qualified and trained researchers. Research needs a high level of intellectual capability and rigorous training in research methods. Obviously, not many police officers posted in training institutions, are interested in serious and sustained research. A methodical research project involves five stages namely, (*i*) choosing the research problem and stating the hypotheses ; (*ii*) formulating the research design of the study; (*iii*) collecting the data ; (*iv*) coding and analysing of these data and finally ; (*v*) interpretation of results so as to test the validity of the hypotheses postulated in the research project. This is a very complex, time consuming and arduous job which requires dedicated professional experts. At present, the Research cells in most of the training institutions are non-existent and dysfunctional due to the apathy of senior officers and non-availability of genuinely motivated and qualified researchers. In order to keep the police training institutions intellectually vibrant and up-to-date in their knowledge of police problems, their research and training needs need to be studied from an integrational approach. The field for police research is quite vast and complex and naturally it involves considerable commitment of resources. The Research cells have been ill-equipped to carry out their assigned functions in the want of professional expertise and experience. Secretiveness of the police force has kept the research cells in a state of non-functional identity. Experience indicates that in most of the training centres, the research cell personnel do not stay long enough to acquire specialisation in research methods. The research work can not be carried out in the absence of a well-equipped library with learned journals, reports and books. The present study discovered that most of the research cells in training institutions all over the country suffer from lack of requisite strength and calibre of their personnel, financial difficulties and lack of co-ordination in effort between police training and police research. The present status of police research units in police headquarters and that of research cells in police training institutions is presented below :

TABLE 8.2

Showing Existence of Research Centres in Police Hqrs. and Research Cells in Police Training Institutions

S. No.	State/UT	Whether Research Unit/Centre in Police Hqrs. functioning	Whether Police Research Cell in Training Institutions established
1	2	3	4
1.	Andhra Pradesh	Yes	Yes
2.	Gujarat	Yes	No
3.	Haryana	Yes	No. proposal pending with Govt.
4.	Karnataka	Yes	No
5.	Kerala	Yes	No
6.	Madhya Pradesh	Yes	No
7.	Maharashtra	Yes	P.T.C., Nasik, P.T.C., Akola have Research Cells.
8.	Manipur	Yes	No
9.	Punjab	No	No
10.	Rajasthan	Yes	No
11.	Tamil Nadu	Yes	No
12.	Uttar Pradesh	Yes	No
13.	West Bengal	Yes	No
14.	Delhi	Yes	No. Proposal sent
15.	Goa, Daman & Diu	No	No
16.	Himachal Pradesh	No	No
17.	Mizoram	No	No
18.	Orissa	No	No
19.	Nagaland	No	No
20.	Tripura	Yes	No

The data reveal that only three training institutions have established research cells so far. Research cell at Police Training College, Anantpur (A.P.) with a staff of one Dy.S.P., one Statistical Officer and one typist has been opened as late as 23rd January, 1981. The Nasic (M.S.) P.T.S. Cell has the staff of one Dy.S.P., one senior public Prosecutor, one public Prosecutor and one police Inspector. The research cell at Police Training School Akola (M.S.) is only three years in existence. One Dy S.P. (Vice-Principal), one Public Prosecutor and one P.S.I. Law Inspector constitute the personnel of this research cell. Thus, the data prove that 90 per cent of the training institutions have no research cells and 30 per cent of the states have no research centres in their police headquarters.

Research Activities at the Institute of Criminology and Forensic Science, Delhi

The two faculties of criminology and forensic science undertake research projects. The Institute has made a beginning by taking up projects such as the one on drug addiction. The project seeks to examine criminological tools and their efficacy in determining the etiology. Immunoassay techniques are employed to identify the extent of addiction and bio-chemical changes brought thereof. In addition to this joint project which is in progress, the two faculties have initiated several other research projects, the prominent of them are being listed below :

(*a*) *The Faculty of Criminology* :

(*i*) Etiology of crime and delinquency

(*ii*) Theories of criminogenesis

(*iii*) Survey of research in deviant Behaviour

(*iv*) Status alcohol and Prohibition

(*v*) Adolescent thieves

(*vi*) A study in socio-cultural dynamics

(*vii*) Criminology : A classified bibliography

(*viii*) Public awareness and opinion about the problems of law enforcement (*ix*) Evaluation of criminal justice policies and programmes and citizens' participation in law enforcement area.

A study on homicide victims is already on the pipe-line and survey on victims of fatal road accidents is in an advanced stage of planning. The relevance of research to police work is highlighted in the training courses conducted by the faculty of criminology, particularly in the course of research methodology. The researchers work on projects which have a bearing on the tasks they have to undertake in the field or which are likely to arise in the foreseeable future. Broadly speaking, such projects have covered job identification, performance, grievances and attitudes.

(*b*) *The Faculty of Forensic Science* :

Guided and supervised by the members of the staff, most of the research projects have been undertaken by the research fellows and the projects sponsored by the Ministry of Home Affairs and by the Council of Scientific and Industrial Research. These projects fall under four categories : viz. (*i*) original, (*ii*) survey, (*iii*) modification of old and (*iv*) development of new techniques. Mention may be made of original researches in the field of photochemical degradation of organic chemicals, immunoassay of potent drugs, enzyme profile of blood samples, drill-bit identification from drilled metal chips and electrophoresis of inks on absorbent loaded filter papers. Similarly, a number of surveys are being undertaken for collecting background information in respect of chemical, physical and biological parameters on printing inks, tranquillizers, blood samples and human teeth. Two new techniques developed during this period are ; (*i*) the use of critical solution temperature for identification of small quantity of a vegetable oil and (*ii*) development of indigenous reflective number plates. The latter has been patented for commercial exploitation.

Research Activities at the Internal Security Academy, Mount Abu

Internal Security Academy, Mount Abu is a premier training and research institution dealing with varied problems of internal security. In August, 1981, the academy constituted a research team to collect data about various aspects of insurgency and counter-insurgency in the country. The purpose was to develop expertise and research awareness in the area. In December, 1981, the academy has initiated a proposal for research affiliation with the Rajasthan University, Jaipur. The objective is to develop a research centre for carrying out research on the problems of internal security and allied police subjects. A "data bank" has also been created in the academy. The field research team has visited Nagaland and Manipur. One officer of the rank of Supdt. of Police and two officers of the rank of Dy. Supdts. of Police constitute the membership of the team. Some useful and informative material has been collected by this field team. The I.S.A. has also prepared a number of case studies which focus on law and order situations. The research activities of the academy are supervised by the Director.

Police Research Training Programmes

The Institute of Criminology and Forensic Science, New Delhi is conducting two short term courses for senior officers of police drawn from the policy-making and managerial levels. The objectives of these two courses as envisaged by their planners are :

(*a*) To highlight the significance of scientific research in the police including its organisation and management ;

(*b*) To identify and formulate research problems and to devise ways and means to evaluate them ;

(*c*) To analyse the scope and limitations of research methods ; and

(*d*) To further develop the facility for planning, implementing and supervising research on police problems.[11]

For Dy. Inspectors-General of Police, a ten-day course on "Orientation to Research Methodology" has been evolved. The course contents are divided in three parts. Part one includes generic considerations such as social research, concept, meaning and major steps, problem identification and formulation of hypothesis. The second part deals with research design : types, concepts and precautions, data collection and its processing. The third part emphasises on mechanical computation of data, use of computers in research, report writing techniques and precautions. The course also includes discussions and symposia on various police problems like traffic accidents, economic offences, police community relations and need for research.

For Superintendents of Police, the Institute of Criminology and Forensic Science, Delhi conducts a six-weeks' course on research methodology. Broadly speaking, the course contents on research methodology include social research viz. concept, meaning and major steps, types of research studies, problem identification and formulation of hypothesis, research design and various other research methods and techniques. During the course, there are discussions and symposia on problems of research in criminology and organisational and financial problems in criminological research in India. The relevance of research to police work is highlighted in both these courses. Under the guidance of the directing staff, the participants work on projects which have a bearing on the tasks they have to tackle in the field or which are likely to arise in the foreseeable future. Broadly speaking, such projects have covered job identification, performance, grievances and attitudes. So far, ten courses on orientation to research methodology have been conducted for the officers of the rank of Dy. Inspectors-General of Police.

Police Research : An Evaluation

Applied research in police organisations is an adventurous undertaking in an environment which is sociologically very rich. The police are the crucial actors in day to day and other formal activities. They are the most visible and represent an active institution of social control. They provide a technological and organisational answer to the Hobbsian question of social control. Due to "secrecy culture" and organisational environment, many police research centres have not published their research studies. A lot of these are available in cyclo-styled or unpublished forms. The B.P.R. & D. as a premier research organisation of the country has completed 47 research projects so far. In the year 1970, it completed its first research project which was a brief analysis of the police arrangements in India. In 1972, three projects on the adequacy of police arrangements during communal riots in Thana, Meerut and Aurangabad districts were completed. Next year, "Specialist Services in the Police Juvenile Aid Police Units" and "Job Analysis at Police Stations and Traffic Department of Delhi and Bombay" were undertaken and completed. The B.P.R. & D. completed nine projects in 1973, seven in 1974, eleven in 1975, five in 1976, seven in 1977 and two in 1978. Some of these research projects are of high quality and are functionally advantageous. Details of research projects completed by the B.P.R. & D. are given in appendix 'B'.

The Police Research Centres of Andhra Pradesh, Gujarat, Karnataka Kerala, Madhya Pradesh, Maharashtra, Rajasthan, Tamil Nadu, Uttar Pradesh and Delhi have also completed a number of small and state level research projects as shown in appendix 'C'. In all ten states out of 22 states of the country are having research centres and their research contribution to police science and police problems in India can be rated as satisfactory. Some of the research projects carried out by police research centres are just compilation of data without application of social research methodology. Some research papers can be regarded as just good "term-papers" prepared by the individuals without having any research orientation. This is partly due to lack of adequate training in research methodology and want of guidance from qualified research guides.

Police Research under Progress and Future Plans

"Professional orientation" of policemen is a pre-requisite for the growth of police research. Police research centres in Andhra Pradesh, Gujarat, Haryana, Karnataka, Kerala, Madhya Pradesh, Maharashtra, Rajasthan, Tamil Nadu, Uttar Pradesh and Delhi have taken up several research projects which are at different stages of preparation and study. The B.P.R. & D. is also having ten research projects in hand at present. In all, ten states are having police research centres which are completing research projects in various areas of police work. The Police Research Centre, Tamil Nadu has four subjects under police science for research with a financial outlay of Rs. 1 lakh. The Police Research Centre, Madhya Pradesh is having seven research subjects under the police science with a financial outlay of Rs. 3,97,061/-. The Kerala Police Research Centre is having five subjects under research in police science with a financial outlay of Rs. 2,00,000/- non-recurring and Rs. 1,00,000/- recurring. Directorate of Civil Police Wireless has a project on setting up of research and development facility in electronics and communications in DCPW under communications with an outlay of Rs. 7,00,000/- non-recurring and Rs. 5,00,000/- recurring. Jammu & Kashmir Research Centre has taken up ten subjects of criminology with a financial outlay of Rs. 1,60,000/- Punjab Police Research Centre has taken up ten projects for research with Rs. 2,00,000/- per annum financial outlay. There is a need for more research projects to make police more effective and improve their performance. The investment made in research and development today in police is extremely meagre. One of the main reasons for starvation of funds in police research and development is that police expenditure itself is a non-plan sector. The police training institutions are however handicapped in taking up research work seriously. Little work has been done by the training institutions in the field of research. N.P.A., Hyderabad and I.S.A., Mount Abu are doing some work by producing periodical syndicate research reports. I.C.F.S., New Delhi is also conducting a number of research projects. The data of the present study reveal that barring these three national level training centres, research activities in most of the training institutions are nominal. Even research cells have not been sanctioned or created in a number of training institutions. This clearly proves the hypothesis that there is an obvious lack of co-ordination between police training and police research in India. The hypothesis that the training enterprise is non-goal oriented in terms of cost benefit has been found partly valid by the present study.

Limitations in Police Research

Indian police has been sensitive to outside research due to variety of reasons. Some of these as pointed out by our respondents are :

(*a*) Bureaucratic rigidity and the threat to personal careers ;

(*b*) Threat to the institutional authority ;

(*c*) Potential tarnishing of the subjectively constructed images and the rhetorics of the organisation ;

(*d*) The threat to the legitimacy of the perspective of the research and the problem of striking a satisfactory research bargain ;

(*e*) Outside researchers do not find a conducive research milieu in the police organisation due to internal schisms of the police department and other aspect of the organisation—secrecy, threat, morale and esteem problems and the problem of security of the state ;

(*f*) Police research presents some special problems of value conflict, role management and danger. The structure of the tactics to be used in this type of research is affected by the problems of access, research style, sponsorship, location and perspective on the action.[12]

Social scientists and researchers have not taken up studies in the field of police administration. Perhaps, the fault lies with the police organisations which have preferred to keep their administrative problems to themselves and even cloak them under a shroud of confidentiality. The traditional factors responsible for all this can be traced to the historical development of the police system in the country.[13] A bold beginning has to be made somewhere to throw the doors of police organisation open to social scientists and social researchers so that a systematic and analytical study of various aspects of police administration can be undertaken with scientific regors. The introduction of professionally oriented, educated and thoughtful policemen to police profession can open a gateway for new knowledge on the working and organisational problems of police administration. The secretive nature of police organisations has made the role of the outsider researcher difficult and sensitive. The police administration in India is almost a virgin soil for social science researchers and if tapped with care, this research can produce gainful results. The reports of the various state commissions of police can at best be regarded an "broad-gauge generalizations". They have indicated areas which need further scientific enquiry and rigorous research. The dual role of police as agents of law and agents of the government, co-ordination between the police and other public agencies, need for organisational and functional changes, police and society and management of police functions are some of the areas which need research by social scientists. To achieve high level professionalism, continuous study and research for improvement and advancement of professional techniques and their application are essential. It is difficult for a researcher to give up his values and attitudes in research exercise. But the quality of social research depends on the personality of the investigator, his professional equipment and training in research methods. His sensitivity to the subtleties of human interaction, his emotional depth and intellectual awareness and his capacity to recognise and counter his own projections help him in developing objectivity. Ability to establish rapport without becoming over-identified and taking things for granted, awareness of ethical considerations and above all, willingness and capability to accept the people on their own terms are characteristics of serious social researcher. Availability of funds and earnest researchers are pre-requisites for high quality research.

Limitations of Police Research Enterprise

One reason for the lack of adequate serious research in police organisation is the non-availability of funds for the purpose. Related to this is the lack of qualified research staff and team work. Fundamental pure research is unlikely to carry much weight in police departments. Applied research, directed by police officials is viewed with some favour though its logical implications are not accepted by the department. Very few scholars have taken up research on police.[14] In India, David

H. Bayley did a commendable job in his pioneering study entitled "Police and Political Development in India" published in 1969.[15]

(There are many serious handicaps in police research in India. Some of these can be listed below :

(a) *Fear of exposure* : Distrust and antipathy of the academic researcher is endemic to most police organisations and researcher is seldom welcomed by the rank and file due to the fear of exposure.

(b) *Public image of the police* : A researcher planning to study police or policing runs the risk of being blinded by the wild image of the Indian police in society as a whole. This casts a long shadow and makes it considerably difficult to identify problems associated with policing.

(c) *Police fraternity and occupational secrecy* : Like the defence services the police in India regard the disclosure of information about their official work as potential threat to their success. Secrecy is important to the police because of the potential embarrasment, a disclosure about mistakes, misguided policies, cover ups and so on might bring to the police organisation. Many policemen generally feel that an outsider has no business to study them unless he too belongs to the police department and such sentiments result in rationalising close-door policy.

(d) *Environmental turbulence* : Many police organisations do have some hodgepodge of cliques, cabals, and conspiracies and since police officers are not expected to trust each other, how can they trust the wisdom of researchers from outside. Danger of exposure of manifold types of corruption, excessive use of force, police brutality, use of third degree methods of interrogation and police lawlessness etc. compel policemen to maintain a close-door policy.

(*e*) *Value conflicts and street level isolation* : The values in the police organisation and the scientific inquiry of social scientists show a wide discrepancy which makes the research situation uncomfortable. The police are marked by political conservatism, a preference for action and decisiveness while the social scientists tend to study political change and its rationale. This sometimes creates value conflicts. The first hand observation of the police in action can often be a frustrating affair. Moreover, the police world is partitioned into several subworlds and it is not easy to see unity of purpose or an underlying strategy behind police actions.

(*f*) *Lack of faith in research* : Most police administrators genuinely believe that social research rarely (if ever) contributes to solution to police problems because no cut and dried solutions are there to complex police problems in the social situations of the developing world.

(*g*) *Paucity of funds* : While in United Kingdom, the budget percentage of investment in research and development is nearly 8 percent, it is only .22 percent in India. The statement given below depicts the overall expenditure on police (including the states/ union territories/central police organisations) and the percentage of expenditure on research and development.

Budget of all states/U.Ts./C.P.Os. in 1976-77	Rs. 83,246 lakhs
Expenditure on police research and development in states and the Centre in 1976-77	Rs. 183.5 lakhs
Percentage or expenditure on police research and development	.22 percent

The approximate expenditure of state police research units comes to about Rs. one crore (recurring). The non-availability of funds is one of the biggest handicaps in police research. No meaningful research is possible without financial inputs. However, some of these obstacles can be and have been overcome by commitment of modern researchers. The police organisations need to be more liberal, open-minded and helpful to these researchers. More and more research units should be sanctioned at all levels and the research set-up of the police organisations should recruit researchers in requisite strength and calibre. Better equipment, scientific training and financial resources can go a long way to make the research enterprise purpose oriented and meaningful.

Police Research and Police Training

Police training and police research apparently need closer coordination and mutual support. Police being engaged in law enforcement deal with human beings. The goal of police research has to be improvement in policy-making, police planning and blending the two with social activities. Utilisation of police can improve meaningfully if the police researcher looks around and uses his scientific training in solving police problems. Police research in the field of police training can be relevant because the skills, knowledge and attitudes of policemen can be shaped through training enterprises. Police research should identify gaps in the expectations and performance of policemen and should suggest new training programmes to bridge these gaps. Research should assist the training effort by providing educative literature. The present study finds a great hiatus between police training and practical field work of the police. Research through empirical studies should pinpoint this and suggest measures to remove this hiatus. To keep the police training institutions intellectually vibrant, practice oriented, realistic and up-to-date in their knowledge of police problems, police research should be considered as one of the basic functions of a police training institution. Actually, all national level police training institutions and state level police training colleges should develop research centres for advanced studies on police subjects.

RESEARCH DIVISION

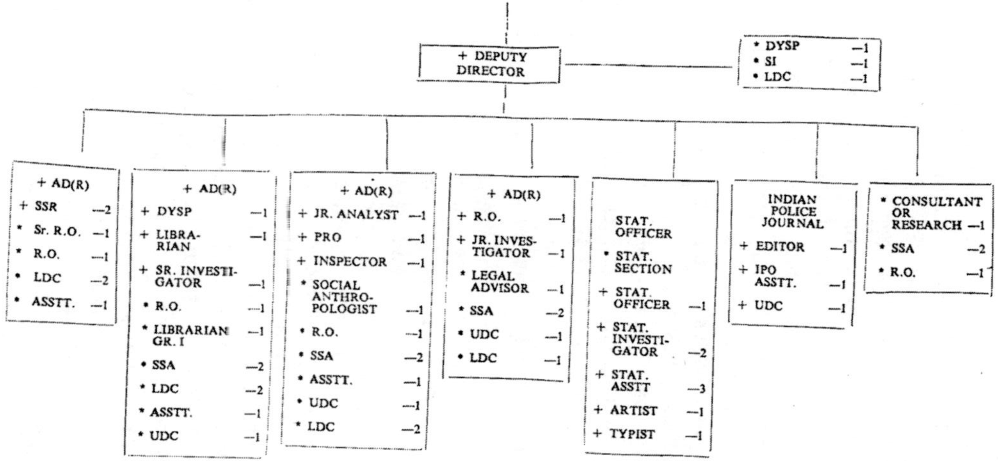

+ EXISTING STAFF
* PROPOSED STAFF

Universities should also come forward to recognise these research centres and permit them to conduct M. Phil. and Ph.D. programmes. Teaching staff of police training colleges should undertake police research leading to a doctoral degree of the university. A beginning in this direction has been made by the Internal Security Academy, Mount Abu and the Institute of Criminology and Forensic Science. Fundamental research should be undertaken by the central and state police research units but these police training institutions at lower levels may also be encouraged to undertake a certain amount of applied research through its instructional staff and senior level course trainees. This will minimise the hiatus obtained between theoretical training and practical police work. At the N.P.A., Hyderabad, every syndicate group of senior officers is assigned a subject for field study and empirical research. The syndicate group reports are published in the pages of "Transactions" published by the academy. They have proved very useful for researchers. In a developing country where the social milieu and administrative reality undergo rapid changes, close co-ordination between police research and police training alone can bring desired results. By taking research work alongwith their training assignments, the police trainers and trainees can improve their competence and credibility in the professional field and cumulatively contribute to the growth of knowledge so very essential to solve police problems of a changing society.

There should be receptivity to ideas and suggestions and willingness to commit resources on the part of the government for the development of research organisations in police. Research Advisory Councils should be constituted at different levels. Police work has scope for fundamental and applied research. The former implies study and development of theories and general principles regarding various aspects of police administration. Applied research represents an exercise to apply such theories or principles to the solution of practical problems. Officers with research aptitude and adequate motivation can carry out sustained work on research projects.

Police research organisations should identify shortcomings, devise solutions and remedies and chalk out long-range plans for improving the police administration. The senior government officials should accept and implement the proposed plans. Receptivity to the suggestions and recommendations of the research organisations and willingness to release funds for the implementation of the same on the part of the government are relevant to the success of the efforts of the research centres. Immediate and spectacular results should not be expected from the research organisations. Research in police work has to be taken up by members working at different levels in different capacities. Research in police work will bring police officials closer to their own world of operations. It will offer deeper insight into hard facts of their professional life. The field of research besides being varied involves commitment to purpose and availability of resources.

There is need for close cooperation between universities and police research centres so that serious research work could be done on police subjects. Police research scholarships for two-and-half years should be sponsored by the B.P.R&D. to encourage scholars to take up research on police matters. Police officers who have research aptitude should be granted study leave with secretarial assistance and financial aid to take up research projects for the Ph D. degree for universities. N.P.A., Hyderabad should have a number of research fellowships to encourage serious research.

Present study indicates that police research in India is not being taken up seriously by the police training institutions viz. Institute of Criminology and Forensic Science, S V. P. National Police Academy Hyderabad, Internal Security Academy. Mount Abu. Police training institutions have not yet taken up research projects seriously and in most of the training institutions, the level of research awareness is fairly low. Research cells in many police training institutions are yet to be established and even in institutions where research cells have been created, trained and competent researchers have not been made available. Then there is lack of co-ordination between the efforts of police training and police research in the country. The Bureau of Police Research and Development and the police training institutions of the country need closer co-ordination in the field of police research. The successful development and implementation of research programmes in police administration will largely depend on the establishment of a closer liasion between police training institutions and police research organisations. All these years, the two lived in two different worlds of seclusion. Attempts have to be made to bring them together for mutual benefit and future growth of police in free India.

REFERENCES

1. Doig, James W., "*Police Problems, Proposals and Strategies for Changes*", Public Administrative Review (Symposium on Police in a Democratic Society) Sep.,-Oct. 1968, p. 393.
2. For composition of Council and detailed functions of Police Research and Development Advisory Council, please, see Police Research and Development Journal Quarter IV-1971, Oct., Dec. 1971, pp. 1-2.
3. Mahmood Bin Muhammad, "*Planning & Research for Crime Prevention*", SVP NPA Mag. Vol. XXV, Nov. 1975, pp 36-7.
4. Tondon, Shrewan, "*Importance of Research and Development in Modernising Police Force*", (Police Research & Development Oct, Dec, 1977), p. 2.
5. Source : B.P.R.&D, "*Strategy for Police Research, Development and Training in India*", 1979, p. 67.
6. For List of 47 projects, see B.P.R. & D. "*Strategy for Police Research, Development & Training in India*", M.H.A., New Delhi, 1979, pp. 61-4.
7. Mahmood Bin Muhammad, "*Planning & Research for Crime Prevention*" SVP NPA Magazine, Vol. XXV, Nov. 1975, p. 37.
8. For details, see B.P.R. & D., M.H.A., Govt. of India, Delhi, "*Strategy of Police Research, Development and Training in India*", 1979, p. 46-60.
9. Report of the Committee on Police Training, M.H.A., Govt. of India, 1973, p. 74.
10. X Symposium of the Heads of golice Training Institutions in India, (SVP NPA Hyderabad, 1981—p. 80).
11. Brochure of Institute of Criminology and Forensic Science, New Delhi, "*Training Courses in Criminology*".
12. Peter Manning, "*The Researcher—An Alien in the Police World—The Ambivalent Force*" (Ed) Arthur Nieder Hoffer & Abraham S. Blimberg, p. 121.

13. Rao, Venugopal S., "*The Present Status and Organisational Future of the Police in India*" in (Ed). Reddy and Seshadri, "*Developing Society and Police*" Osmania Univesrity, Hyderabad, 1972, p. 27.
14. In USA, a number of Scholars have done research on Police subjects. For details, see "*Policing—A View from the Street*" (Ed.), Manning Peter K. and Maanen John Van—Good Year Publishing, California, 1978, pp. 350-59.
15, Others in the field are :

    Dr. Anand Swarup Gupta : did his research work on "*Crime and Police in India upto 1861*" and later on "*The Police in British India 1861—1947*".

    Sri Bhupinder Singh has done research on "*Police Administration in Assam 1874 to 1947*" and has been awarded Ph. D. degree by Gauhati University in 1974.

    J.C. Madan got his Ph. D. degree from the University of Delhi on his Thesis "*The Police Administration in British India 1861-1902*".

CHAPTER NINE

PART I

SARDAR VALLABHBHAI PATEL NATIONAL POLICE ACADEMY, HYDERABAD : A STUDY

THE S.V.P. N.P.A., Hyderabad is the premier police Academy of India and can be well compared with the Federal Bureau of Investigation Academy of United States and Bramshill Police Academy of Great Britain.[1] It represents the greatest effort at police training designed to develop leadership of the I.P.S. (Indian Police Service). Today all the top positions in the police organisations in the states and in Central police Organisations are manned by the personnel who had their initial training in this training institution. The N.P.A., administratively speaking, lies under the care and control of the Ministry of Home Affairs, Government of India. The Union Govt. created this Central Police Training Institution by taking upon itself the responsibility of providing facilities for training of senior police officers of the Country.[2] The constitution of the I.P.S. as an All India Service necessitated a common pattern of police training for all the officers and the same has been met by establishment of this premier police training institution. Apart from the obvious advantage of highly qualified staff and equipment, a central institution was created with a view to develop espirit de corps, professional competence and national outlook with dedication to unity of the country.[3] Before 1947, the direct recruits of the Indian (Imperial) Police were trained in the police training colleges in their respective provinces. With a view to achieve a measure of uniformity in the system of policing in different parts of the country and fostering an all India outlook at the initiative of the late Home Minister Sardar Vallbhbhai Patel, the Central Police Training College was started in the year 1948. It was a momentous decision to provide for a centralised and uniform all-India training for the I.P.S. officers with the aim of fostering a sense of national belonging among young I.P.S probationers who were drawn from all corners and differing states of the country and society. Development of mutual understanding among the I.P.S. probationers was the prime objective because this was to stand them in good stead in the performance of their future task of police leadership in different parts of the country. The academy was vested with responsibility of bringing about a desired degree of uniformity in the system of policing in various parts of the country.[4]

Sri P.L. Mehta, I.P. was the founder Commandant of the institution and remained Commandant of the Central Police Training College from 15.9.1948 to 31 January, 1954. On September 15, 1949, the Central Police Training College got started and the first batch of I.P.S. officers presented their charge reports on a sheet of plain paper. The instructional staff consisted of the following :

(*i*) Shri S.H.J. Pratt (Dy. S.P. and Chief Drill Instructor)

(*ii*) Shri R.N. Banerji (Dy. S.P. and Chief Law Instructor)

(*iii*) Shri T.K. Lawai, Scientific Aids Instructor.

(*iv*) Shri Bahadur Singh, Riding Master.

(*v*) Hd. Const. Kanchan Singh, Drill Instructor.

(*vi*) Sri J.R. de Chazal I.P.—joined as the first Asst. Commandant on 5.10.1948 and left the institution on 14.10.1949.

SARDAR VALLABHBHAI PATEL NATIONAL POLICE ACADEMY

ORGANISATIONAL CHART

DIRECTOR

Deputy Director (Admn.)

Hospital

- Staff Surgeon —1
- Nurses —2
- Lab. Technician —1
- Compounder —1
- Nursing Orderly —4

Library

- Librarian —1
- Librarian Grd. III —1
- L.D.Cs. —2
- Book Binder-c-Attendant —1

(Admn/Genl/R. Sec)

- Supdt. (Min.) —1
- U.D Cs. —2
- L.D.Cs. —4
- Tele. Optr. —2
- Multi. Optr. —1
- Jr. Gest Optn —1
- Daftry —2
- Peon —1

Accounts

- Accountant —1
- U.D.Cs. —5
- L.D.Cs. —3

Store Sec.

- U.D.C. I/C —1
- U.D.C. —1
- L.D.C. —1

- RI/QMI —1
- Sanitary Inspr. —1
- Inspr. (Band) —1
- S. Is. —2
- SI (Band) —1
- HC (Genl) —9
- HC (Band) —3
- Constables —82
- ,, (Band) —15
- Cooks —2
- Sweepers —14
- Bhisties —5
- Mali —7

(M.T./Sec.)

- Inspr. —1
- S. Is. —2
- Head Mech. Jamedar —1
- Drivers —15
- Helpers (Const) —4

(W.TS. Sec.)

- Inspector (Commn) —1
- Radio Tech. Grd. II —1
- Wireless Oprts. —2
- Sr. Projectionist. —1
- Jr. ,, ,, —1
- Jr. Engineer —1(Elec.)
- Painter-cum-Artist. —1

A.D. (O) — For Senior Officers Course.

A.D. (C)

A.D. (L)

A.D. (S)

PA & STENOGRAPHERS — 12

(1 PA, 4 Sr. Stenographers & 7 Jr. Stenographers)

PA to Director	Steno to A.D. (.)/A.D. (L-II)
Sr. Steno to D.D. (Trg.)	Steno to A.D. (OD)/A.D. (L-III)
Sr. Steno to D.D. (Admn.)	Steno to A.D. (C)/A.D. (C-II)
Sr. Steno to A.D. (O)	Steno to A.D. (S)/A.D. (Sc. Aids)
Sr. Steno to A.D. (L)	Steno to Profesor in Business Management & Readers in Behavioural Sciences & Teaching Methodology.
	Steno to A.D. (Trg. Methodology)/ Research Officer.
	Steno to A.D (A)/A.O.

SARDAR VALLABHBHAI PATEL NATIONAL POLICE ACADEMY

ORGANISATIONAL CHART

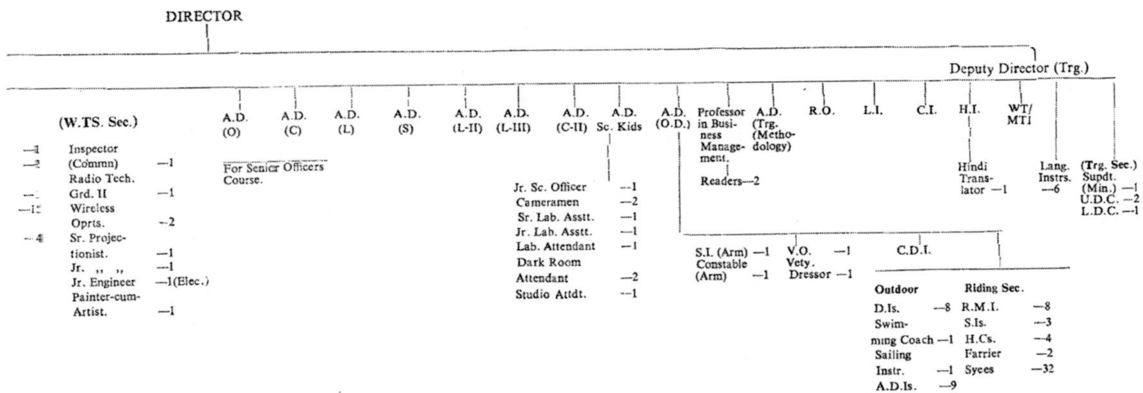

SARDAR VALLABHBHAI PATEL NATIONAL POLICE ACADEMY

ORGANISATIONAL CHART

DIRECTOR

Deputy Director (Admn.)

Hospital

- Staff Surgeon —1
- Nurses —2
- Lab. Technician —1
- Compounder —1
- Nursing Orderly —4

Library

- Librarian —1
- Librarian Grd. III —1
- L.D.Cs. —2
- Book Binder-c-Attendant —1

(Admn/Genl/CR. Sec)

- Supdt. (Min.) —1
- U.D.Cs. —2
- L.D.Cs. —4
- Tele. Optr. —2
- Multi. Optr. —1
- Jr. Gest. Optr. —1
- Daftry —2
- Peon —1

Accounts

- Accountant —1
- U.D.Cs. —5
- L.D.Cs. —3

Store Sec.

- U.D.C. I/C —1
- U.D.C. —1
- L.D.C. —1

A.D. (A)

- RI/QMI —1
- Sanitary Inspr. —1
- Inspr. (Band) —1
- S.Is. —2
- SI (Band) —1
- HC (Genl) —9
- HC (Band) —3
- Constables —82
- ,, (Band) —15
- Cooks —2
- Sweepers —14
- Bhisties —5
- Mali —7

(M.T./Sec.)

- Inspr. —1
- S. Is. —2
- Head Mech. Jamedar —1
- Drivers —15
- Helpers (Const) —4

(W.T. Sec.)

- Inspector (Commn) —1
- Radio Tech. Grd. II —1
- Wireless Optrs. —2
- Sr. Projectionist. —1
- Jr. ,, ,, —1
- Jr. Engineer —1(Elec.)
- Painter-cum-Artist. —2

A.D. (O) A.D. (C) A.D. (L) A.D. (S)

For Senior Officers Course

PA & STENOGRAPHERS — 12
(1 PA, 4 Sr. Stenographers & 7 Jr. Stenographers)

PA to Director	Steno to A.D. (L)/A.D. (L-II)
Sr. Steno to D.D. (Trg)	Steno to A.D. (OL)/A.D. (L-III)
Sr. Steno to D.D. (Admn.)	Steno to A.D. (C)/A.D. (C-II)
Sr. Steno to A.D. (O)	Steno to A.D. (S)/A.D. (Sc. Aids)
Sr. Steno to A.D. (L)	Steno to Professor in Business Management & Readers in Behavioural Sciences & Teaching Methodology.
	Steno to A.D. (Trg. Methodology)/ Research Officer.
	Steno to A.D.(A)/A.O.

Training Programme conduc

- Basic Course of IPS Probatione
- Senior Officers Course
- C.B.I. Cadets Course
- B.T.T. Course

ƆAR VALLABHBHAI PATEL NATIONAL POLICE ACADEMY

ORGANISATIONAL CHART

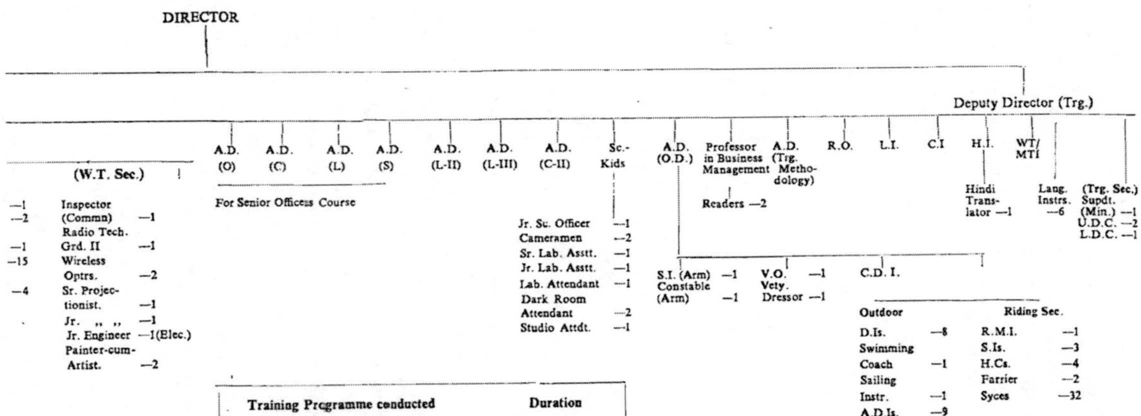

Training Prcgramme conducted	Duration
Basic Course of IPS Probationers	11½ Months
Senior Officers Course	14 Weeks
C.B.I. Cadets Course	9 Months
B.T.T. Course	1 Month

The I.P.S. probationers training was heavily weighted in favour of outdoor training in the shape of physical training, equitation and drill. Initially the administrative block, class-rooms, library and the mess were all accommodated in the M.E.S. Barracks at Mount Abu. Later administrative block and the class-rooms were shifted to a small C.P.W.D. building known as "Springfield". The officers' mess we shifted to Rajputana Hotel Estate with effect from 1st December, 1949. Again within a short period, Springfield had to be vacated and the administrative block and the class-rooms were moved to the buildings of "Abu Lawrence School," Mount Abu. A proposal was made in 1953 for starting a special refresher course for the I.P.S. officers who have put in eight years of service in the field. It was started in June, 1960 and was later named as advanced course with a six months' duration. This course was redesignated as senior officers' course in 1969. From April, 1973, the duration of the course has been cut down to 14 weeks and the syllabus was also modified in view of the recommendations of the Gore Committee on Police Training.

From October 1965, the posts of Commandant, Deputy Commandant and Assistant Commandant were redesignated as Director, deputy Director and Asst. Director respectively. The Central Police Training College was renamed as the National Police Academy in May, 1967. The post of a D.I.G. was created in 1957 and Sri E.L. Stracey took over charge as the first Deputy Commandant of the School. Consequent upon the recommonations of the B.N. Mullik Report, there was an increase in the strength of the directing staff. The recommendations of the D.P. Kohli Report augmented the strength further in 1966 resulting in the addition of posts of one Dy Director (D.I.G.) and five Asst Directors (Ss.P.) to its faculty.

On February 5, 1975, the N.P.A. shifted to its present campus at Hyderabad. The new campus is situated on the Hyderabad Bangalore National Highway at a distance of about eight kms from Charminar. The Academy was given its present name i.e. "Sardar Vallabhbhai Patel National Police Academy" at its new campus which is spread over an area of 202 acres of land. The building complex comprises an administrative block, messes for probationers and trainees, an auditorium, a stadium, a gymnasium, a squash court, a hospital and residential quarters for the faculty.

Basic training to the Sub-Inspectors cadets of the Central Bureau of Investigation was started in the year 1965. Originally it was a six month course but subsequently it was raised to 11 months. 139 C.B.I. cadets have passed out of this institution between 1965 and 1972.

The Andhra Pradesh Conference Hall of the Academy has been constructed by a munificent grant of Rs. 2.25 lakhs by the Andhra Pradesh Government. The Hall was formally inaugurated on 23rd August, 1977. In 1979, three new types of training programmes were introduced during the year. The first Top Management Development Course of two weeks was conducted from 21 Feb to 6 Mar. 1979. The first Basic Terminal Course was conducted from 5th Mar. to 4th April, 1979. The First Crime Prevention Course was conducted in April, 1979. Thus, the N.P.A. introduced three new courses for senior police officers during 1979.

There is a high level advisory board headed by the Union Home Secretary which periodically reviews the syllabi and the training methodology of various courses run at the Academy. The following members constitute the advisory board :

(*i*) Financial Adviser, M.H.A.

(*ii*) Prof M.S. Gore

(*iii*) Director, I.I.P.A., New Delhi

(*iv*) Principal Admin. Staff College of India, Hyderabad

(*v*) Director, I.B.

(*vi*) Director, C.B.I.

(*vii*) Director-General, C.R.P.F.

(*viii*) Director-General, B.S.F.

(*ix*) I.G.P., Tamil Nadu

(*x*) Director, S.V.P., N.P.A., Hyderabad

(*xi*) Jt. Secretary (Trg.) Cabinet Secretariat, D.P. & A.R.

The Director (Trg.), B.P.R.&D., New Delhi is the Member Secretary of this board. The board is required to pay a visit to S.V.P.N.P.A. Hyderabad at least once every calender year, as may be arranged in consultation with the Director of the Academy to undertake annual stock-taking of the work of the Academy. It makes recommendations to the M.H.A. for improving the training of the I.P.S. officers. The functions of the board are (*i*) to review every three years the syllabi of various courses. (*ii*) to examine the adequacy of educative material and (*iii*) to recommend on matters which has relevance to the effectiveness of training or improvement in the physical facilities at the Academy.

Organisation and Staff

National Police Academy has a sanctioned strength of 335 members. The staff position of the Academy is as given at page no. 292 The Academy staff is divided in two wings, administrative and training wing, each under a Dy Director of the rank of Dy. Inspector-General of Police. The organisational chart is given at page no. 292.

Training Programmes at N.P.A.

The Academy is currently conducting the following courses :

(*a*) Basic course for I.P.S. Probationers (duration 11½ months)

(*b*) Besic Training Terminal Course for the I.P.S. probationers (duration one month)

(*c*) Senior Officers' Course for 14 weeks duration

(*d*) Basic Course for Sub-Inspectors of the Central Bureau of Investigation (duration nine months)

(*e*) Crime Prevention Course (duration ten days)

(*f*) Top Management Development Programme (two weeks duration)

(*g*) Junior Management Course

(*h*) Senior Management Course

Senior Officers' Course has now been stopped and in its place, three management courses have been started.

The Academy plans to start courses for training of trainers of three different durations for the officers of the rank of D.Is.G.

TABLE 9.1

Showing Staff Position of N.P.A. Staff Position (Sanctioned Strength) of the Academy

S. No.	Name of Post	Sanctioned strength	Existing strength	Vacancies
	1	2	3	4
1.	Director	1	1	—
2.	Deputy Directors	2	2	—
3.	Assistant Directors	11	10	1
4.	Staff Surgeon	1	1	—
5.	Professor in Business Management	1	—	1
6.	Research Officer	1	—	1
7.	Readers in Behavioural Science & Teaching Methodology	2	2	—
8.	Chief Drill Instructor	1	1	—
9.	Law Instructor	1	1	—
10.	Hindi Instructor	1	1	—
11.	Crime Instructor	1	1	—
12.	M.T./W.T. Instructor	1	1	—
13.	Administrative Officer	1	1	—
14.	Jr. Scientific Officer	1	—	1
15.	Veterinary Officer	1	1	—
16.	Superintendents	2	2	—
17.	Inspectors	10	10	—
18.	Swimming Coach	1	—	1
19.	Sailing Instructor	1	—	1
20.	Inspector (Com/Tech.)	1	—	1

Sl. No.	Name of post	Sanctioned strength	Existing strength	Vacancies
	1	2	3	4
21.	Inspector (M.T.)	1	1	
22.	Inspector (Band)	1	—	1
23.	Language Instructor	6	2	4
24.	P.A. to Director	1	1	—
25.	Accountant	1	1	—
26.	Stenographer Grade-I	4	4	—
27.	Painter-cum-Artist	1	1	—
28.	Junior Engineer (Electronic)	1	1	—
29.	Nurses	2	1	1
30.	Librarian	1	1	—
31.	Lab. Technician	1	1	—
32.	Hindi Translator	1	1	—
33.	Sanitary Inspector	1	1	—
34.	Sub-Inspectors	6	6	—
35.	Sub-Inspector (MT. Tech)	2	1	1
36.	Sub-Inspector (Band)	1	—	1
	B.F.	73	58	15
37.	Radio Technician Gd. II	1	1	—
38.	Librarian Grade-III	1	1	—
39.	Senior Lab. Assistant	1	1	—
40.	Junior Stenographers	7	6	1
41.	Upper Division Clerks	11	11	—
42.	Lower Division Clerks	10	10	—
43.	Telephone Operators	2	2	—
44.	Hindi Typist	1	1	—

	1	2	3	4
45.	Compounder	1	1	—
46.	Camera men	2	—	2
47.	Jr. Laboratory Assistant	1	1	—
48.	Senior Projectionist	1	1	—
49.	Junior Projectionist	1	1	—
50.	Wireless Operators	2	2	
51.	Multigraph Operator	1	1	—
52.	Head Mechanic Jemadar	1	1	—
53.	Head Constables (including MT/RT)	37	34	3
54.	Head Constables (Band)	3	—	3
55.	Book Binder-cum-Attendant	1	1	—
56.	Constables	87	80	7
57.	Constables (Band)	15	15	—
58.	Daftries	2	2	—
59.	Peon	1	1	—
60.	Syces	32	31	1
61.	Farriers	2	1	1
62.	Lab. Attendant	1	1	1
63.	Jr. Gestetner Operator	1	1	—
64.	Nursing Orderlies	4	4	
65.	Dark Room Attendant	2	+	—
66.	Veterinary Dresser	1	1	—
67.	Studio Attendant	1	—	1
68.	Malies	7	7	
69.	Cooks	2	2	—
70.	Sweepers/Bhisties	19	18	1
	Total	335	297	83

Ss.P. and Dy Ss.P. as soon as the additional faculty is sanctioned and training materials prepared. Similarly, it is proposed to start training course for state police officers who are included in the select list of I.P.S. The Centre has already taken a decision and even the syllabus has been worked out and sent to the state governments for their comments and suggestions. The Union government has decided about the refresher course for the state police service officers to be inducted into the I.P.S. and states have been directed to bring in suitable notifications making such a course compulsory for promotion of state officers to the rank of Superintendent of Police.

The I.P.S. Probationers Course

The training pattern and contents of this course have been reviewed several times. Mr. B.N. Mullik I.P. (Retd.) then Director, I.B. went into the question of training of I.P.S. officers and submitted a comprehensive report in the year 1960. Subsequently Mr. D.P. Kohli I.P. (Retd), then Director, C.B.I. was asked to examine the training of I.P.S. officers. He submitted his report in 1966. Mr. Kohli suggested a programme of practical training which was approved by the Ministry of Home Affairs and was enforced in the states in 1970. Later, the Gore Committee on police training again reviewed the syllabus and contents of the probationers' course and Post N.P.A practical training which has been now implemented. Thus, the course contents and syllabus of I.P.S. probationers course have undergone careful revisions. At present the I.P.S. (Probationers' Final Examination) Regulations 1979 are in vogue and the syllabus for outdoor and indoor subjects has been laid down under rule 5 of the said regulations. The curriculum of training and study for the basic course for the I.P.S. probationers is determined by the N.P.A. board and the board has the power to make such amendments and alterations in the curriculum as may be found necessary and appropriate, from time to time, to bring the curriculum of training and study in consonance with the developments and changes relevant to police work in the country. In the revised syllabus, outdoor work iucludes physical fitness, swimming, equitation, weapons training and drill. For the course, 1128 working periods have been allotted for teaching indoor subjects and 683 working periods have been allotted for outdoor training. This shows clearly a definite emphasis for indoor training for I.P.S. probationers. The Indoor subjects comprise a number of subjects as recommended by the Gore Committee on police training. There are few minor changes in the marks which were suggested by the Gore Committee, for various subjects and which have been laid down in I.P.S. (Probationers' Final Exam.) Regulations 1979. The differences can be noticed in the table given below :

TABLE 9.2

PART I INDOOR

S. No.	Subject	Gore Committee M.Marks	Gore Committee Duration Hrs.	I.P.S. Regulations M.Marks	I.P.S. Regulations Duration hrs.
1	2	3	4	5	6
1. a.	Modern Indian and Role of Police				
b.	Police Org. office records and procedure	50	2	50	2
2.	Law (with books)				
	Paper I I.P.C.	100	3	100	3
	Paper II Cr.P.C.	100	3	100	3
	Paper III Indian Evidence Act & Minor Acts	100	3	100	3
3.	Police Science				
	Paper I Crime Prevention	50	2	50	2
	Paper II Crime Investigation	75	3	75	2
	Paper III Forensic Medicines	25	1½	25	1½
	Paper IV Forensic Science	50	2	75	2
	Paper V Maintenance of Order, Traffic Control and security of foreigners	75	2	75	2

1	2	3	4	5	6
	Forensic Science practical	25	—	50	—
4.	Criminology	50	2	50	2
	Total marks	700			
5.	Management concepts & techniques	75	—	50	2
6.	Human behaviour and police attitudes	75	—	50	2
	Total	150			
	Grand Total	850			

PART II OUTDOOR WORK

1	2	3	4	5	6
1.	Physical fitness	50	—	40	—
2.	a. Personal performance in squad drill, arms drill and sword drill including turn-out	25	—	30	—
	b. Command and Control	25	—	20	—
	c. Field craft	10	—	Not given	
	d. Crowd Control	15	—	20	—
3.	Weapons Drill	50	—	40	—
4.	Equitation (optional)	25	—	25	—
5.	Swimming	Not suggested		15	—
	Total	200		200	

I.P.S. Regulations have adopted Gore Committee Recommendations as given in Appendix IX of the Report with very few minor alterations. While Gore Committee suggested 75 maximum marks each for Management Concepts and Techniques and Human Behaviour and Police Attitudes, I.P.S. Regulations 1979 have allotted 50 maximum marks for each subject. When the Gore Committee suggested that instructors should maintain observation/evaluation sheets carrying marks depending on rating scales, regulations have included these subjects in final examination scheme. Again while Gore Committee suggested 10 marks for field craft, Regulations have not included it in final examination scheme and while the Committee allotted 50 marks for physical fitness. Regulations have allotted only 40 marks. However, except for the above mentioned minor alterations, the final examination scheme of I.P.S. probationers is broadly based on the recommendations of the Gore Committee.

Keeping in view of the recommendations of Gore Committee, the question papers are divided into two parts, part I consists of objective type of questions in which acquisition of knowledge understanding and application are tested. It consists of true/false tests, multiple choice tests, matching test, completion items. short answer questions etc. Part II of the paper consists of essay type questions. Pass percentage in all the subjects i.e. indoor and outdoor and qualifying tests in the examination has been fixed 40 in accordance with the ruling of U.P.S.C. and M.H.A. A probationer who fails in a subject is awarded 'O' in that particular subject and the probationer is required to clear this examination subsequently. It is affecting his inter-se-seniority which is having its bearing to his promotion prospects and confirmation. To assess a probationer, the Director, N.P.A. with the help of senior members of his faculty, awards his marks out of 100 to a probationer and the assessment is based on his performance in the examinations, games and sports, his mess and club activities, his punctuality and attendance and his activities in other associations. Since 1969, the Director has been made incharge for conducting I.P.S. probationars' final and re-examination which is conducted by the examination cell.

The passing out parade is an important ceremony for the I.P.S. probationers and the Academy. Full one week is declared passing out week and delegates from all the states are invited to attend the passing out parade and various other ceremonial functions. Generally, a three days' seminar on some topical subject is held on the passing out parade day the chief guest awards trophies, cups, medals and prizes for the meritorious performance of I.P.S. probationers. There are 20 awards which are awarded on the passing out parade day by the chief guest. The procedure and sequence of events are quite impressive. The passing out parade is generally presided over by an eminent person who delivers the address to the probationers and awards prizes and trophies on the occasion. I.P.S. probationers get an opportunity to attend "Seminar" which is held during passing out week. The researchers had an opportunity of looking at the feed-back and evaluation given by the probationers about their course.

Most of the trainees interviewed for the present study felt that the training given to them was quite adequate and useful. About 65 percent of the probationers stated that the standard of training was reasonably high. About 20 percent of respondent trainees of the sample said that the outdoor training still receives too much importance and they get completely exhausted by this. 15 percent of them maintained that there were certain overlapping subjects between basic I.P.S. probationers training and the Foundation course and this could be looked into and rectified. The researcher interviewed a few I.P.S. probationers on the day of their passing out from the Academy. 90 percent of them were generally very much satisfied with the training they received. The views of some probationers were worth mentioning : "Training is useful and perhaps for professional career but too much authoritarian atmosphere with emphasis on discipline and smartness builds up mental tension in trainees". Another probationer confessed, "I purposely did not take much interest as I am not interested in police job and will appear for I.A.S. examination again". One trainee felt that "the training atmosphere was better at L.B.S. National Academy of Administration, Mussorie and training atmosphere at N.P.A. is full of tension and stress". Many I.P.S. probationers found quality of instruction at N.P.A. quite high and physical facilities better than Mussorrie. In probationers' course at N.P.A., the academic curriculum is quite ponderous. So many subjects are taught simultaneously and with such speed that one hardly has time to think over what one has just been taught. One I.P.S. probationer felt that the scope and sphere of the subjects are in utter disproportion to the time available. This makes the pressure of the probationers unduly heavy. One trainee held the view that training helped in "developing an integrated outlook in administrative behaviour and professional outlook" Another trainee said "I have learnt to shed many angularities and the attitude of irresponsibility which were the legacies of the University life."

Basic Training Terminal Course

A short rounding off course for I.P.S. probationers after they have completed their practical field training in the states has been started in the Academy. The month long basic terminal course is conducted for probationers from 28 the I.P.S. batch who passed out of the Academy in 1976. The first such terminal course was conducted from 5th March to 4th April, 1979 and 23 I.P.S. officers/probationers of the 28th and 29th batch participated in it. Eleven such courses have been conducted by the N.P.A. so far. It was envisaged that in the first two years, there would be six courses in a year to cater 30 officers in each course. Thereafter the number of courses may be reduced to once in three months or once in six months, depending on the number of officers passing out of the Academy. This one month's rounding off training would be mainly by way of discussions in groups on problems faced by the trainees in the field during their field exposure. Through panel discussions and syndicate work, solution to problems should be arrived at. It has been envisaged that each officer returning to the N.P.A. after field training would submit a report of his experience in the field. They would also be asked to bring with them at least two case studies as well as the case diaries of one case which they had handled and at least one problem situation which they might have faced in the field of law and order, management or police administration. During the period of rounding off training, the officer would be expected to do P.T. every day and attend the parade once a week and participate in all sports and games activities. They are also expected to do a minimum of one hours library work and submit a study paper during their one month's stay in the Academy which will form the basis for the case study library which will be built up by the guide officers for training future batches of probationers. They are also expected to participate in all mass activities, cultural and other group activities in the Academy. The course contents highlighted the following :

(*i*)	Charge report writing	2	periods
(*ii*)	Submission of report of field experience and discussion	4	,,
(*iii*)	Individual discussion with guide officers case studies	8	,,
(*iv*)	Interaction with faculty members and senior members/course officers	4	,,
(*v*)	Interaction with visiting lecturers	8	,,
(*vi*)	Syndicate work		
(*vii*)	Book/Syndicate Study review		
(*viii*)	Film show and discussions		
(*ix*)	Morning P.T.	1	daily
(*x*)	Sports	1	do

There will be no special input during this course but syndicate work will be to concentrate on problems-oriented exercises on investigation and supervision of cases, public relations, inter-personal relationships, personnel management, group dynamics, leadership styles, communication in the organisation, law enforcement and social perspectives crises management, grievances enquiry and redressal. Experienced officers having wide knowledge of different fields of police work are invited for these interaction sessions.

The basic training terminal course for I.P.S. probationers is expected to be relevant to the officers as they are expected to harmonise theoretical knowledge with practical field life and the gap between the two has to be bridged through this course. A close evaluation of this course is, therefore, necessary. Informal discussions with a few officers who had recently undergone the course, were studied and it was discovered that most of these trainees found it useful and educative. The case studies which were presented by the course trainees, were also regarded as useful. There were practical problems which the trainees brought out for discussion with the faculty and several useful conclusions were arrived at after discussions. Thus, the overall practical utility of Basic Training Terminal Course was felt by 75 percent of the trainees who were interviewed by the researcher.

The X B.T.T. (Basic Training Terminal) Course was attended by 18 officers who came from different parts of the country and attended the course from 2 March to 4 April, 1981. Nine officers interviewed for the case study. Out of these, five found the course very useful and four rated it as useful. Some of the general points brought out by these respondents were as under :

(*a*) There is a gap between the teaching in N.P.A. and the field experience.

(*b*) The teaching in N.P.A. is too theoretical and during training, the probationers should be exposed to real practical situations.

(*c*) There should be more exposure to the field conditions but the teachings of theoretical part at N.P.A. is useful.

(*d*) Syndicate papers should be discussed rather than reviewed.

The B.T.T. Course provided an opportunity to the probationers to meet their batch mates and exchange their experiences of professional life in the states. This course was rated as useful as the senior officers could get their concepts crystallised by academic discussions with faculty members and among themselves.

Senior Officers' Course

Senior officers course was earlier called advanced course and had the duration of six months. From 1 April, 1973, the duration was reduced to 14 weeks and I.P.S. officers with six to ten years of service and Dy Supdts. of Police who have been promoted to the post of Supdt. of Police, are required to attend this course. Police officers from foreign countries also attend this course under Technical Cooperation Scheme of the Colombo Plan and the special Common-wealth African Assistance Plan. The objective of the course has been to provide an opportunity to the trainees to keep abreast of innovations in police techniques and investigation, relevant advances in management techniques and administration and to provide them with an orientation in modern behavioural concepts. The overall objective is to develop a dynamic and dedicated leadership for the police service. The syllabus of studies covers public order and security, crime, law, application of science and technology to police work, research and training, management concepts and techniques, human behaviour and police attitudes and other topics of general interest. The outdoor training consists of P.T., Yoga and games. Each participant has to submit a brief write-up about himself giving a narration of his academic background and work done in other fields after leaving the schools/colleges. Each participant is also required to deliver a talk of 20 minutes duration on the subject of his choice. In addition, each officer is required to prepare and submit an individual paper on a subject of his choice. The participants are divided into syndicate groups of 4/5 officers for studying topical problems with the help of a guide and carry out research including a field study of the subject. Trainees have the option for drawing the standard rate of allowance of Rs. 170/- per week. This was brought parity in the allowance of trainees who attend the senior officers course. The participants are exposed to the problem of rural dynamics and a number of lectures of specialist guest speakers are arranged to give them an awareness of the relevant subjects. Trainee officers alongwith their guides, visit a number of places as a part of the study tour and carry out an empirical study of their syndicate subject with the help of a questionnaire and interviews of the public. Senior officers' course trainees also visit various other training institutions located at Hyderabad. More than 550 trainees have so far attended senior officers' course.

Every participant during the last week of the course is required to fill up the course evaluation form. These course evaluation reports are compiled by the course coordinator and put up to the Director, N.P.A. The researcher carried out a survey of course evaluation of 50th senior officers' course held at N.P.A. from 1st June to 5th September, 1981. The course was attended by 24 officers. Regarding duration of the course 14 officers wanted it for 14 weeks, five officers for ten weeks and one officer each for eight and 20 weeks duration. The majority of the trainees felt that 14 weeks is an ideal duration. Regarding the question whether study tour to distant places should be retained or dropped, 16 respondents wanted to retain the present practice, two trainees wanted increased duration of tour and two wanted study tour to be dropped. The rating of overall design of the course was as under :

TABLE 9.3
Course Rating by Participants

		Excellent	Very Good	Good	Fair	Poor
1	2	3	4	5	6	7
1.	Range of subjects covered	4	15	3	—	—
2.	Concepts and Principles discussed	4	18	—	—	—
3.	Practical approaches explored	—	12	9	1	—
4.	Sequence of topics and exercises	1	13	6	1	—

Regarding time table, the trainees showed their responses as under :

TABLE 9.4

		Just Right	More or less Right	Needs major changes
1	2	3	4	5
1.	Duration of work-day	18	3	—
2.	Time allotted to various in-puts, generally speaking	12	6	3
3.	The ratio between lectures and discussion sessions	8	10	3

Responses partaining to overall grading of the course were as under :

Extremely Useful	Very useful	Useful	Some what useful	Not useful at all
1	2	3	4	5
5	14	3	Nil	Nil

Regarding outdoor work, it was suggested that P.T. should not be compulsory and Yoga should form a regular feature. It was held that individual talk should be given more duration. Subjects like tele-communication, computerization of crime and finger-print records, rural dynamics need be given more emphasis. It was also suggested that trainees need to take course little more seriously and to motivate a system of test/ examination should be introduced and performance evaluation must go in officers' confidential reports.

Top Management Programme

The top management course is of two weeks' duration for the officers of the level of Dy Inspectors-General of Police. The primary aim of this programme is :

(*a*) To show the participants both the need and the possibility of planned change in organisational structures, systems and procedures ;

(*b*) To impart to them the knowledge and skills which would help them function effectively as internal change agents and optimise the use of organisational resources, including skill in the use of outside experts ;

(*c*) To stimulate them to overcome their inertia and complacency barrier ("it does not really apply to our organisation", "how can we change anything unless the circumstances change" etc) and start their own self-development through analysis of their day to day experiences ; and

(*d*) To give the participants a chance to stand back and see their jobs and roles in society in perspective.

Top Management Development Course was held in the Academy from 21st February to 6th March, 1979 with the assistance of specialists in various management and behavioural science fields, from the Administrative Staff College of India and the small Industries Extension Training Institution in addition to the serving and retired senior police officers of India. Ten senior faculty members of A.S.C.I. Hyderabad, were employed as resource personnel. 15 Senior police officers of the rank of D.Is. G.P. attended the course. Two such courses were held in 1981 in two months of January and September. The five objectives of the programme, as enunciated to the participants were :

(*a*) To analyse both internal and external environment problems and strategies of police ;

(*b*) To acquaint with the quantitative techniques of management including system analyses and operational research, information gathering and processes and performance budgeting ;

(*c*) How the management and behavioural science concepts and techniques can be applied to get the best out of the people ;

(*d*) To allow the participants to stand back and look at the organisation objectively ; and

(*e*) To sensitise the participant himself to the work group and environment.

The scrutiny of feed-back from the 14 participants indicating the extent to which the training programme succeeded in achieving the above objectives has indicated thus :

TABLE 9.5

Objective attainment		To a great extent	Some what	Not at all
1	2	3	4	5
Objective	1	8	6	—
,,	2	6	8	—
,,	3	9	5	—
,,	4	6	8	—
,,	5	9	4	—

The participants' overall ratings of the programme design were indicated as below :

TABLE 9.6

S. No.	Course Design	Rating of Course Design				
		Excellent	Very Good	Good	Fair	Poor
1	2	3	4	5	6	7
1.	Range of subject matter covered	1	9	4	—	—
2.	Concepts and Principles discussed	2	6	5	1	—
3.	Practical approaches explored	1	—	7	5	—
4.	Sequencing of topics and exercise	—	5	4	5	—

The data received from response of the participants regarding the various aspects of the programme work schedule can be presented as under :

TABLE 9.7

S. No.	Elements	Rating: Just Right	More or less Right	Needs major Change
1	2	3	4	5
1.	Duration of a work-day	4	6	4
2.	Time alloted to various in-puts	2	10	2
3.	The logical position of various in-puts in the time table	2	12	—
4.	The ratio between the lectures and discussion sessions	4	8	2

The rating of the participants on the various aspects of the programme methodology was as follows :

TABLE 9.8

S. No.	Methodology	Rating: Very effective	Fairly effective	Not effective
1	2	3	4	5
1.	Talks (generally)	4	10	—
2.	Group discussions	3	10	1
3.	Plenary sessions	2	9	2

Nine participants found the material as very useful and five found it somewhat useful. The course provides a good exposure of management concepts to the participants.

C.B.I. Sub-Inspector Basic Training

The Academy has been conducting basic training for Sub-Inspectors of I.B. and C.B.I. in the past. 43 batches of I.B. cadets have been trained at the Academy and after 1974 the training of I.B. cadets have been stopped at the Academy. The duration of the course was six months and the number of cadets trained in the last seven batches are as under :

TABLE 9.9

Batch	Year of passing	No. of trainees
1	2	3
37	1970	45
38	1970	50
39	1971	55
40	1971	51
41	1972	38
42	1972-73	34
43	1973	40

So far 17 batches of C.B.I. Cadets have been trained at the Academy. The duration of C.B.I. cadets basic training is now nine months. The number of C.B.I. cadets trained during the last ten years batch-wise are as under :

TABLE 9.10

Batch	Year	No. of trainees
1	2	3
7	1970	19
8	1971	25
9	1972	25
10	1973	25
11	1974	20
12	1975	24
13	1976	21
14	1977	14
15	1978	19
16	1979	12
17	1980	15

The cadet sub-inspectors course is organised for directly recruited sub-inspectors of C.B.I. Under this programme, officers recruited as Probationer Sub-Inspectors undergo initial professional training for nine months, with a slant on special investigation work. The cadets are mainly trained in substantive and specific laws which their organisation is expected to enforce and the techniques of investigation of crimes. The course is designed in such a way that they are able to concentrate their attention in developing their aptitudes and skills as the investigating officers utilise the scientific aids and techniques of investigation to the maximum.

Crime Prevention Course

This 10-day course is meant for I.P.S. officers with four to seven years of service. Crime prevention course provides required knowledge and skills to the officers relating to various aspects of crime prevention and social defence.

Symposia and Seminars

As the premier police training Academy of the Country, it has been regularly conducting symbosia of heads of the Police Training Institutions and has been organising Workshops, Seminars on various subjects. In the Symposium of heads of police training institutions, the problems of police training are discussed and recommendations are made on important points. This symposium highlightens various problems of the police training institutions. During the passing out parade week of I.P.S. probationers, a three days seminar on some topical subject is organised every year. On the issues framed in the working paper, background papers are invited from eminent police officers and academicians. Proceedings are later issued to the concerned in the form of a cyclostyled book. The subjects on which seminars have been held during the last ten year are given below :

The proceedings of the Seminar alongwith working paper and background papers form very good training material on the subject. At present, seminar proceedings are published in cyclostyled form.

TABLE 9.11

Year	Subject	Duration
1	2	3
1970	Promotion Policies & the Concept of Meritocracy	3 days
1971	Public Order: Scope and Extent of Effective Police Action	3 days
1972	Need for Motivational Techniques in Police Service	3 days
1973	Personnel Development Programme in Police Services in the Country	3 days
1974	Need for structural Change in Police organisation in the Country	3 days
1975	Role of Police in Redressal of Grievances of Weaker Sections of the Society	3 days
1976	Optimising Human Resources	6 days
1977	Identifying the requirements of Police in the field of Management	4 days
1977	Police at the Cross Roads	3 days
1978	Rule of Law and Role of Police	3 days
1979	The Protection of Human Rights in Criminal procedure	3 days
1980	Training Requirements of Management Concepts and Techniques	3 days
1980	Police Unrest	3 days
1981	Police and Mass Media	3 days

Research and Publication Work at the Academy

The sanctioned strength of research cell of the Academy is one Research Officer and one Stenographer. The post of research officer is yet to be filled in by the U.P.S.C. However, officers of the senior course are carrying out useful research through syndicate group with the assistance of members of the staff who act as guides to the syndicate groups. A number of syndicate reports prepared by now have been published in the form of N.P.A. Transactions. N.P.A. has been publishing Transactions yearly (now half-yearly) since 1961 in which certain selected syndicate and individual Research papers prepared by participants of the senior course are also published. These research papers throw light over various facets of police organisation and work in India. These papers have been found very useful and contain primary materials in many respects. As these papers are published by field officers who have mature experience of police work, there is a good blending of theory with pragmatic touch of a professional. The utility of these syndicate reports can be judged by the facts that some knowledgeable academicians and scholars have quoted these syndicate reports in their books.[6]

Training Aids and Material

N.P.A. has procured all available latest training aids and equipments. Academy has a number of very useful films on management, police, training, medical and general subjects. Latest instructional techniques and methods are being employed by the trainers at the N.P.A. The pattern of pedogogy has undergone a change in a salutary shift of emphasis from traditional lecture method to latest training techniques like syndicate work-workshops, seminars, brainstorming and others. Audio-visual aids like close-circuit Television are commonly being used to supplement the drab lecture method which can hardly be eschewed when lot of skills information and knowledge has to be given to the trainees in a short period. Short skits, role plays and mock court scenes on legal issues are video-tapped and later exhibited to the trainees of various courses. This in followed by discussions which create an awareness in the minds of the trainees about the perils that are involved in the violation of civil liberties and fundamental rights of the citizens. Academy has developed a large number of indigenous case studies, role playing exercises and human relations training materials which are extensively used in its professional courses for the young entrants as well as for the refresher courses of the senior police officers. The methods of training besides lecture, include group discussions, self-study, case studies, book review, tutorial class, panel discussions, mock-court, concurrent field exposure and capsule courses on specialised subjects e.g., rapid reading, report writing, effective public speaking, yoga training, rural dynamic and agrarian life, work study etc. Workshops on leadership and training of trainers are very useful and effective training techniques are used by the Academy. N.P.A. is doing a pioneering job in utilising the latest training techniques and aids in police organisation.

Co-Curricular Activities, Recreation and Welfare

The Academy provides for various co-curricular activities to develop total personality of trainees. To inculcate healthy social, cultural and moral values in the trainees, the Academy promotes extra-curricular activities such as shramdan, sports and games, films and plays, photography, fine-arts etc. All these activities have substantially enriched the corporate life of the campus and have built up a congenial atmosphere for training. The Library, Professional and Current Affairs Circle, organise meetings addressed by experts and luminaries on various subjects of professional and topical interest. To strengthen the moral fibre, a series of lectures by scholars of various religions are also organised. A very lively event organised periodically by this society is the Quiz Competition. The Reporters' Club is publishing an interesting house journal called the Academy Reporter. This is in addition to the regular Academy Magazine which is published annually. A number of welfare institutions provide amenities to the staff and trainees of the Academy and also form the model to the trainees to study such activities. The trainee officers are included on the management bodies of all these institutions by which technique they get an opportunity to actively handle and get a feel of such welfare activities. The N.P.A. Co-operative stores, managed by the staff and trainees, sells a wide range of commodities including uniform articles at reasonable rates. The Academy runs a Thrift and Savings Society with a share capital of Rs. two lakhs. The main object of the Society is to encourage the habit of thrift by enabling the members to save part of their earnings, which also earns good dividends. The Welfare Society, run on the subscriptions raised from its members and with a small subsidy from government, organises various welfare measures including help in the matter of higher education of children, medical care, providing gainful employment to the families in their spare time etc. Welfare Centre where fabrication of uniforms and garments is done by the family members of the N.P.A. staff with 30 sewing machines given to them on easy instalment facility, helps in supplementing family income. The Welfare Centre, the recently opened Nursery and the Creche, work under the auspicies of the N.P.A. Mahila Mandali which consists of a band of dedicated ladies who work in an honorary capacity. It is proposed to appoint a lady doctor on part-time basis for health promotion activities such as family planning and child-care. A canteen and a fair price grain shop are also run on the Academy premises.

The Environs of the Academy

The environs of the N.P.A. present a model for the other police training institutions of the country. The campus atmosphere of the Academy is most conducive for effective training for the Indian Police Service officers. The community life of the Academy presents a multi-mix of cultures furthering emotional integration among all who live in the campus. The Academy campus with young I.P.S. trainees from all over India and officers of various courses makes it a mini-India. The administrative block, conference hall, auditorium, library block, Tamil Nadu Guest House, gymnasium hall, parade and sports grounds, stadium with six lanes and the bronze statue of Sardar Vallabhbhai Patel give the Academy campus a real pride of being the premier police training institution of the country. The Academy has become a cynosure of many developing neighbouring countries which often send their representatives to visit the Academy before they start setting up their own police training institutions in their countries. The physical facilities now available at the Academy are more or less ideal for all the training institutions of the country though it is fastly developing its facilities further. The complex of Academy has an administrative block which is utilised for offices, S.B I. branch, C.I.S.F. Training College, N.P.A. Library, Class-rooms and Co-operative shop. The Academy has a well-equipped auditorium with a capacity of 583 seats where films are screened by the Academy Cinema Club. The A.P. Conference Hall is used for conducting seminars and important joint sessions of trainee officers. The Govt. of Andhra Pradesh gave a grant of Rs. 2.5 lakhs for its construction and Andhra Pradesh Government has made a further donation of Rs. 2 lakhs to enlarge the Conference Hall by constructing two more seminar-rooms. In 1980, on 31st October, a bronze statue of Sardar Vallabhbhai Patel at the cost of Rs. one lakh was installed in the Academy campus. A well equipped and rich Library, a gymnasium-hall, riding groups, M.T. Training grounds, play fields, squash court, tennis grounds provide other physical facilities to the trainees of the Academy. The Tamil Nadu Guest House built at the cost of Rs. 2 lakhs has been donated by the T.N. Govt., and is used by visiting guest lecturers and officials visiting the Academy. The state government of Uttar Pradesh and Sikkim as also the Border Security Force have donated a sum of Rs. 75,000 and Rs. 50 lakhs respectively for construction of Guest Cottages which are under construction now. The Chief Minister of Bihar has donated Rupees 5 lakhs for the construction of a Bihar Guest House in the campus and laid the foundation stone for the same Plans for the construction of Science block as also the development of cricket and hockey grounds are under way and are being taken up in a phased programme. More guest cottages will be constructed in the near future as governments of Uttar Pradesh, Sikkim and Bihar have donated funds for construction of the same in the campus. The I.P.S. officer's mess is the centre of corporate life of the institution and has been furnished at a cost of about Rs. 2.25 lakhs. Adequate residential accommodation for all members of the faculty is not available due to the fact that number of faculty members has increased during the last four years and construction of quarters has not kept the pace with it. There is a proper hospital with a qualified medical officer and other staff. They Academy Library is located in spacious library block with more than 20,000 books and 133 periodicals on various subjects. Cornerstone for a swimming pool was laid in 1978 but so far construction work has not started. The physical facilities of the Academy are ideal in the existing circumstances.

Expenditure of the Academy

The final grants and the actual expenditure of the N.P.A. during the last ten years are as under :

TABLE 9.12

Year	Final grants in Rs.	Actual expenditure in Rs.
1	2	3
1971-72	24,77,700	24,11,942
1972-73	24,29,000	26,41,842
1973-74	24,89,500	26,75,826
1974-75	35,95,000	34,20.496
1975-76	44,37,000	46,10.447
1976-77	50,18,000	53,13,667
1977-78	55,93,000	57,39,023
1978-79	56,39,000	57,26.120
1979-80	51,01,000	51,02.004
1980-81	58,87,000	58,20,872

There is a general trend of increasing expenditure during the last decade and the actual expenditure has more than doubled itself. Table indicates that actual expenditure is generally exceeding the final grants except in 1980-81. The budget for 1981-82 is Rs. 57.71 lakhs. The estimates are likely to grow up in the coming two years in view of certain items of stores and equipment sanctioned to the Academy in the form of an X-ray plant, additional vehicles, cine projector, a laboratory, colour close-circuit television, a movie camera and projector etc. The state and central governments are liberally sanctioning amounts for the Academy so that it may continue to expland and become an ideal police training institution of the country.

Problems and Prospects

Problems of the Academy are manifold and can be divided broadly into five categories. The first relates to trainers, the second to trainees, the third about administrative problems, fourth about physical facilities and the fifth is of miscellaneous nature. The researcher had long interviews with the Director of the Academy and informal discussions with the other members of the staff to get the proper dimensions of the various problems and difficulties of the Academy. Regarding trainers, the researcher was told that state governments are reluctant to spare good and experienced officers who have proper aptitude for training jobs. When demands are sent to the states and central police organisations, very few names are recommended by the state governments and central police organisations. Thus the field of choice for selection of staff for the Academy becomes very limited. For outdoor staff, deputation of members of the Central Reserve Police Force and Border Security Force is not easily accepted by the respective Directors-General. Good officers with training background are not made available by the CRP/BSF. Due to low scales of pay for Professors and Readers, Academy has not been able to get eminent academicians on their faculty and the posts are lying vacant. Trainers of higher intellectual calibre are required in the Academy but it is difficult to get such trainers from amongst the serving police officers. Probationers have no respect for those teachers who have no in-depth knowledge of the subject because probationers are generally quite inquisitive. Probationers who are eligible for appearing in the next I.A.S. and allied service examinations continue to prepare for the combined U.P.S.C. examination and do not take interest in training. In order to prepare for next I.A.S. examinations, they are inattentive in classes and absent themselves from classes on flimsy grounds. Many officers nominated for various courses try to avoid training because during training period, they are generally posted out on transfer from their present job. Therefore, the actual attendance on courses is generally low. The figures given below will indicate the facts.

The administrative problems of the Academy are numerous.

TABLE 9.13
Showing Capacity and Attendance in Senior Officers' Course at the N.P.A. Hyderabad

Year	Duration and frequency of course	Capacity	Nominations	Actual atten-dance	Average
1	2	3	4	5	6
1979	14 weeks		81	54	50%
1980	and three	35 per	91	63	60%
1981	courses	course (105)	98	60	57
	per year	per year			

The financial powers of the Director, N.P.A. are not equivalent with the powers of the Director-General, C.R.P.F. and B.S.F. When Director, N.P.A. refers cases to the government of India, these cases are bound to get delayed. Public Service Commission takes a very long time in filling up vacancies of the trainers and when suitable persons do not come forward, the posts remain vacant. The proposals sent for the improvement of the faculty are pending for a long time with the government. Problems regarding physical facilities are particularly in respect of shortage of residential quarters for the non-gazetted staff. There is no sanction for swimming pool so far though corner-stone was put in 1978. There is no shooting range for the pistol and rifle firing. Even foot-ball and hockey grounds are yet to be developed Academy does not have required number of vehicles and for various functions Academy has to seek help of Director General, Andhra Pradesh Police and the I.G.P., C.R.P.F. Transport available with the Academy is inadequate. Man-power available with the Academy was not sufficient to provide man for training demonstrations and for campus maintenance. The post of Director is lying vacant for more than last six months. However, the Academy has done very commendable job in imparting useful training to the senior police officers of the country.

REFERENCES

1. For details about F.B.I. Academy and Bramshall Police Academy, see—Baddeley Fred, American British National Police College, The Police Chief, May, 1981, Vol. XLVIII, No. 5, p. 25 ; Kenneth EJ and O. Connors J.A. The F.B I. Academy 1984, F.B.I. Law Enforcement Bulletin July, 1979, p. 24 ; Gammage Allen : "*Police Trg. in the U.S.A.*", Charles C. Thomas Springfield, 1963, p. 23.
2. For similar visws, see Misra, S.C., "*Police Administration in India*", N.P.A. Magazine, 1970, p. 174.
3. See Stracey, E.L., "*A Century of Police Training*", (Central Police Training College Magazine, Vol. XI, Oct. 1961, p. 7) ; Jayawant, A.R., "*A Century of Police Training*, (Indian Police Journal, Centenary Issue, 1961, p. 166-94).
4. Mukerjee, A.P., Twenty Five Years of our Alma Mater, N.P.A. Magazine, Vol. XXIII, Nov. 1973, p. 6.
5. Chawla, G.S., "*Police Forces in State—Centre to spend Rs. 100 crores for modernisation*"—Indian Express, Monday, July 27, 1981.
6. a. Bayley, David H., "*The Police and Political Development in India*", (Princeton University Press, 1969), pp. 72, 64, 291, 352.
   b. Sharma, P.D., "*Indian Police : A Development Approach*", Research Delhi, 1977, pp. 98, 99.
   c. Sharma, P.D., "*Police, Polity and People in India*", (Uppal Publishing House, New Delhi, 1981) pp. 62, 155, 175.
7. Muhammad, Mohamood Bin, "*Training in Development Administration*" (S.V.P.N.P.A. Magazine Vol. XXVII, Nov. 2, 1977), p. 73.

PART II

INTERNAL SECURITY ACADEMY, MOUNT ABU

THE INTERNAL Security Academy is located at the beautiful hill station in the Aravallies at the height of about 1230 meters above the see level at Mount Abu. Mount Abu is situated at a distance of about 30 kms. from Abu Road, the nearest railway line of the Western Railways. Mount Abu is 210 kms. from Udaipur and 260 kms. from Ahmedabad and both these places are connected by air services. Thus, it is roughly four to five hours' journey by car from both these places. The place has a very pleasant climate and is famous for Dilwara Jain Temples which are only two kms. away from Abu. It is a summer tourist hill resort and is an ancient historical place, said to have been established by Rishi Guru Vashist.

Internal Security Academy (I.S.A.), Mount Abu is a training institution of the Central Reserve Police Force and comes under the supervision of the Director-General, C.R.P.F., New Delhi under the Ministry of Home Affairs, Government of India.

The I.S.A. conducts the following courses at Mount Abu :

(*a*) Basic training course for directly appointed gazetted officers of the C.R.P.F. and other para-military organisations.

(*b*) Professional in-service training to the C.R.P.F. officers/ central police organization officers.

(*c*) Internal security courses for District Magistrates/ Superintendents of Police and Deputy Superintendents of Police and officers of equivalent ranks of public sector undertakings.

(*d*) Various seminars and special training programmes on internal security for senior police officers of the level of Dy. Inspector-General of Police and others.

The Academy was established at Mount Abu on February 1st, 1975 consequent upon the shifting of the National Police Academy from Abu to Hyderabad. The basic training course for the C.R.P.F. appointed Deputy Superintendents of Police was shifted from the Central Training College I, C.R.P.F., Neemuch alongwith the faculty and was accommodated in some of the buildings vacated by the N.P.A. During 1975-76 the Academy continued functioning on ad hoc basis without any sanctions of posts by the Government of India by attaching various ranks from various C.R.P.F. units. The Ministry of Home Affairs, Government of India, formally sanctioned 161 posts for the Academy in November 1976 and the postings came into existence with effect from December, 1976. Thus, the Academy functioned on ad hoc basis for almost two years. According to a study group report of the Ministry of Home Affairs, the aim of the Internal Security Academy, Mount Abu is to train police officers in the area of internal security and handling of widespread disturbances involving law and order problems thereby supplementing and strengthening the national training efforts.

The Academy is divided into administrative and training wings for the purpose of functional cohesiveness and clarity. Training wing has three faculties—faculty of internal security and insurgency; faculty of management and behavioural sciences and faculty of public administration and legal studies. Social science research forms a part of the faculty of management and behavioural sciences. Administrative wing covers office management, hospital, adjutant office, quartermaster office and the accounts. This organisational pattern has been in vogue since October, 1981 and has made the faculty members somewhat free from routine chores of administrative work. It has further enabled them to concentrate on training exercises exclusively. One service company has also been attached to the Academy for administrative purposes.

Faculty

Officers of the rank of Asst. Directors and below are selected from the C.R.P.F. Force whereas Director and Deputy Director are I.P.S. officers on deputation. The gazetted officers of the C.R.P.F. posted in the Academy do not get any special pay nor are they entitled for free accommodation. The non-gezetted ranks of the C.R.P.F. posted in the training centres as instructors get special pays at the rate of Rs. 40 for Inspectors, Rs. 30 for S.Is. and Rs. 20 for H.Cs. The Academy has on its panel of guest faculty members 50 specialists from different academic disciplines. Retired police officers and other civilians are also invited for speaking assignments. A variety of serving officers from the Intelligence Bureau, Central Industrial Security Force, National Police Academy, Hyderabad and other state police organisations are also invited to deliver lecture and share their experiences with the trainees. The number of guest speakers who delivered lectures to the trainees during the last three years is as under :

TABLE 9.14

Year	Guest Faculty of				Total
	Aca-demicians (I.A.S.)	Police Officers from States	Officers from C.R.P.F.	Specialised Police Officers from I.B.	
1	2	3	4	5	6
1979	4	13	4	7	28
1980	12	21	34	7	74
1981	24	26	23	10	83

Generally, speakers deliver three talks on three different subjects to the trainees. These trainers with their different backgrounds share their expertise with the trainees. The table indicates that there is increasing utilisation of guest speakers.

The Trainees

There are different type of trainees attending courses in the Academy. The C.R.P.F. officers and officers of other central police organisations like I.T.B.P. and members of Cabinet Secretariat attend in-service training. The internal security courses are attended by officers of state police forces, officers from the Central Police Force including C.R.P.F. and officers from public sector undertakings. The state police participation in the training programmes of I.S.A. can be presented by the table that follows :

TABLE 9.15

S. No.	States/C.P.Os./ U.T.	D.M.S./ Ss.P. on I.S.	Course	Dy. Ss.P. on I.S.	Course	Total
		1980	1981	1980	1981	
1	2	3	4	5	6	7
1.	Andhra Pradesh	—	3	2	6	11
2.	Assam	—	1	—	—	1
3.	Arunachal Pradesh	1	—	2	—	3
4.	A.&N. Islands	—	—	—	1	1
5.	Bihar	—	—	1	—	1
6.	B.S.F.	2	3	8	2	15
7.	C.R.P.F.	3	4	13	13	33
8.	Delhi	—	2	7	4	13
9.	Gujarat	—	3	2	1	6
10.	Haryana	—	1	4	3	8
11.	Himachal Pradesh	1	—	—	—	1

1	2	3	4	5	6	7
12.	I.T.B.P.	5	2	15	2	24
13.	Jammu & Kashmir	—	1	—	3	4
14.	Kerala	—	—	1	—	1
15.	Maharashtra	1	1	4	5	11
16.	Madhya Pradesh	—	1	1	—	2
17.	Mizoram	2	—	—	—	2
18.	Nagaland	—	—	—	1	1
19.	Orissa	—	—	5	—	5
20.	Punjab	1	3	6	5	15
21.	Rajasthan	2	—	2	4	8
22.	Sikkim	—	—	1	—	1
23.	S.S.B.	—	2	—	3	5
24.	Tamil Nadu	1	3	—	2	6
25.	Uttar Pradesh	2	7	10	12	31
26.	West Bengal	—	—	—	1	1
27.	C.I.S.F.	2	2	6	9	19
	Grand Total	23	39	90	77	229

The table indicates that almost all the state governments, union territories and central police organisations are utilizing the courses. Uttar Pradesh is sending maximum trainees in the courses after the C.R.P.F., I.T.B.P. and C.I.S.F. are also regularly sending their trainees.

The table given on the following page indicates that more and more public sector undertakings are sending their trainees. Indian Airlines and F.C.I. are the two undertakings which are, at present, making maximum utilisation of the course.

An analysis of the data indicates that officers from various state police organisations and various public sector undertakings are attending the courses. The present study undertook a detailed analysis of the capacity for each course, nominations

TABLE 9.16

Showing Trainee Participation in Internal Security Courses from Public Sector Undertaking (1979-81)

S. No.	Name of Undertaking	Year 1979	1980	1981	Total
1	2	3	4	5	6
1.	Air India	—	6	—	6
2.	Bharat Heavy Movers, Banglore	1	—	—	1
3.	Central Coal Fields	—	1	—	1
4.	Eastern Coal Fields	—	2	—	2
5.	F.C.I.	1	5	3	9
6.	H.M.T.	—	2	3	5
7.	Indian Airlines	2	8	5	15
8.	Instrumentation Ltd., Kota	—	1	—	1
9.	Indian Oil Blending Ltd.	1	—	1	2
10.	I.A.A.I.	—	—	2	2
11.	Joseph & Co. Ltd., Calcutta	—	1	—	1
12.	Mecon Ranchi	—	1	1	2
13.	N.T.C. Bombay/Nagpur	2	—	—	2
14.	O.N.G.C., Dehradun	—	—	1	1
15.	Western Coal Fields	—	—	2	2
	Total	7	27	18	52

sent for the course and trainees who finally attended the course for Dy. Supdts. of Police at the I.S.A. The analysis indicates that during 1979, 60 percent of the course capacity was utilised while during 1980, the figure was only 27 percent. During 1981, it again remained at 28 percent. Thus, the trainees who attend the course fall short of the total capacity and optimum utilisation of the training facilities is not being obtained. There are several reasons for this under-utilisation of training opportunity. The study could discover the following :

(*a*) The trainees are not interested in attending courses which do not have much relevance to their promotions.

(*b*) Some states fail to spare trainees due to law and order problems.

(*c*) Some trainees feel apprehensive of their transfer if they go for the course and, therefore, they try all possible means to avoid their nomination to the course.

The analysis of data about C.R.P.F. courses indicates that 95 percent of the trainees nominated for the courses attend it because in C.R.P.F. the training exercise is given greater weight age and most of the courses are career courses. In commando course conducted during 1981, the percentage of trainee participants who could attend the course to the total number of trainees nominated for the courses was as high as 80 percent. The analysis of data about seminars held for Dy. Inspectors-General of Police leads to conclude that the response to the course during 1980 and 1981 was rather poor as very few participants attended these seminars. The reluctance on the part of the D.Is. G.P. to attend the seminars is obvious. Some trainees feel reluctant to come for these courses because their family life is disturbed and there is the possibility of transfer from the post they hold at present.

The Training Programmes

The I.S.A. conducts three different types of internal security courses for the officers of the ranks of (*i*) Dy. Superintendents of Police, (*ii*) District Magistrates and Superintendents of Police and (*iii*) Dy. Inspectors-General of Police. The working duration of these courses is 18 working days, 10 working days and 6 working days respectively. The terminal objectives of these courses are ;

(*a*) To provide participants with the historical background and fundamental knowledge of civil disturbances, law and order problems and problems of internal security ;

(*b*) To provide a hightened awareness of the need for professional expertise for initiation of proper preventive and preparatory measures and employment of functional management techniques during actual handling of various problems of internal security and during actual confrontation management ;

(*c*) To enable participants to appreciate and understand the respective capacities, resources and responsibilities of various agencies and organisations involved in the difficult task of dealing with internal security problems ;

(*d*) To expose them to the latest theories, doctrines, principles of insurgency and counter-insurgency, terrorism, hijacking, left extremistism, violence and other such problems of internal security of a democratic society ; and

(*e*) To enable participants to share theit field experiences with others thus enabling cross-fertilization of ideas relating to internal security problems and to enable them to provide case studies and lessons from the various internal security problems handled in the past.

In these internal security courses, topical subjects like law and order, communal riots, industrial disputes, linguistic and regional agitations, political agitations, weaker sections of the society, V.I.P. security, youth unrest, agrarian unrest, problems of police accountability in a democratic society, violence in Indian society, rule of law, laws relating to internal security and many other subjects are covered. The trainees prepare an evaluation feed-back of every course on the closing day. The course appreciation attempted by the Dy. Supdts. of Police on internal security course of 18 working days for the last three years is presented on the following page.

The data reveal that trainees are generally satisfied with the

TABLE 9.17

Showing Internal Security Course Appreciation by Trainees

Year	Total no. of trainees	General Impression About Course (in percentage)			
		Very Good	Good	Satisfactory	Poor
1	2	3	4	5	6
1979	115	50	30	20	—
1980	110	39	48	13	—
1981	100	43	52	5	—

course contents and they find the course useful. The data also indicate that in 1979, 50 percent trainees found course very good while 30 percent rated it as good and only 20 percent put it as satisfactory. In 1980, 39 percent trainees considered the course as very good, 48 percent regarded it as good and only 13 percent checked it as satisfactory. In 1981, 43 percent trainees regarded the course as very good, 52 percent graded it as good and only 5 percent graded it as satisfactory. No trainee during the last three years checked it as poor or sub-standard.

The Internal Security Course for District Magistrates and Superintendents of Police was analysed and studied on the basis of the course evaluation sheets received from the trainees. This evaluation in tabular form is given on the following page. The data show that trainees are generally satisfied with the training and find the course useful. The general impression indicated in the feed-back indicates that in 1979 as many as 49 percent trainees considered the course as very good. In 1980, 40 percent of them regarded the course as very good but in the year 1981 only 22 percent trainees could appreciate it as very good. As low as 4 percent trainees regarded the courses as satisfactory in 1979 while in 1981 this figure touched as high as 8 percent.

TABLE 9.18

Showing Evaluation of Internal Security Course by Dist. Magistrates & Supdts. of Police

Year	Total Trainees	General Impression About the Course (in percentage)			
		Very Good	Good	Satisfactory	Poor
1	2	3	4	5	6
1979	48	49	47	4	—
1980	32	40	60	—	—
1981	49	22	70	8	—

A six working days seminar for Dy. Inspectors-General of Police on internal security is the major highlight of I.S.A. training programmes. Three such seminars were held in 1979, one in 1980 and one in 1981. The evaluation of the trainee participants of the seminars about this training programme can be tabulated as under :

TABLE 9.19

Showing Evaluation of Seminar Programme by Dy Inspectors-General of Police at the I.S.A.

Year	Total Trainees	Genera' Impression About the Course (in percentage)			
		Very Good	Good	Satisfactory	Poor
1	2	3	4	5	6
1979	21	34	66	—	—
1980	9	28	62	10	—
1981	8	35	65	—	—

The table shows that officers found the course good and useful for their work. No officer rated the course as poor in quality. The evaluation given by the Dy. Is.G.P. indicates that in 1979, 34 percent checked the course as very good while in 1980 only 28 percent could regard it as very good and in 1981 as high as 35 percent found it as very good. For all the three years, more than 60 percent participants checked it as good. For all the three years, the seminars attracted a number of eminent serving and retired senior police officers and academicians as faculty.

Besides conducting internal security courses, the Academy conducts several training programmes for C.R.P.F. officers. Directly appointed Dy. Supdts. of Police of the C.R.P.F. are given basic training for 52 weeks. Three such courses have so far been conducted by the Academy and the last batch of 38 officers completed their basic training in December, 1977. For the last five years, no direct recruitment of the Dy.Ss.P. has taken place and, hence no such course has been conducted during the last five years. In-depth interviews with trainee officers of the last three batches were carried out for the present study to evaluate the course. Responses were varied and interesting. One officer remarked, "There was too much emphasis on weapons and field craft and too little attention on jobs which are required to be carried out by directly appointed Company Commanders (Dy.Ss.P.)". Another officer hesitatingly said that "there was too much emphasis on teaching of law, C.R.P. Act and Rules, C.R.P. Manuals and office procedure but little practical training for Coy. Commander's role and job". One trainee felt that his Academy training was very useful and set a good base for his future role as a police officer. Generally, officers spoke very high about the quality of instructors who trained them at the Academy. The scrutiny of syllabus and course contents of directly appointed Dy.Ss.P. course reveals that subjects like political, economic and social frame-work of India, management concepts and techniques, behavioural science and implications of the changing social scene for the role of police, were not covered in the syllabus and the Gore Committee's recommendations regarding revision of syllabus were not adhered to. Informal interviews with the superiors of these directly trained officers were held and most of them held the view that directly appointed officers trained at the Academy were better trained as compared to those who were trained at the CTC I C.R.P.F., Neemuch.

The Academy also conducts Assistant Commandants Refresher Course, Company Commanders Refresher Course, Senior Subedar (Inspector) Refresher Course, Medical Officers Combatisation Course, Commando and Rock Climbing Course for the C.R.P.F. Officers.

Asst. Commandants' and Senior Dy.Ss.P. refresher courses have been attended by 22 officers in 1977, 72 in 1978, 23 in 1979, 17 in 1980 and 29 in 1981. The duration of the course is ten weeks. The evaluation of the course given by the trainees of the last batch indicates that 38 percent trainees considered the course as very useful, 46 percent found it just useful and 16 percent said that it was inadequate and merely satisfactory.

Company Commanders' Refresher Course of 8 weeks duration was held in the Academy to reorient the Coy Comdts. having four to five years of service in the rank. The Coy. Comdr. Ref. Course syllabus is based on the recommendations of the Gore Committee Report on police training and subjects like management concepts and techniques, behavioural science, political, economic and social framework of India form part of the syllabus. The number of officers who attended the course with their results is given on the following page.

The facts indicate that big percentage of trainees in course work hard and get qualified. The evaluation attempted by the trainees shows that 30 percent of the trainees found the course very good, 62 percent good and 8 percent useful and satisfactory.

Senior Subedar (Inspector) Refresher Course is a promotion course and qualifies an Inspector of the C.R.P.F. for promotion to the rank of Dy.S.P. Earlier, the duration of the course was 14 weeks but in 1981 it was reduced to 10 weeks. The number of officers who attended the course with their results is also given on the following page.

During 1981, due to large number of vacancies in the rank of Dy.Ss.P., simultaneous two courses were conducted at a time by the Academy and the duration of the course was also

TABLE 9.20

Showing Evaluation of Coy. Comdrs. ref. Course

Year	Total trainees attended	Passed/qualified	Failed
1	2	3	4
1975	63	57	6
1976	77	73	4
1977	43	41	2
1978	20	18	2
1979	42	42	—
1980	55	54	1
1981	39	38	1

TABLE 9.21

Year	Total trainees attended	Passed	Failed
1	2	3	4
1978	41	36	5
1979	41	38	3
1980	53	43	10
1981	244	226	18

reduced. Analysis of the data received through evaluation sheets of the officers of senior subedar refresher course demonstrates that 60 percent found it very good, 24 percent rated it as good and 16 percent said that it was satisfactory and useful. The analysis of evaluation materials of the course indicates that 54 percent trainees found it very good, 36 percent found it good and 10 percent found it satisfactory and useful.

C.R.P.F. Medical Officers' Combatisation Course is conducted at the Academy for training medical officers who join the force in various gazetted ranks. 12 M.Os. were trained in 1977, 14 in

1978, 14 in 1979, 8 in 1980 and 11 in 1981. The duration of this course was earlier four weeks, but was gradually increased to eight weeks and now it has been extended to 16 weeks. This course enables the medical officers to familiarise themselves with the C.R.P. Act and Rules and office procedure and gives them physical outdoor training foı the tough life. Interviews with the M.Os. who were trained in the last course were held by the researcher. One doctor respondent said, "They went to make us tough police officers but in the process, we will lose the grey material". Another officer respondent said, "Course is of too long a duration and this training is going to deprofessionalise us as we will lose touch with our professions." One M.O. with N.C.C. background felt that training of medical officers is going to make them tough officers who can rub shoulder to shoulder with other C.R P.F. officers and will benefit them in the long run. The reaction of various officers was of a mixed type, however, all of them felt that the duration could be reduced to 10 weeks or so.

Commando and Rock-Climbing Course is one of the most difficult outdoor training courses conducted by the Academy. The first course of Commando and Rock Climbing was conducted in April-May, 1979 wherein 27 young Dy.Ss.P. of last directly appointed Dy.Ss.P. course were trained. The second course was conducted in Oct., Nov. 1979 wherein 49 constables/under officers/subordinate officers of the C.R.P.F. were trained. During 1980, 25 subordinate officers/under officers were trained and in 1981 13 GOs/SOs were trained. This course is for trainees who are below 35 years of age. Unarmed combat, rock-climbing, confidence jump from 40 feet height in water, two days' living off the land and long route marches culminating in 40 kms. march form the part of outdoor curriculum. This course instils lot of confidence in young officers and prepares them for commando mission of highly difficult nature. The duration of the course is eight weeks. Commandos are physically conditioned in P.T. and battle obstacles in which they have to cross 1,100 meters and 20 obstacles in 15 minutes. They are given training in anti-hijacking drill, swimming, boating and relief & rescue operations and trained for commando missions.

Training Aids and Techniques

The Academy has prepared training material for all courses and on arrival for the course trainees are given compendium of background papers for the course. It has published a number of monographs and articles on various subjects of internal security. While guest speakers adopt lecture and discussion methods, faculty members are using latest training methods and techniques, Audio-visual aids like over-head projectors, slides, charts, films and recorded cassettes etc. However, about 75 percent of the training is carried out by lecture and discussion method in most of the courses. Academy has purchased 12 training films on map reading, motivation and leadership and ten recorded cassettes on management subjects. Besides lecture method, syndicate groups prepare syndicate reports on various assigned subjects. Case studies and incident methods are used in analysing communal riots cases with the help of group discussions. Role play exercise is organised for providing practice to participants in confrontation managemant. In-basket exercises are given in C.R.P.F. In-service courses to find out their decision-making and administrative capabilities. Panel discussions are held with the help of trainees on various controversial issues like police associations and campus police. Workshops are organised for carrying various practical projects and behavioural science exercises. Delphi method, micro lecture method, micro-lab method and other training methods and techniques are also used in the Academy. The Academy has also published a number of papers in the form of articles/monographs on various topics to benefit the trainees.[1]

The Director of the Academy and other members of the staff feel that the myth of non-availability of guest speakers has been exploded during the last two years when 74 guest lecturers visited the Academy in 1980 and 83 guest speakers in 1981. The Academy is facing no shortage of guest speakers. Location of the Academy, according to the present Director, is ideally suited for academic pursuits. Physical facilities in the Academy could not be developed due to the indecision of the Government about its permanent location. However, recently the Director-General, C.R.P.F. has finally decided to continue the

Academy at Abu. Some buildings which were handed over by the N.P.A. at the time of its shifting to Hyderabad were taken over by the C.R.P.F. and these buildings have not yet been renovated. The maintenance of the existing buildings leaves much for improvement but so far no major repairs and renovations have been undertaken. Every time proposals for major works were sent to the government, but these were returned with the remarks that till location of Academy is finally decided, no expenditure sanction can be granted and things continued on ad hoc basis. The residential facilities for the trainees seem quite inadequate and unsatisfactory. These buildings are old and in dilapidated conditions and unsuitable for a training institution of national level.

However, the atmosphere and environment on the campus seem conducive for academic work both indoor and outdoor. The members of the faculty were found in friendly and affectionate relationships with the trainees. Adequate training ground for drill, P.T. sports and games is not available. Also, adequate accommodation is not available for library and reading-room. The I.S.A. does not have an auditorium where all the trainees and staff can sit at one time. Adequate residential accommodation has not been provided to instructional and supervisory staff. Medical Officer and Signal Officer are living in mess which is for single officers. Thus, the Academy has inadequate and unsatisfactory physical facilities. During rains, ceilings of most of the buildings leak. Academy has a sanction of ten-bedded hospital but no proper hospital building is available. This validates the general hypothesis that police training institutions in India are in a general state of neglect and particularly in respect of physical facilities. The absence of these minimum physical facilities make the general environment somewhat unconducive for effective and job-oriented training. The Academy has a very well equipped and rich library having more than 13,000 books and subscribes to 45 professional journals and magazines. The documentation has also been started in the library and all standard reference books are now available for consultation. The overall environs are conducive for study, training and reflections and trainees do not find many distractions. The cordial relationship of instructional staff with the trainees and the stress-free training build up a congenial atmoshere for training and learning.

Research Work at the I.S.A.

The Academy has recently set up a research cell to collect data on various aspects of insurgency and counter-insurgency in the country and to develop expertise on relevant subjects. A research field team consisting of one Asst. Commandant and two Dy. Supdts. of Police visited Nagaland, Mizoram, Manipur and other places and have collected valuable materials on insurgency and counter-insurgency. The data-bank is being established at the Academy for analysing and processing this data collected by the research team of the Academy. Efforts are afoot to get the Academy affiliated to the University of Rajasthan, Jaipur and get recognised as a research centre. This will enable the researchers to carry out their work at the Academy for the award of the degrees of Ph.D. or M. Phil of the University of Rajasthan, Jaipur in areas relevant to police work.

Publications

The Academy has prepared compendiums for almost all courses conducted therein. Besides, I.S.A. has published proceedings of the various D.Is.G.P. seminar and background papers for the seminars. It has published the following main monographs :

(*a*) The Problems of Police Accountability in a Democratic Society.

(*b*) Political Agitations, Public Protests and the Role of Police.

(*c*) Social Responsibilities of the Police : Scope and Limitations.

(*d*) Crowd and Mob Psychology—the Concept of Confrontation Management.

(*e*) Improving the Police Image.

(*f*) Policy Planning for Internal Security.

(*g*) Weaker Sections of the Society : The Problem, the Scenario and the Perspective based on eight Case Histories.

Moreover, during the last three years, many case studies on law and order situations have also been prepared in the Academy. About a hundred articles on various aspects of internal security, police and other allied subjects have also been prepared by the members of the Academy faculty. These articles are incorporated in the compendium of background papers in various courses.

Training Costs

The present study has endeavoured to work out the cost of training in terms of expenditure per trainee per day. This has been worked out by calculating the working days of various courses and multiplied by the total number of trainees for various courses conducted by the Academy. D.Is.G. Seminar, D.Ms. and Ss. P. course on I.S., Dy.Ss.P. course on I.S and other various C R.P.F. courses conducted during last seven years have been taken into consideration for evaluation. The total training days depict the working days and cost per day per trainee for last seven years has been worked out. The cost per training per day for last seven years has been depicted in the diagram given and table appended below :

TABLE 9.22

Year	Total training days	Total Expenditure in Rupees	Cost training day in Rupees/ps.
1	2	3	4
1975	16436	55448	3/37
1976	16436	435746	26/51
1977	14250	571182	40/08
1978	13321	1454354	109/18
1979	14093	1733854	133/11
1980	20357	1875913	92/15
1981	25330	2248490	88/77

The data indicate that cost is declining during the last three years though there is inflationary trend in market prices. Thus, if it is worked out in terms of base year, it will show still more downward trend of cost per trainee day per during the period.

The researcher has gone through the evaluation of the internal security courses as given by the trainees. The number of increase of trainees from public sector undertaking are gradually increasing and this is a clearly visible trend showing the utility of internal security courses. For I.P.S. officers, internal security course is now a career course and, therefore, it is bound to be more and more subscribed in the years to come. The I.S. seminar meant for the D.Is.G.P. has been found very useful by 35 percent of the participants and 65 percent as good. The C.R.P.F. courses are generally fully subscribed because surrender of vacancies is generally not permitted by the officers of the ranks of Is.G.P. Officers of the I.T.B.P., C.I.S.P., S.S.B. and other para-military organisations are attending C.R.P.F. refresher courses meant for Commandants and Asst. Commandants. Thus, the Academy is doing very good work by organising useful refresher courses for the gazetted officers of the police.

Like other police training institutions, the present staff of I.S.A. is inadequate to cope with the increasing demands of the trainers for various courses. The strengthening of core staff of the Academy by appointment of academicians and police officers with aptitude for training can go a long way in improving effective training. Rent free houses have not been allowed to the gazetted officers. The various internal security courses do not get adequate number of trainees and courses remain undersubscribed. In C.R.P.F. courses, however, position is very good as surrender of seats is done very seldom. More than 90 percent trainees attend the C.R.P.F. courses and only in very exceptional and compassionate cases, seats allotted are surrendered. The response in D.Is.G.P. seminar and I.S. courses for D.Ms. and Ss.P. is unsatisfactory. Though research work is being taken up in right earnest and the field research team has collected data of immense utility, the officers of field research team attached to the Academy have been returned to the unit with effect from April, 1982, and thus field research team has been practically disbanded. No separate staff has been sanctioned so far for research cell. The trainees coming to the Academy particularly for the I.S. courses were found worried as they feared transfer from their present places of postings. The researcher found that more officers of higher ranks were required for taking classes in D.Ms. and S.sP. courses, Commandant Refresher Course and Asst. Commandants Refresher Course. It was observed that many senior officers attending seminars were not seriously involved in the training process and had not done their home work well. It was observed that members of the faćuity, junior to the trainees in rank do not get required acceptability in the class-room. There is a need for a Professor of Management for the Academy to teach management concepts and techniques. Similarly, a Professor of Behavioural Sciences is also needed in the Academy to give input of behavioural sciences in various training programmes. A qualified Research Officer, having police background should be in-charge of the research cell of the Academy so that he may co-ordinate the research work and may guide officers who are interested in doing research for their M. Phil or Ph. D. degrees on police subjects. The Academy atmosphere at present is strees-free and there is very cordial trainee-trainer relationship in the campus. The sports facilities are being utilised by the trainees who are interested in sports and games. In the Academy, there is greater emphasis on refresher courses than on basic courses. Actually, at present, only refresher and specialised courses are being conducted by the Academy.

The Academy has started ethical training by inviting religious speakers who speak on various moral and ethical principles. An effort is being made in the Academy to develop a secular outlook for the police officers and this particular subject is being given due attention. Training efforts are being directed to bring about attitudinal change in the trainees. The Academy has during last six years prepared a number of training monographs, compendiums of background papers and articles on various subjects and has, thus, made valuable contribution in building up training literature. Latest training techniques and instructional methods are being utilised in the Academy. Periodical review of training programmes is being carried out and new subjects are added from time to time to keep up training in tone with the changing requirements of the society. Trainees are being oriented towards the sensitivity to the ambiguities and ambivalences of group and individual action and insight into the trainee's own ideological conflicts by exposing them to the talks of various eminent academicians from various disciplines. Internal Security Academy is doing a commendable job in training state police officers in internal security matters and will ultimately pave the way for professionalism in the police force.

REFERENCE

1. For details, see "*Proceedings of the Tenth Symposium of the Heads of the Police Training Institutions in India*", Patna, 1981, (SVP NPA Hyderabad—Appendix II), pp. 46-51.

CHAPTER TEN

EPILOGUE

TRAINING in police is a teaching and learning process aimed at making lasting improvements in the role enactment capabilities of the trainees as well as developing their ability to assume higher levels of responsibilities. In particular, it prepares them for effective performance of their roles as :

(*i*) Law enforcing agency ;

(*ii*) Executive arms of the government ;

(*iii*) Protection of the rights and liberties of the citizens ;

(*iv*) Agents of social change ; and

(*v*) Formative role in political development.

It also prevents the police officers' obsolescence and keeps them fully aware of the situational context of their operational, politico-economic social environment. The present study was launched with the following tentative hypotheses for testing their validity by a field survey and empirical study of police training enterprise in India :

(*a*) The police training instituions in India are inadequately staffed for purpose of administration of training of the police force of the country.

(*b*) The police training institutions in India are concentrating more on basic training programmes rather than on the refresher training courses for various ranks.

(*c*) The expenditure incurred on police training in various states of India is percentage-wise low in proportion to the total costs of police budgets of the states.

(*d*) The police training institutions in India are in a general state of neglect and more so in respect of the physical facilities obtained on their campuses.

(*e*) Training tools and equipment for police training are outdated in most of the training institutions of police. Very little innovative effort has been made to render them functional.

(*f*) There is lack of coordination between police training and police research in India with the result that the training enterprise is non-goal oriented in terms of cost benefit.

These hypotheses have been put to the empirical tests for validity or otherwise in the present study.

The Police Trainers

The training of policemen in India is the basic responsibility of the state governments though Central Government is providing guidance, help and finance to improve police training. The research has shown that the instructional staff of most of the police training institutions in India has been inadequate. The survey of 25 training institutions revealed that 72 percent of the training institutions suffer from shortage of trainers. Most of the police trainers neither have the interest nor the capacity to train. Posting to police training institutions is regarded as a punishment because of loss of power and privileges and, therefore, usually police officers of the right type and aptitude are not posted to training institutions and in many cases, the training institutions have become the dumping grounds for the inconvenient, disgruntled and unwanted police officers. Police trainees, particularly in refresher training, find vast gap between role enactment, role expectation and role ideal and regard training as redundant. They do not pay proper attention to training and the trainers do not get proper response particularly in refresher courses from trainees and this causes frustration to the trainers. This dissatisfaction is transferred to enumerating such deficiencies which are beyond his control, may be, real or imaginery. It ultimately results in transference of guilt to the inadequacy of trainees and job dissatisfaction to the trainers. Majority of the instructors were found to be unhappy, disgruntled and apathetic to their training assignments. Right type of police officers are not posted in training institutions because there is a general neglect of training institutions by the higher authorities. Trainers do not get job satisfaction in training institutions because of the non-applicability of training to actual field work and non-acceptance of their teachings by the trainees. 45.90 percent of the respondents of the sample agreed that the police trainers in most of the police training institutions are not qualified, motivated and competent to teach and train policemen. The inadequacy of staff is further compounded by the inability of the police training institutions in attracting and retaining experienced, competent and highly motivated trainers. The instructor to trainee ratio compiled by the researcher also shows that 75 percent of the institutions have inadequate outdoor staff. Thus, research has proved the hypothesis that the police training institutions in India are inadequately staffed for the purpose of the administration of the training of the police force of the country.

The Police Trainees

Two types of trainees generally come to police training institutions. The first category consists of newly appointed police officers at various levels who undergo basic training courses for a given period of time in the training institutions. There they learn basic skills and knowledge of their job and also get primary occupational socialisation in police sub-culture and the second category of trainees consists of those police personnel who come to training institutions for refresher, specialised or advanced training. This category of police trainees have field experience and, therefore, they are aware of the gap between role expectation, role enactment and idealized role. Police training prepares them for only idealised role and, hence, is of little practical value and thus, they do not have sufficient motivation to undergo refresher or advanced courses.

Basic and Refresher Training

In the opinion survey of police personnel of various ranks, 53.10 percent of the respondents felt that basic police training given to them was adequate while 35.90 percent felt that it was partly adequate.

Refresher training for I.P.G. officers is mostly conducted at S.V.P., N.P.A. Hyderabad, I.S.A. Mount Abu and I.C.F.S., New Delhi. Each state police college is conducting refresher training for Dy. Ss. P., Inspectors, Sub-Inspectors and other ranks. Refresher courses of constables and head constables is generally carried out at District police lines and forms part of annual training programmes. Thus, the hypothesis that police training institutions in India are concentrating more on basic training than on refresher training is disproved.

Training Tools and Instructional Techniques

The Study found that lecture method, demonstration drill and use of black-boards are used in all police training institutions, whereas other modern methods of instructions are not very popular with the trainers. As many as 58.18 percent of the respondents were even not aware of the new training techniques and methods. Though equipments like tape-recorders, 16 mm projectors and over-head projectors were available in some police training institutions, the police trainers themselves did not have any training in handling or utilising them. Moreover, may of the trainess had no faith in the efficiency of these newer techniques of training and they considered them as too exotic for Indian conditions. However, modern training techniques are being used in varying degree in some of the progressive training institutions. In the present changed circumstances, there is greater emphasis on police role and which can be fulfilled by bringing about changes in training techniques. Due to various psychological and organisational factors, these changes are being implemented in only a few training institutions and thus the hypothesis stands only partly proved.

Environs of Police Training Institutions

The environs of a police training institution consist of tangible and intangible constituents. Physical facilities, trainers, administrative and supporting staff, organisational and administrative set-up, type and level of trainees, training techniques and methods, training contents and programmes, financial allocation and supervision of training are the main tangible constituents. The duration and season of training courses, location of training institutions, organisational sub-culture and value system, psychologies of administrative authorities, trainers, interpersonal relationships and motivation for learning are its major intangible constituents. The overall physical facilities are inadequate in various training institutions and the study has amply validated the hypothesis that the police training institutions in India are in a general state of neglect and more so in respect of physical facilities obtained on their campuses. The physical training conditions in the form of residential, academic and training facilities were not conducive enough to promote a congenial atmosphere for learning.

Police Research

According to the date of the present study, the Bureau of Police Research and Development has completed 47 research projects and has 10 projects in its hand. Out of 20 states/union territories studied by the researcher, 14 states have research centres in police headquarters and only two state police colleges in states have research cells. Thus, 90 percent of the training institutions have no research cells and 30 percent of the states have even no research centre in their police headquarters. Thus, the hypothesis that there is lack of coordination between police training and police research in India with the result that the police training enterprise is non-goal oriented in terms of cost-benefit analysis has been partly proved by the present study.

Financial Costs of Training

It has been established in the present study that one percent of the total budget should be regarded as adequate expenditure on training. As 50 percent of the states are spending less than one per cent of the total police budget on training, the hypothesis that the expenditure on police training in various states of India is percentage wise low to the total costs of police budget of the state is partly proved.

National Academics

Both S.V.P. National Police Academy, Hyderabad and Internal Security Academy, Mount Abu have special nature. The present strength and competence of the faculty is not adequate to handle various advanced courses. Some officers posted in these academies did not have the necessary training, academic and field background and were misfits for their training assignments. Senior officers attending training workshops, seminars and symposia were usually non-serious and professionally uninvolved and their contribution and participation was marginal. They were also rank concious and were unwilling to be taught by persons junior in rank. Nearly thirty to sixty percent of the trainees nominated to these academies try to avoid coming because of personal and other reasons. In both the institutions, no separate funds exist for police research nor research cells have been established. The study has revealed that latest methods and instructional techniques have been introduced in both these Academies. In contrast to other police training institutions, the atmosphere in these two police academies was stress-free and relaxed.

Recommendations and Suggestions

Police training in India needs to be revitalised and reorganised so that it may produce efficient and competent police officers having appropriate attitudinal change in their life styles necessary to meet the complex challenges of a modern society. Police officers should build up a thinking apparatus of the social-bling who can properly deal with the decent citizens in the process of sorting out social deviants and criminals. Police training should try to usher in a new era of policing where policemen are loved and adorned by the citizens and they may become their true friends, philosophers and guides. The political environment of lawlessness and corruption, the economic environment of super-inflation and economic crises, the social environment of social disorder and conflict should be properly understood by the police trainees. This will enable them to handle correctly the difficult and intricate situations of a democratic society. Training has to completely bridge the existing gap between role enactment, role expectations and the idealised role of the police.

National Police Training Commission

A high-power National Police Training Commission can be a useful agency for the coordination of police training and police research activities all over the country. It can be an effective agency to formulate and implement a well-designed, concrete, comprehensive and institutionalised national policy of police training.

Identification of Training Needs

In the fast changing socio-economic political framework in which police have to operate, training must bridge the gulf between role expectation and role enactment. For this, identification of training needs should be an exercise carried out by research centres in collaboration with Universities every five to seven years. Training needs for police officers at action level, supervisory level and policy level must be identified separately.

Administration and Organisation of Training

Administration of police training in India comprising of planning, organising, staffing, directing, coordinating, reporting and budgeting needs a managerial approach to make it goal-oriented. The training cycle of sponsoring of trainees, training, feed-back, modification of training and sponsoring again has to be well coordinated.

Restructuring of Training Division and Training Institutions

Training Division of the Bureau of Police Research and Development should be strengthened so that it can function effectively. Training institutions should also be restructured so that there is harmonious blending of the staff because, at present, the non-police staff find themselves in an alien environment and have difficulty in adjusting themselves in the stiff heirarchial system of the police. This may be further aggravated when active collaboration of the Universities will be obtained. State police headquarters and training division should coordinate nomination of trainees in various courses to make optimum utilisation of training facilities to prevent waste of resources resulting from unused facilities of training institutions. Reserves should be kept ready to attend courses if the nominated persons are unable to attend the training. There should also be specialisation of training courses in earmarked institutions to prevent overlapping of efforts. The impetus and support for training activity should come from the highest points in central and state governments.

Staff of Training Institutions

Posting to training institutions of staff should be more advantageous in terms of pecuniary benefits, status and career prospects as compared to their posting in field formation and elsewhere. In this, both the apparent and hidden benefits should be taken into account and the advantages in the training institutions should be considerably more. Stigma attached to posting in training institutions should be removed by posting willing and competent police officers and qualified academicians in training institutions. They should be entitled to rent free accommodation, special pay and other incentives like preference in deputation for training abroad. As an incentive and with a view to increasing their training capability, the instructional staff should be given preference in selection for training abroad. After training abroad, they should be posted back to the training institutions. There should be careful placement of personnel in training institutions as trainers and willingness of personnel must be obtained before a person is posted to a training institution. Trainers should visit various important places regularly so that they do not lose touch with the field. Mobile training teams from training centres must study important events by visits and exchange of ideas with the field officers. There is a need to have a behavioural scientist in the faculty of police training institutions to take up the work of identifying positive attitudes and developing methodology for bringing about change in the attitudes of the trainees. Behavioural scientists can also teach behavioural science to the trainees and help the authorities in carrying out research in some specified areas. There should be exchange of personnel among training institutions within India and abroad for cross-fertilisation of ideas and optimum utilisation of personnel resources. Instructional staff posted in training institutions should undergo "training of trainers" course so that they may learn the art of teaching. To provide incentive to instructional staff, Government of India should institute "Dronacharya Medal" to be conferred to all those who serve in training institutions for one year or more.

Training Programmes and Syllabi

Training programmes and syllabi should bridge the gap between role enactment and role expectations and the idealised role and cater for the actual practical needs of the trainees. Training syllabi should be modified to cover the new areas such as economic offences, computer abuse, computer management and corruption in public life.

Training for Computer Crime Investigation

In the modern age, computer crime has been called by various names : computer-abuse, computer-fraud, computer-related crime or automatic data-processing crime (ADP) and computer offences. The Law enforcement officers should be trained to investigate successfully these offences. The training needs of the computer crime investigator can be stated in terms of three training levels :

(*i*) An awareness level—general level

(*ii*) A comprehensive level

(*iii*) A specialist level

Police trainees should be given understanding about the vulnerability of computer crime. Law enforcement officers should be trained to investigate computer offences by an intensive training programme and it will include teaching the investigator how to obtain evidence and has to stress on terminology, recognition and understanding of source documents, availability of information from console logs, evidence problems, sources, recognition, obtaining and preservation with an adequate comprehension of computer crime scheme and the manipulation of auxiliary storage. Training courses for investigators of computer crimes have to be carefully designed and administered in India in collaboration with the C.B.I. and some officers can be sent to the F.B.I. Academy for getting four weeks' comprehensive level training for investigating computer crimes. For computerisation of crime/criminal records, finger traffic records, pay and allowances, it is necessary that S.Is prints, under training at police training colleges should be given basic knowledge of computer and its working so that when they go to the police stations, they may know the importance of feeding computer expeditiously and correctly. 15 days' familiarisation course should be arranged for all senior ranks in computer working so that they get proper organisation.

Training Tools and Techniques

Training tools and techniques should conform to the training needs and training objectives. Indianisation of training techniques and tools should be carried out and they should be oriented to Indian culture and ethos. It is not necessary to use latest training techniques unless they are found useful and effective for imparting training. For effective training, all the instructional staff should be imparted specialised training in use of various training tools and techniques so that they can utilise latest available facilities for training. Guide system should be introduced in all training institutions and every trainee should, on the first day of arrival, be attached to a member of the faculty who should act as guide for him. For senior courses, generally, officers of higher ranks or at least of same rank with more experience should be detailed as guide. These guides are of immense use in guiding trainees about preparation of individual papers and syndicate reports. Training films on Indian police should be made by the B.P.R.&D., in collaboration with the Films Division of the Govt. of India. There is a need to promote greater collaboration between training institutions by exchange of adequate teaching material, equipments and training films. A brochure should be published periodically by the B.P.R.&D. giving names of training institutions, objects of various courses conducted by them, capacity of the course, details of syllabi, duration, cost of training and other facilities so that all state police personnel may utilise the available training facilities to its maximum extent. Specific strategy should be devised to sensitive the police force to develop and sustain a most secular out-look particularly, while operating in sensitive communal riot-prone areas. Exposure of trainees to various religious and comparative religions by eminent theologicians and academicians can bring out a change in the out-look of trainees. Training in secular out-look for lower ranks must be ensured by training institutions particularly in communally sensitive states. Training programmes for various ranks should be constantly evaluated and modified after carefully analysing the functional contents of various jobs and role expectations of the police and the tools and techniques for training should have relevance with the training programme.

Training Material

Police officers having experience and aptitude should be given monetary incentives to prepare training material for various ranks. Trainers should be encouraged to prepare 'case studies' and other material useful for training and they can be liberally sanctioned honorarium for this purpose. There is a great pacucity of training material for use by the police trainers. Intensive efforts need to be made to develop other training material for use in the training programmes. In every course, the trainees need to be provided with adequate up-to-date indigenously developed and culturally relevant background material. N.P.A. Hyderabad and I.S.A., Mt. Abu are doing some pioneering job in the field of developing training material. The state training institutions should give a list of publications and other training material available with them to the B.P.R.&D. for complication and circulation. S.V.P. N.P.A. Hyderabad has brought out in cyclostyled form agenda and notes of the X Symposium of the Heads of the Police Training Institutions in India held in Patna in October, 1981, and list of training material has been brought out as appendices II to IV. Monographs on training methodology should be published by all major training institutions and each training institutions should develop a publication cell to bring out relevant training material. The instructional material should meet the needs of various levels of trainees and should be suffused with environmental realism and indigenous experience. There is a need for co-ordination in preparation of methodical distribution of teaching material between institutions so that all can draw from the total pool available in the country. There should be frequent exchange of training equipment and material and utilisation of expert staff by the training institutions other than those where it is located. Training Division B.P.R.&D. should act as a clearing house for training material available at the country as well as abroad.

Environs of Training

Environs of police training need greatest attention and particularly the physical facilities. Both tangible and non-tangible constituents of environs need improvement in police training institutions. Requisite buildings for administration, faculty, hostels, residence of instructional staff and other important amenities have to be sanctioned in all the training institutions and more funds be provided under the modernisation scheme of the Govt. of India. Only qualified, willing and committed people should be posted as heads of the police training institutions. Cent percent residential accommodation for staff be sanctioned in an incremental manner for all ranks. More incentives and motivations should be made available for trainers. Swimming-pools should be sanctioned in police academies and state police training colleges so that various ranks may be taught swimming and life-saving techniques during in-service and basic training courses. Adequate land for sports, games, equitation and outside parade should be made available in the institutions. Rifle range and pistol firing range should be located in close vicinity of training institutions and adequate funds should be made available to equip firing ranges with latest sophisticated equipments. Each training institution should be provided with spacious and well furnished auditorium where all staff and trainees may assemble for witnessing cinema, cultural shows and other literary functions of the institution.

Model police stations, model police controlroom, traffic point sand model and sand model of crowd control at V.I.P. meeting are essential physical facilities which should be provided in all the institutions. Environs of training institutions should be conducive for stress-free and effective job-oriented training.

Financial Allocations

Each state should spend one percent of the total police budget on police training and should spend 5% of the budget on research and development of the organisation. Liberal modernisation grants should be made available to the training institutions for improving their physical facilities. Annual allotment of funds for purchase of library books, magazines and journals of professional interest should be raised liberally and efforts should be made to equip the college libraries and district police libraries with books on police subjects available in India and other countries where a lot of advancement has been made in police work. More funds should be made available to the state police training centres by the states and the centre for improving the physical facilities. Govt. of India should accord sanction for diverting some of the funds available in the modernisation grant for construction of buildings for police training institutions of the states. The states should utilise the modernisation grant for providing equipment and training aids to police training institutions. The funds under the modernisation grant scheme should be allowed to be diverted for the construction of buildings for training institutions.

Evaluation and Feed-back

An effective feed-back system to judge and evaluate the impact of training should be established in all the states which should be responsible for assessing and testing the responses and impact of training with reference to professional, organisational and personnel improvements in the trainees. The system of evaluation and follow-up should be carried out by an expert independent body so that impartial and objective assessment of trainees, trainers and the training system as a whole may be effectively carried out. Principals, heads of various faculties and senior members of the training institutions should visit various districts and areas during vacation or at certain intervals to check up how far the training imparted in the training institutions helped the trainees in their police work in their actual work/life. A scientific and objective evaluation of each training programme alongwith cost-benefit analysis should be carried out by the research centres of the police headquarters in collaboration with Training Division of the B.P.R.&D. and the Universities.

Trainees

Trainees who are nominated for training course should not be transferred during the training and should be posted back in the previous place of posting. During training period uniform special training allowance to all trainees be given so that they get some monetary incentive for training. Daily allowance should be adequate enough to cover all the expenses of the trainees. Trainees who get good gradings and positions in various courses be suitably rewarded/commended by their superior officers and these gradings should be taken into consideration at the time of promotion. As an incentive, officers obtaining research degrees on police subjects should get special allowance of Rs. 100 p.m. Even certain useful courses should carry special allowances at sliding rates. Selection of trainees for various training programmes should be purposive and the aim should be to choose the best available material and not the unwanted ones. After training, trainees should be posted in such a way that the training imparted to them may be utilised.

Research and Training

Certain selected police academies and colleges should be affiliated to Universities as research centres and research facilities should be provided by the police training institutions to researchers who can carry out independent research work on police subjects for their M. Phil or Ph.D. degrees. To carry out meaningful research, it is imperative to strengthen the organisational infra-structure itself and diversify its activities itself to achieve predetermined goals. Fellowships should be instituted by N.P.A. Hyderabad and I.S.A. Mt. Abu for two years for officers who are interested in research. There is a need to bring police research development and training in the plan sector to accelerate the growth and development of this neglected area of public life. Adequate and willing competent staff should be posted in research centres and research cells of the training institutions. Research centres of police headquarters should be headed by a Research Officer who has requisite research degree in social sciences and who has aptitude for research work. Research cell of training institutions should have one D.I.G. or S.P., one Research Officer, one statistical officer, two investigators and complementary staff of stenographers and clerks. Financial assistance should be provided for publication of papers and theses of approved quality which could be used as a suitable teaching material on police subjects. The old and rare reports should be republished by the B.P.R.&D. for training purposes. All material collected and reports and papers prepared by the National Police Commission should also be made freely available to training institutions. There should be coordination in research in various training institutions by bringing out a bibliography on police research already conducted and topics on which research is in progress. Research centres should send their research projects to B.P.R.&D. which in turn should publish its gist/abstract in quarterly journal of it and copies sent to all the training institutions and police libraries.

Police Training and Education

It is difficult to train all police officers in training institutions and, therefore, correspondence courses for various ranks should be organised by police headquarters in each state for officers upto the rank of Inspectors. B.P.R. & D. should conduct correspondence course for gazetted ranks. Certain selected police training institutions should also introduce suitable correspondence courses for the benefit of serving personnel. Jawahar Lal Nehru University, Delhi ; Osmania University, Madras University and a few other Universities should start a chair for police science. Police science should be taken as a subject for Bachelor of Arts and Master of Arts degrees.

B.P.R. & D. should also take up the case with the University Grants Commission and the Academic Boards of the Universities. Universities should introduce specialised studies in Police science criminology and criminalistics at graduate and post-graduate levels. Police training and education be given further impetus by providing monetary and other motivations to police officers to acquire higher education in various disciplines closely connected with police work. Management, behavioural sciences, sociology, psychology are some of the areas where police officers should acquire more knowledge so that they may ultimately build up the faculties of the training institutions.

Recommendations about N.P.A.

National Police Academy, Hyderabad should become a repository of knowledge and expertise on police. Staff of the Academy should be upgraded and restructuring proposal pending with the Government of India should be approved and sanctioned so that more experienced and professionally sound staff may be available for conducting training of senior police officers. Syndicate reports and proceedings of various seminars/symposia/workshops be published by the publication cell of the Academy and should be priced for sale. Research cell of the Academy should be reconstituted and one D.I.G. (D.D.), one A.D., two Research Officers, four field research investigators and supporting secretarial staff should be sanctioned for the Academy. Academy library should introduce institutional library issue system so that state police training institutions may get books from N.P.A. Training of trainers' wing with one Dy. Director, two Asst. Directors and one psychologist with supporting staff should be sanctioned. Physical facilities for additional courses like training of trainers course and state police officers (I.P.S.) Selection course should be catered for. Additional lecture halls, hostel, furniture and other requirement for additional courses should be sanctioned. N.P.A. should start correspondence course on crime prevention and police management.

Recommendations about Internal Security Academy

The staff of the Internal Security Academy, Mt. Abu, should

be upgraded to make it self-sufficient. I.S.A. should have two Dy Directors, four Asst. Directors, one Reader in Behavioural Science, one Professor in Management Science and one Research Officer on the staff to form the core faculty of the Academy. I.S.A. should be restructured to cope with the increasing demand for specialised training. All existing hired buildings should be purchased and necessary renovation, alteration and additions should be carried out. A senior officers' hostel for forty officers with dining hall, lounge and other mess facilities should be built up. Auditorium, seminar hall, four lecture halls, hospital and other necessary buildings should also be sanctioned for the Academy. Research cell should be created with a full time staff of one Asst. Director, one Research Officer, two Research Investigators and other supporting staff for carrying out various duties laid down for the cell. A comprehensive master-plan for the buildings required by the Academy should be drawn up and the Government of India should sanction the required funds for construction of these buildings and other physical facilities. Internal Security Academy should become a store-house of all expertise on internal security subjects.

General Recommendations

Non-institutional training in the form of circulars, training bulletins, training keys should be introduced. Training Division should issue training bulletin every month and it should be sent to all offices upto the level of station house officers in which developments should be incorporated. "Training Key" published by International Association of Chiefs of Police, Washington should be subscribed by all training colleges and academies. Training Division should also publish book reviews of all good books published in foreign countries. Informal on the job training by the supervisory officers should be ensured. Informal training should also find a place of pride in the training programme of the police. Members of the training staff should be encouraged to provide training in an informal setting to their trainees. Political leadership should be convinced to provide support for the police training in India. State governments and Central Government should provide support for the training in terms of adequate allocation of resources. Top police leadership should also provide full support and help to police training institutions by posting efficient and good administrators and by providing other requisite infrastructure. Police training should be incorporated as a separate head for discussion in the All India Police Science Congress. National level library for police personnel on the pattern of defence services should be established and police officers should be able to get books through postal facilities. All police training institutions should be able to get books, magazines and journals from N.P.A. on institutional basis. N.P.A., Hyderabad should also build up a library of police films and all the training institutions should be able to get films on institutional basis. Various training courses for all ranks should be linked with career planning and promotions on the pattern of the Indian Army and certain courses could be made compulsory for further *rank promotions at various levels. State government should prepare five year development plan regarding police training* and states should carry out perspective planning projecting future training need for a period of five years and should work out requirements of various physical facilities that are required to meet the future needs of training. In view of the magnitude of the training tasks, correspondence courses in training for jobs not requiring conceptual skills may be explored and certain correspondence courses on the pattern of courses organised abroad, should be started by the national level training institutions for senior police officers. Study leave should be liberally sanctioned to the personnel to give a fillip to self-training programmes and research projects. Subject to suitable variations in individual cases, ten per cent of the total period of service in the career span of police officers should be ear-marked for training in all the states. India should evolve a police training policy at national level to cope with the increasing challenges in police work. It should reflect a concerted, rational and well-planned policy in the field of training at both the state and union levels. Perspective long-term training policy for atleast two decades should be drawn in a pragmatic manner and training facilities should be expanded on the same lines. Police training in India should be revitalised by reorientation towards (*i*) sensitivity to the ambiguities and ambivalences of group and individual action, and (*ii*) insight into the trainee's own ideological conflicts and ambivalences. Sensitivity here means an openness to recognising the complexity, ambivalence and subtlety of emotions, feelings, thoughts and life styles other than one's own. Both the N.P.A., Hyderabad and I.S.A., Mount Abu should be made repositories of knowledge for their specialised fields and should be able to provide consultancy. These Academies should become research and experimental centres where new training methodologies should be experimented and Indianised. These training academies should become model police training institutions for the third world countries and their libraries should get the status of national police libraries. These suggestions are in the nature of a package deal in that they are inter-connected and inter-dependent. If few suggestions are implemented in isolation, they will not result in the general improvement of the training efforts and, therefore, comprehensive, all round implementation alone will produce desired results. Indian police needs to be adequately trained and oriented in their skills and attitudes for the effective and efficient management of the changed and fast changing situation with all its in-built dimensions of conflict. This process needs drastic overall organisational changes with appropriate man-power planning, modernisation and effective utilisation.

Vistas for Future Research

The researcher has tried to study some aspects of police training in India but certain very useful and important areas of police training have remained undiscovered and untouched. It is hoped that some other social scientists would take the following issues and would help to fill in the gaps existing in the literature on police training :

(*a*) Training needs of Indian police ;

(*b*) A cost-benefit analysis of training programmes of State and Central level training institutions ;

(*c*) Evaluation of training programmes of various police training institutions ;

(*d*) Motivation and attitudes of police trainers and their job satisfaction in India ;

(*e*) Motivation and attitude of police trainees and their involvement in training programmes in India ;

(*f*) Areas of application of modern training tools and Equipment in police training ;

(*g*) Problems of police training institutions in different states ;

(*h*) Instructional material for police training in India and its evaluation ;

(*i*) Police training programmes and its follow-up ;

(*j*) Financial administration and police training in India ;

(*k*) Comparative study of police training of various states ;

(*l*) Evaluation of police research in India ;

(*m*) Identification of methodology for training in behavioural modification and change ;

(*n*) Training of police women in India ;

(*o*) An evaluation of specialised police training courses of India ;

(*p*) Training in central police organizations like C.R.P.F., B.S.F., C.I.S.F., I.T.B.P. ;

(*q*) Evaluation and in-depth study of police training institutions of each state ;

(*r*) Human relations training in police organisations in India ;

(*s*) Trainee-Trainer relationships in police training and institutions in India ;

(*t*) Impact of training on police sub-culture.

Concluding Remarks

It has been endeavoured in this study to analyse the administration of police training in India in an objective, scientific and rational manner on the basis of empirical data from the field. Police profession in India has to develop dynamism and viability to cope with the changing needs of the modern society. For this, a policeman has to be professionally efficient, competent and well-informed. Education and training must humanise the police in the democratic values of thesociety and should solidify foundations for a mutually supportive police-public relationship ensuring secularism, socialism and social justice.

APPENDICES

APPENDIX A

LIST OF POLICE TRAINING INSTITUTIONS IN INDIA

Name and Location of Training Institutions

1. Border Security Force Academy, Tekanpur, Gwalior, Madhya Pradesh.
2. Border Security Force Training Centre & School, Hazaribagh, Bihar.
3. Border Security Force Training Centre, Jammu, Jammu & Kashmir.
4. Border Security Force Training Centre, Jullundur Cantt., Punjab.
5. Border Security Force Training Centre, Kadamtala
6. Border Security Force Training Centre, Jodhpur, Rajasthan.
7. Border Security Force Training Centre, Shillong, Meghalaya.
8. Central School of Weapons and Tactics, Indore, Madhya Pradesh.
9. Central School of Mechanical Transport, Sagar, Madhya Pradesh.
10. Central Bureau of Investigation Training Centre, New Delhi.
11. Central Detective Training School, Calcutta.
12. Central Detective Training School, Hyderabad.
13. Central Detective Training School, Chandigarh.
14. C.F.P.B., Calcutta.
15. C.I.S.F. Training Centre, Hyderabad.
16. C.I.S.F. Training School, Bhilai.

17. Institute of Criminology and Forensic Science, New Delhi.
18. Internal Security Academy, C.R.P,F., Mount Abu.
19. C.R.P.F. Central Training College-I, Neemuch.
20. C.R.P.F. Central Training College-II, Avadi, Tamil-Nadu.
21 Recruits Training Centre-I, C.R.P.F., Barwaha, Madhya Pradesh.
22. Recruits Training Centre-II, C.R.P.F., Avadi, Tamil Nadu.
23. S.V.P. National Police Academy, Hyderabad.
24. North East Police Academy, Barapani, Shillong.
25. Police Training College, Anantpur, Andhra Pradesh.
26. Police Recruits School, Vijayanagaram, Vishakapattanam, Andhra Pradesh.
27. Police Recruits School, Amberpet, Hyderabad, Andhra Pradesh.
28. Police Training School, Anantpur, Andhra Pradesh.
29. Police Training College, Dergaon, Assam.
30. Recruit Training School, Dargaon, Assam.
31. Armed Police Training Centre, Dargaon, Assam.
32. Police Radio Training School, Gauhati, Assam.
33. Assam Police Radio Organisation, Training School, Jalukbari, Gauhati, Assam.
34. Elementary Fire Fighting Training School, Maligaon, Assam.
35. Police Training College, Hazaribagh, Bihar.
36. Constables Training School, Nathnagar, Bihar.
37. Advance Training School, Patna, Bihar.
38. B.M.P., Training Centre, Patna, Bihar.
39. Police Training College, Junagarh, Gujarat.
40. Police Training School, Baroda, Gujarat.
41. Police Training School (For S.R.P.), Chowkey, Junagagh, Gujarat.
42. Police Training College, Madhubn, Haryana.
43. Armed Police Training Centre, Madhuban, Haryana.

44. Police Training School, Junga, Simla, Himachal Pradesh.
45. Recruits Training Centre, Chamba, Himachal Pradesh.
46. Police Training School, Udhampore, Jammu & Kashmir.
47. Police Training College, Trivandrum, Kerala.
48. Police Training School, R.V. Puram, Trichur, Kerala.
49. Police Training School, Tamavaramapuram, Kerala.
50. Main Training Centre, Malapuram, Kerala.
51. Police Training College, Mysore, Karnataka.
52. Mysore State Police Training School, Channapatna, Karnataka.
53. City Armed Reserve, Bangalore, Karnataka.
54. Police Driving and Maintenance School, Yelhanka, Karnataka.
55. Traffic Training Institute, Briand Sqare, Bangalore, Karnataka.
56. S.B. Training Institute, Utility Building, Bangalore, Karnataka.
57. M.P. Police Training College, Sagar, Madhya Pradesh.
58. Armed Police Training Centre, Indore, Madhya Pradesh.
59. Police Training School, Indore, Madhya Pradesh.
60. Police Training School, Rajnandgaon, Madhya Pradesh.
61. Police Training School, Tigra, Madhya Pradesh.
62. Police Training School, Pachmarhi, Madhya Pradesh.
63. Police Training School, Rewa, Madhya Pradesh.
64. I Training Bn. S.A.F., Indore, Madhya Pradesh.
65. VI S.A.F. Training Bn., Ranchi.
66. Radio Training School, Indore, Madhya Pradesh.
67. Police Training College, Nasik, Maharashtra.
68. Police Training School, Naigan, Bombay, Maharashtra.
69. Recruit Police Training School, Akola, Maharashtra.
70. Regional Police Training School, Nagpur, Maharashtra.
71. Regional Police Training School, Khandale, Maharashtra.
72. R.P.T.S., Jaina, Maharashtra.

73. Special Branch Training Institute, Dadar, Bombay, Maharashtra.
74. Traffic Institute, Bombay, Maharashtra.
75. S.R.P.F. Group I Pune, Maharashtra.
76. Manipur Police Training Centre, Pangei, Near Imphal, Manipur.
77. Police Training School, Chumukedima, Nagaland.
78. N.A.P. Training, Chumukedima, Nagaland.
79. Police Training College, Angul, Orissa.
80. Police Training School, Nayagarh, Orissa.
81. Orissa Police Signals Training School, Cuttack, Orissa.
82. Police Training College, North Zone, Phillaur, Punjab.
83. Police Recruits Training Centre, Jahankalan, Punjab.
84. Refresher Training Centre, Patiala, Punjab.
85. Punjab Armed Police Training Centre, Jullundur Cantt., Punjab.
86. C.I.D. Training Centre, Sec. 36, Chandigarh, Punjab.
87. Wireless Training Centre, S.A.S. Nagar, Punjab.
88. Recruits Training Centre, Ladha Kothi, Sangrur, Punjab.
89. Rajasthan Police Academy, Jaipur, Rajasthan.
90. Police Training School, Kishangarh, Rajasthan.
91. Police Training School, Udaipur, Rajasthan.
92. R.A.C. and A.P. Training Centre, Jodhpur, Rajasthan.
93. Police Training School, Jodhpur, Rajasthan.
94. Security Training School, Jaipur, Rajasthan.
95. Wireless Training School, Jaipur, Rajasthan.
96. Police Training College, Ashok Nagar, Madras, Tamil Nadu.
97. Police Recruits School, Vellore, Tamil Nadu.
98. Police Recruits School, Coimbatore, Tamil Nadu.
99. S.A.P.I. Bn. Madras, Tamil Nadu.
100. Railway and Armed Police Regimental Centre, Avadi, Tamil Nadu.

101. Police Transport Workshop-cum-Training School, Avadi, Tamil Nadu.
102. Police Training College-I, Moradabad, Uttar Pradesh.
103. Police Training College-II, Moradabad, Uttar Pradesh.
104. Police Training College-III, Sitapur, Uttar Pradesh.
105. Recruits Training School, Moradabad, Uttar Pradesh.
106. Armed Training Centre, Sitapur, Uttar Pradesh.
107. Recruit Training School, Sitapur, Uttar Pradesh.
108. Recruit Training School, Shajahanpur, Uttar Pradesh.
109. Police Training School, Chunar, Mirzapur, Uttar Pradesh.
110. Recruit Training School, Gonda, Uttar Pradesh.
111. Recruit Training School, Ghazipur, Uttar Pradesh.
112. Recruits Training School, Fatehgarh, Uttar Pradesh.
113. Intelligence Department Training School, Lucknow, Uttar Pradesh.
114. Police Motor Transport Centre, Sitapur, Uttar Pradesh.
115. Police Training College, Barrackpore, West Bengal.
116. Police Training School, Calcutta, West Bengal.
117. Police Training College, Agartala, Tripura.
118. Police Training School, New Delhi.
119. Recruit Training Centre, New Delhi.
120. Police Training School, Volpoi, Panaji, Goa Doman. & Diu
121. Police Training Centre, Lungverh, Mizoram.
122. Police Training Centre, Bandesdewa, A.C.P.
123. Police Training School, Shillong, Meghalaya.
124. Recruit Training Centre, Gangtok, Sikkim.

APPENDIX B

RESEARCH PROJECT COMPLETED BY B.P.R. & D.

Year

1973

1. Enforcement of Arms Act, Explosives Act etc.
   - (*a*) Leakage of Potassium Chlorate to unlawful elements.
   - (*b*) Leakage of Arsenic Disuiphide to unlawful elements.
   - (*c*) Leakage of Picric Acid to unlawful elements.
   - (*d*) Leakage of high explosives to unlawful elements.
2. Reasons for decline in the percentage of successful prosecutions in cases of kidnapping in West Bengal and Union Territories.
3. Texicological Effects of C.S. gas.
4. Thefts of copper wire.
5. Reluctance of the public to aid the police in the detection of crime and crime reporting at police station.
6. Organisation and system of policing in medium size cities in India.
7. Adequacy of police arrangements in tribal districts.
8. Police arrangements on the Indo-Nepal Border—(Separate reports on the Intelligence set-up and the set-up of police stations and outpost).

	9. Impact of democratic decentralisation on rural crime.
1974	1. Study of the causes of increase in crime in Delhi.
	2. Theft/losses of Explosives in rail transport.
	3. Need, structure and functions of crime prevention units in the police.
	4. Women police.
	5. Study of traffic inforcement by police authorities in Kanpur.
	6. Reorganisation of the Bihar Armed Police.
	7. Security and law order problems in collieries of Bihar.
1975	1. Automobile theft and deficiencies in the existing law and procedure.
	2. Systems study of Bihar Police.
	3. Prosecution at the sessions level.
	4. Use of fire arms in riot control.
	5. Cost effectiveness of Home Guards.
	6. A Survey of institution buildings of the Delhi Police.
	7. Survey of research in forensic science.
	8. Growing trends of violence and use of fire arms and explosives in crimes of violence.
	9. Police fatalities.
	10. Impact of the Revised Code of Criminal Procedure (Committee Report).
	11. A scheme for motor transport workshop for Delhi Police.

1976

1. Police Management at the top level.
2. police personnel—Recourse to courts in administrative and disciplinary matters—A pilot study.
3. Fleet Management for the police.
4. Enforcement of Untouchability (Offences) Act 1955.
5. Economisation of manpower through modernisation—A case study of the Delhi Police.

1977

1. Performance appraisal in police.
2. Kidnapping of children.
3. Rural policing.
4. A study of Technical Armed Police Battalions of Haryana.
5. Survey of private detective agencies and commercial security services.
6. Some aspects of horse racing in India.
7. Beat patrolling in urban areas.

1978

1. Adequacy of police and other administrative arrangements in some industrial areas in and around Delhi.
2. Criminality amongst women in India (A study of female offenders and female convicts).

Appendix 'C'

POLICE RESEARCH CENTRES IN INDIA

Name of the State/UT and strength of the Centre	Research projects completed	Research projects in hand
1	2	3
1. **Andhra Pradesh**		
Sanctioned strength of the Centre :	1. Faction in Rayalaseema (Kurnoch). Cuddapah and Anantpur Districts.	1. Extension of up to date study of factions crime in Rayalaseema District.
Addl. S.P. — 1 Inspector — 2	2. Corruption amongst the police officers	2. The problem of wire thefts in the State.
Sub-Inspector — 2	3. Implications of Panchyat Raj set up (AP)	
Head Constable — 4 Constable — 8	4. Problem of ex-criminal tribes.	
2. **Gujarat**		
Sanctioned strength of the Centre :	1. Reasons for increase in offences of murders in the State in 1965	1. Acquittal of murder cases in the State in the year 1970

1	2	3
Dy. S.P. — 1	2. Temple thefts.	2. Wholesale acquitted in gambling cases upto 4-5.
Inspector — 1	3. Kidnapping of children for the purpose of begging.	3. Acquitted in gambling cases in Surat city in the year 1970.
Sub-Inspector — 1	4. Fall in the percentage of conviction in the State and possible remedies.	4. Bail and heinous crime.
Unarmed Police — 1	5. Chapter cases and their effects in curbing the crime.	5. Extent of property offences in the area of urban, semi-urban and predominantly rural area in Jamnagar District.
Head Constable — 1	6. Effect of Externment cases in crime.	6. Disposal of cases u/s 107 Cr. P.C. Analysis of—in Jamnagar District.
	7. Problems of Sikh Rakhas in the state.	7. Acqnittal in cases u/s 4-5 of gambling Acts in Baroda City.
Peon — 1	8. Problems of Bharuads and damage to crops in the state.	8. Increase of hurt cases in Baroda Range.

1	2	3
	9. Thefts of atomizers	9. Study of cases of misappropriation.
	10. The prevention of the type of crim.nality resulting from special changes and impact of industrialisation of crime.	10. Minutes of the DIG's conference held in 1972-machinery for collection of statistics of police.
	11. Fall of conviction in chapter cases for the years 1968 & 1969 at Ahmedabad Railway Station.	
	12. Copper wire thefts on Surat Broach Sections in the year 1970.	
	13. Crime due to superstition.	
	14. Problems of thefts and illicit export of cultured property.	
	15. Grant of bail and incidence of heinous crime.	
	16. Acquittal in chapter cases u/s 109 Cr. P.C. from Surat District.	

1	2	3
	17. Illicit manufacture, sale and possession of fire arms. 18. Fatal motor accidents. 19. Acquittal of murder cases of Surat and Broach Districts. 20. Test cases under Prohibition and Gambling Act without Panchas in Baroda Range in the year 1970-71. 21. Cycle thefts in Surat city in the year 1970.	
3. **Haryana** Sanctioned Strength of the Centre Dy. S.P. — 1 Sub-Inspector — 1 Steno-typist — 1 Constable — 1	No research project has been completed.	1. Investigation of cases and disposal of complaints by NCOs at police stations to find out causes of interruption in the investigation. 2. Juvenile Delinquency.

1	2	3
		3. Kidnapping of children for begging purposes.
		4. Handling, labelling and packing of exhibits pertaining to criminal cases.
		5. Different kinds of thefts.
		6. Activities of Ex-notified criminal tribes.
		7. Study of traffic accidents vis-a-vis working of traffic police.
4. Karnataka		
Sanctioned strength of the Centre	1. Juvenile delinquency, its measures for combating juvenile delinquency	1. Causes for delay in service of process project. Report is completed and is pending approval of higher authorities.
Suptdt. of Po lice — 1	2. An analysis of road accidents in	2. Study of missing person in

1		2	3
		Mysore State 1958-1966.	Karnataka State for four years from 1972-1975. Draft report has been prepared and is pending final approval.
Dy. S.P.	— 2	3. Report on the study of cheating by bogus firms in India.	3. Misappropriation in co-operative institutions in Karnataka State for years from 1966-1975. An additional questionnaire has been sent to all the unit offices and replies are awaited from some offices.
Inspector	— 2	4. An analysis from road accidents in Mysore State 1958-1967.	
Sub-Inspector	— 2	5. Scope for data processing of crime records through automation.	
Constable	— 12	6. An analysis of road accidents in Mysore State for 1968—comparison with those of 1958-1967.	

1	2	3
FDC — 1	7. Police morale and public relationship and public complaints against police in Mysore State for the year 1952-67 (An analysis).	
SDC — 1	8. An analysis of road accidents in Mysore State for 1969—comparison with those of 1958-1968.	
Steno — 1	9. Guidelines for the investigation of several types of offences.	
Typist — 2	10. Causes of the pendency of police cases in courts in Karnataka State.	
Librarian — 1	11. Causes for high incidence of murders in the districts of Dharwar, Bijapur and Belgaum during the years 1972-1973 and 1974.	
Sr. Statistical Asstt. — 1	12. Socio-economic study of the XX batch of Armed Police and Constable recruits.	

1	2	3
Dalyath 1 —	13. Socio-economic study of the XVII Batch of Armed Police Constable recruits.	
	14. Socio-economic study of XXXI Batch of Civil Police Constable recruits.	
	15. Socio-economic study of XIX Batch of Armed Police Constable recruits.	
	16. A comparative study of suicides in Bangalore city during the years 1972, 1973 and 1974.	
	17. A study of suicides at "Tippus Drop" Nandi Hills, Kolar District 1966-75.	
	18. Death of suspects in police custody in Karnataka State during the years 1972, 1973 and 1974.	
	19. Work load in police stations	

1	2	3
	conducted for one week of Ulsoor Gate police Station, bangalore city.	
	20. Socio-economic study of XVIII Batch of Armed Police Constables.	
5. Kerala		
Sanctioned strength of the Centre :	1. Study of Juvenile delinquency in Kerala.	1. Study of the incidence of burglary in Trivandrum city from 1964-69.
S.P. — 1	2. Copper wire theft in Kerala.	2. Study of the scriptory work in police stations.
Dy. S.P. — 1	3. Crime in logical survey of Sabarigiri project area.	3. Study of the new petition enquiry system in Central region.
Inspector — 1 Statistical officer — 1	4. Study on the production and distribution of Potassium Chlorate in Quilon District in Kerala State.	4. Study of the working of the police-public relations office in police hrs.
6. Madhya Pradesh		
Sanctioned strength	1. Problems of thefts and illicit	1. Action under Cr. P.C. to

1	2	3
of the Centre :	export of the cultural property in M.P.	prevent breach of peace.
Dy. S.P. — 1	2. Ex-criminal tribe Kanjars.	2. Difficulty and execution of warrants on truck/bus drivers.
Inspector — 1	3. Cheating by false offers of employment.	3. Escape of prisoners from police custody.
Sub-Inspector — 1	4. Ex-criminal tribe other than Kanjars.	
L.D.C. — 1	5. Crime due to superstition in M.P.	
Orderly Const. — 2	6. Traffic & road safety in respect of four cities of M.P.; Gwalior, Bhopal, Jabalpur and Indore.	
Statistical Officer		
Computer (UDC) — 1		
L.D.C. — 1		
Librarian — 1		
7. **Maharashtra**		
Sanctioned strength of the Centre :	1. Compensation for the victims of crimes of violence.	1. Delay in the disposal of criminal cases in the courts of law.

1	2	3
S.P. (Law & Research) — 1	2. Sample survey regarding delinquent behaviour in children from Pune and Sholapur.	2. Diagnostic study of atrocities on Harijans.
Dy. S.P. (Research) — 1	3. Impact of industrialisation on crimes in Thana District.	
Statistical Officer — 1	4. Suicides and attempted suicides.	
Detective Police Inspector — 1	5. Indebtedness among police constabulary in Pune Rural District.	
Inspector — 1	6. Democratic decentralisation and its impact on rural crime.	
Detective Police Sub-Inspector (Research) — 1	7. Tenancy law and its impact on Rural crime.	
	8. Increase in cases of dacoity in Aurangabad District.	
Detective Police Head Constable — 2	9. Abstraction of cheques, drafts and valuable documents during postal transit.	
Junior Grade Clerk-cum-typist — 1		

1	2	3
8. Manipur		
Sanctioned strength of the Centre :	Not available	Not available.
A small unit consisting of—		
Inspector — 1 Sub-Inspector — 1 Asstt. SI of Crime — 1 Branch CID has — 1 been set up under the supervision of S.P. CID Manipur.	I.G.P. Manipur has in one Communication to the researcher intimated that there is no research cell/centre till date (Letter dtd. April, 1982)	
9. Rajasthan		
Sanctioned strength of the Centre :	1. Lok Sabha Election in Rajasthan (1971)—A research study.	1. Study of traffic probiems in Jaipur city.
Addl. S.P. — 1 Inspector — 1	2. Study of agitations in Rajasthan (Jan-Sept., 1972).	2. A study of copper wire theft.

1		2	3
Inspector	— 1	3. Police in the eye of public.	3. A study of police station response to modus operandi work.
Sub-Inspector	— 1	4. Public reaction to a police situation—A study	4. A scheme for computerisation centre of police crime record.
Steno	— 1	5. Draft scheme on 'Students' security organisation.	5. A study on night burglaries in Jaipur city (under completion).
U.D.C.	— 11	6. To properly deal with the cases of child lifting and begging, a booklet of instructions, prepared in vernacular captioned 'Bal Apharadh Bhiksha Vritti—Police Ka Kartavya'.	6. A history of action against dacoits is being compiled, letters have been addressed to the concerned for eliciting information.
L.P.C.	— 3		7. Compilation of letters issued by police hqrs. 8. Study of Meenas of District police is also in hand. Thefts/recoveries of cultural properties, idols, antiquities in Rajasthan.

1	2	3
10 Tamil Nadu		
Sanctioned strength of the Centre :	1. A report on the sociological survey conducted at Neyveli regarding crime and its relation to industrial development and growth of population.	1. "Wire Thefts"—A study of wire thefts in Tamil Nadu for 5 years from 1971 to 1976.
Dy. S.P. — 1	2. A criminological survey of Thottia Naiks crimes.	2. "Idol Thefts"—A study of idol thefts for 10 years from 1967 to 1976.
Inspector of police — 1	3. Report on the sociological survey conducted at Sathanur Dam site (North Arcot District) with particular reference to crime and its relation to developmental activities and growth of agriculture.	3. "Rehabilitation" Rehabilitation of Ex-convicts who were provided with bank loans in the Districts in Tamil Nadu—to examine a sampling in a year's time and see the percentage of perseverance and success.
Sub-Inspector — 1	4. Report on sociological survey con-	4. "Housing conditions of

1	2	3
	ducted at the Krishnagiri Dam site (Salem District) with particular reference to crime and its relation to developmental activities and growth of population.	policemen in Chengalpattu (East) Police District and Madras City."
Constable — 2	5. Criminological survey of Valeya Crimes.	5. "The pattern of petty cases booked the circumstances, motivations and other values".
Stenographer — 1	6. Juvenile delinquency in Madurai distt.	6. "The effects and results of D.O. letters and circulars issued by the Inspector General of Police in 1977 to all police officers in the State on the toning up of police administration with special reference to police-public relationship."
	7. Juvenile delinquency in Salem District.	7. "The Police-Public Relationship"—A study of cross section of the public

1	2	3
		opinion survey by constabulary under in-service training (19200 persons from four groups, viz. teachers, students, labourers and Harijans) being conducted in 24 batches all over the State.
	8. Prevention of criminality resulting from social changes accompanying economic development in less developed countries.	
	9. Criminological survey of the Kundah Project area in the Nilgiries District.	
	10. A study of Kepmari crimes in India.	
	11. Suicides and attempted suicides in Madras State.	

1	2	3
	12. A study of crime trends in Madras State during the year 1962 and 1967—General Elections.	
	13. A study on "Wire Thefts" with particular reference to Chengalpattu District.	
	14. Incidence of wire thefts in Madras State 1960-1965.	
	15. Research on "Idol Theft".	
	16. A study of incidence of burglaries in Tanjavur District.	
	17. Manpower utilization in Madras city police.	
	18. Study of the enforcement of prohibition.	
	19. A survey report on the problem of eve-teasing, intimidation and mischief in general by juveniles in certain wards of Madras city.	

1	2	3
	20. Research Report on cheating by false offers of employment in Tamil Nadu during 1966-70.	
	21. A note on the problem of traffic accidents in Tamil Nadu.	
	22. Preparation of draft format for Case Docket Sheet.	
	23. A study of explosive cases occurred in Tamil Nadu during 1976 and measures suggested to minimise them.	
	24. Discontinuation of daily and Weekly Crime and occurrence sheet in the districts and replacement in its place a Daily Flash through V.H.F.	
	25. A note on "The Genesis of Dy. Suptdts. Of Police cadre and its present growth in Tamil Nadu."	

1	2	3
	26. Introduction of standardized format of cases Diary Part-I streamlining the investigation all over the State.	
	27. Standardized proforma (Inspection Notes) for the visits and inspections of police stations by Circle Inspectors and Sub-divisional Officers.	
	28. A Study on "Counterfeit cases in Tamil Nadu."	
	29. A study of "Analysis of types of prisoners involved in trivial cases and confined in Central Jail, Madras and four sub-jails in Chengalpattu East Police District during the last quarter 1976."	
11. Uttar Pradesh		
Sanctioned strength for the Research Cell		
Suptdt. of Police — 1	1. Child lifting in UP	1. Law & order problem connected with elections.

1		2	3
Dy Suptdt. of Police	— 1	2. Road hold-up in UP.	2. Road robberies in urban & rural areas of UP.
Inspector	— 1	3. Juvenile delinquency.	3. Acquittal in murder cases in UP.
Statistical Asstt.	— 2	4. Crime during elections.	4. Wonton & mallicious destruction of railway property.
D.I. (M)	— 1	5. Preventive measures in use and their relationship with crime.	5. Posting of Inspectors I/c at police station.
Clerk	— 2	6. Robberies & dacoities in running trains.	6. More deterrent punishment under section 363/354 IPC.
Peon	— 1	7. Murders in UP.	7. Reocrds at police station in UP.
		8. The impact of communal disharmony on law & order situation in the State.	8. Study regarding bombs used during 1978, 1979 and 1980 in commission of crime in UP.

1	2	3
	9. Premature release of hardened criminals.	9. Study regarding sanction of Reserve Contingent Reserve Fund for the future of police department.
	10. Problem of unlicensed weapons in UP.	
	11. Theft of cultural property in UP.	
	12. Bail and the incidence of heinous crimes.	
	13. Theft of copper wire.	
	14. Juvenile Aid Pureaux.	
	15. Prosecution at the sessions level.	
	16. Statistics regarding daily average population of convicts and under-trials in jail.	
	17. Punishment awarded under UP. Excise cases.	

1	2	3
	18. Adequacy of punishment under Arms Act cases.	
	19. Denotified tribes in transition.	
	20. Strength and expenses on police.	
	21. Use of illicit fire-arms.	
	22. Arms and ammunition falling into unlawful hands.	
	23. Steps to curb manufacture of illicit arms.	
	24. Antiquities and Art objects.	
	25. Democratic decentralization and its impact on rural crimes.	
	26. Forged court Fee stamps.	
	27. Illegal traffic in girls from M.P. and their sale in Banda.	

1	2	3
	28. Amendment necessary to be enforced in UP Gambling Act.	
	29. Meeting threats of announced agitation by advanced arrests.	
	30. Law & order situation in UP.	
	31. Road accident on Sitapur-Kanpur Road.	
	32. Present communal trend and activities of members of ex-criminal tribes.	
	33. Collection of statistics in Kumbh Mela 1977.	
	34. Mysterious disappearances of persons during 1972.	
	35. Delay in disposal of cases in courts of sessions and Magistrates of UP.	

1	2	3
	36. Study regarding married women killed by their husbands or their in-laws due to inadequate dowry or presents.	
	37. Cases of high incidence of murders during 1978.	
	38. Reducing scriptory work at all levels in police department.	
	39. Study regarding working of Police Central Rooms in UP.	
	40. Utilization of Section 400/401 IPC.	
	41. Utilization of Section 75 IPC.	
	42. Copper wire & copper equipment thefts in UP.	

1		2	3
12 **Delhi**			
Sanctioned strength of Centre :		1. Study of the crime in Excise cases (Liquor cases) in Delhi.	1. Car thefts in Delhi.
Dy SP	— 1	2. Study of the incidence of burglary in Delhi.	2. Supply of guards on "Pay-days" and its effect on man power resources.
Inspector	— 1	3. Study of the cases of snatching in Delhi.	3. Quantum of punishment awarded by the courts u/a 116 Delhi Police Act. A sample survey of 20 cases of Acquittal/discharged by the courts.
Sub-Inspector	— 1	4. Study on the crime in cycle theft cases in Delhi	4. Procedure being followed at the police stations on a report of any untoward incidents or loss of child.
Constables	— 5	5. Study on the crime of pick-pocketing in Delhi.	5. Functions of SHO.
		6. Study of the cases of cheating and fraud in Delhi.	6. Accidental deaths & suicides in India—1981.

1	2	3
	7. Study of motor vehicle lifters active in Delhi.	7. Crime in India—1981.
	8. Study on auto lift in Delhi.	
	9. Study on the problem of use of drugs and narcotics in Delhi.	
	10. Study on crime in Railways in Delhi.	
	11. Study on incidence of robbery and snatching in Delhi.	
	12. Economisation of man-power through modernisation—A Case Study of Delhi Police.	
	13. Study on robbery-dacoity and knifers bad characters fit for maintenance of history sheets.	
	14. Standard of reception in	

1	2	3
	Reporting rooms of police stations/police posts.	
	15. Beat patrolling in police stations of Delhi with special reference to Swain System of patrolling.	
	16. Cars reported stolen but subsequently found Abandoned during 1980.	
	17. Deployment of police force for handling agitations etc. during the Winter Session of Parliament 1980.	
	18. A study note on the first International Symposium on the protection of financial establishments against robbery and burglary.	
	19. Information regarding protection of banking/financial	

1	2	3
	establishments against robberies and burglaries.	
	20. A Research Study regarding time spent by the police in dealing with non-cognizable matters with special reference to landlord-tenant disputes and dowry cases.	
	21. Security proceedings for keeping the peace and good behaviour (u/ss 107/151 & 107/150 Cr.P.C.)	
	22. Crime against women in Delhi.	
	23. Evaluation of the use of the amended provisions of the core of criminal procedure through ordinance No. 12 of 1980, Now Act No. 63 of 1980.	
	24. Suicides in Delhi 1980.	

1	2	3
	25. Security proceedings for keeping the peace and good behaviour Iu/ss 107/151 & 107/150 Cr P CI.	
	26. Police Karamchari Ek Vardidhari Nagrik He Jabki Ek Nagrik Bina Vardi Ke Police Karamchari He. (The policeman is a citizen in uniform while a citizen is a policeman with uniform).	
	27. Causes of murder cases in Delhi.	
	28. Quantum of punishment awarded by the courts for violation of exterment orders under sections 46, 47 and 48 of Delhi Police Act.	
	29. Mafia type crime in Delhi.	
	30. Incidence of crime in some major cities of the world (1978-79-80).	

APPENDIX D

SHOWING STATE AND UNION TERRITORIES WITH AREA, POPULATION POLICE/POPULATION RATIO, POLICE AREA RATIO ETC.

Sl. No.	States/U.Ts	Area (Square Kilometres)	Population 1981 (in thousands)	Total strength of State Police Force	Civil Police/ Population Ratio (per ten thousand of population)	Civil Police/ Area Ratio (per 100 square Kilometres)
1	2	3	4	5	6	7
STATES						
1.	Andhra Pradesh	2,76,814	53,593	56,358	8.81	17.06
2.	Assam	78,523	19,903	21,526	8.26	20.93
3.	Bihar	1,73,876	69,823	66,483	7.50	30.11
4.	Gujarat	1,95,984	33,961	62,485	14.41	24.97
5.	Haryana	44,222	12,851	21,497	12.15	35.31
6.	Himachal Pradesh	55,673	4,238	8,857	15.61	11.88
7.	Jammu & Kashmir	2,22,236	5,954	24,379	29.24	7.83
8.	Karnataka	1,91,773	37,044	45,109	10.71	20.69

9. Kerala	38,864	25,403	33,072	10.46	68.36
10. Madhya Pradesh	4,42,841	52,139	80,266	10.75	12.65
11. Maharashtra	3,07,762	62,715	1,07,818	10.67	21.75
12. Manipur	22,356	1,411	8,534	25.13	15.86
13. Meghalaya	22,489	1,328	6,475	22.13	13.07
14. Nagaland	16,527	773	15,431	31.27	14.62
15. Orissa	1,55,782	26,272	32,901	9.82	16.56
16. Punjab	50,362	16,670	35,156	17.44	57.72
17. Rajasthan	3,42,214	34,108	46,918	9.09	9.06
18. Sikkim	7,299	315	1,802	41.49	17.91
19. Tamil Nadu	1,30,069	48,298	50,562@	9.22	34.25
20. Tripura	10,477	2,047	8,472	18.84	36.81
21. Uttar Pradesh	2,94,413	1,10,886	1,42,557	9.39	35.36
22. West Bengal	87,853	54,486	75,614	8.30	51.49
TOTAL (STATES)	31,68,409	6,74,218	9,52,272	10.20	21.70

1	2	3	4	5	6	7
UNION TERRITORIES :						
23.	A & N Islands	8,293	188	1,882	100.11	22.69
24.	Arunachal Pradesh	83,578	628	2.268	36.11	2.71
25.	Chandigarh	114	450	2,535	56.33	2223.68
26.	D & N Haveli	491	104	148	7.40	15.71
27.	Delhi	1,485	6,196	31,050	32.81	1369.02
28.	Goa, Daman & Diu	3,813	1,082	2,644	17.90	50.80
29.	Lakshadweep	32	40	286	71.50	893.75
30.	Mizoram	21,087	488	2,813	34.22	7.92
31.	Pondicherry	480	604	1,700	16.56	208.33
	TOTAL (U.Ts)	1,19,373	9.780	45,326	32.70	26.79
	GRAND TOTAL	32,87,782	6,83,998	9,97,598	10.52	21.89

NOTE :

1. Figures are provisional
2. *(as on 31.12.83)
3. @(as on 31.12.84)

APPENDIX E

SHOWING POLICE STRENGTH, POLICE, RANGES, POLICE STATIONS AND POLICE DISTRICTS

Sl. No.	States/U.Ts	Strength of Civil Police	Strength of Armed Police	Total strength of State Police Force	Number of Ranges/ Zones	Number of Police Districts	Number of Police Stations
1	2	3	4	5	6	7	8
STATES							
1.	Andhra Pradesh	47,238	9,120	56,358	8	25	988
2.	Assam	16,436*	5,090*	21.526*	4	13	153
3.	Bihar	52,361	14,120	66,483	16**	46	1,071
4.	Gujarat	48,936	13,549	62,485	4	25	400
5.	Haryana	15,617	5,880	21,497	4	12	145
6.	Himachal Pradesh	6,615	2,249	8,857	2	12	76
7.	Jammu & Kashmir	17,407	6,972	24.379	2	14	110
8.	Karnataka	39,685	5,421	45,109	6	20	617
9.	Kerala	26,568	6,500	33,072	3	15	352
10.	Madhya Pradesh	56,027	24,230	80,266	16***	45	991

11. Maharashtra	66.937	40,881	1,07.818	6	33	756
12. Manipur	3.546	4,988	8.534	2	8	49
13. Meghalaya	2,939	3,536	6,475	1	5	22
14. Nagaland	2,417	13.014	15,431	1	7	37
15. Orissa	25,803	7,098	32,901	6	17	384
16. Punjab	29,069	6.080	35,156	3	12	214
17. Rajasthan	31,015	15,900	46,918	7	30	594
18. Sikkim	1,307	495	1.802	—	4	20
19. Tamil Nadu	44,551@	6,011@	50.562@	6	26	956
20. Tripura	3,857	4,615	8,472	1(Z)	3	37
21. Uttar Pradesh	1,04,092	38,465	1,42,557	17&	57	1,303
22. West Bengal	45,239	30,375	75,614	4	25	378
TOTAL (STATES)	6,87,662	2,64,610	9,52,272	119"	454	9,653

1	2	3	4	5	6	7	8
UNION TERRITORIES:							
23.	A & N Islands	1,882	—	1,882	—	1	12
24.	Arunachal Pradesh	2,268	—	2,268	1	10	30
25.	Chandigarh	2,535	—	2,535	—	1	8
26.	D & N Haveli	77	72	148	1	1	3
27.	Delhi	20,330	10,729	31,050	2	6	69
28.	Goa, Daman & Diu	1,937	707	2,644	N.A.	3	23
29.	Lakshadweep	286	—	286	—	1	11
30.	Mizoram	1,670	1,143	2,813	1	3	31
31.	Pondicherry	1,000	700	1,700	4	1	29
	TOTAL (U.T.s)	31,985	13,341	45,326	9@@@	27	216
	GRAND TOTAL	7,19,647	2,77,951	9,97,598	128££	481	9,869

NOTE:

1. Figures are provisional
2. NA stands for 'NOT AVAILABLE'
3. *(as on 31.12.83)
4. @(as on 31.12.84)
5. **(Zones-5, Ranges-11)
6. ***(Zones-4, Ranges-12)
7. @@(Regions)
8. @@@(4-Regions, 5—Ranges)
9. (Z) Zone
10. & (Zones-5, Ranges-12)
11. [11](15—Zones, 104-Ranges)
12. ££(15-Zones, 109 Ranges & 4-Regions)

APPENDIX F

SHOWING POPULATION AND CRIME FIGURES

Sl. No.	States/U.Ts	Population 1981 (in thousands)	Total IPC Cognizable crime reported in 1984	Rate of Criminality (Rati of Cognizable Crime/Population per lakh)
1	2	3	4	5
STATES				
1.	Andhra Pradesh	53,593	53,268	99.39
2.	Assam	19,903	38,926	195.58
3.	Bihar	69,823	1,11,733	160.02
4.	Gujarat	33,961	83,927	247.13
5.	Haryana	12,851	17,662	137.44
6.	Himachal Pradesh	4,238	5,065	119.51
7.	Jammu & Kashmir	5,954	17,122	287.57
8.	Karnataka	37,044	79,235	213.89

1	2	3	4	5
9.	Kerala	25,403	48,044	189.13
10.	Madhya Pradesh	52,139	1,67,945	322.11
11.	Maharashtra	62,715	1,64,424	262.18
12.	Manipur	1,411	2,529	179.23
13.	Meghalaya	1,328	1,605	120.86
14.	Nagaland	773	1,427	184.61
15.	Orissa	26,272	41,164	156.68
16.	Punjab	16,670	12,831	76.97
17.	Rajasthan	34,108	71,672	210.13
18.	Sikkim	315	283	89.84
19.	Tamil Nadu	48,298	1,03,297	213.87
20.	Tripura	2,047	6,025	294.33
21.	Uttar Pradesh	1,10,886	1,68,425	151.89
22.	West Bengal	54,486	72,161	132.44
	TOTAL (STATES)	6,74,218	12,68,770	188.18

UNION TERRITORIES ;			
23. A & N Islands	188	739	393.09
24. Arunachal Pradesh	628	960	152.87
25. Chandigarh	450	1,806	401.33
26. D & N Haveli	104	250	240.38
27. Delhi	6,196	30,773	496.66
28. Goa, Daman & Diu	1.082	3,090	285.58
29. Lakshadweep	40	23	57.50
30. Mizoram	488	1,821	373.16
31. Pondicherry	604	2,613	432.62
TOTAL (U.Ts)	9,780	42,075	430.23
GRAND TOTAL	6,83,998	13,10,845	191.64

NOTE :

1. Figures are provisional

BIBLIOGRAPHY

BOOKS :

Arora, Ramesh K. and Kukar, Jagdish C. (Eds) : *Training and Administrative Development*. The H.C.M State Institute of Public Administration, Jaipur, 1979.

Bayley, David H. : *Forces of Order, Police Behaviour in Japan and United States*, University of California Press, Berkeley, 1976.

Bayley, David H. : *The Police and Political Development in India*, Princeton University Press, 1969.

Banton, Michael : *The Policeman in the Community*, Basic Books Inc New York, 1964.

Bhanot, M.L. and Misra, Surat : *Selected Readings on Police*, B.P.R&D., New Delhi, 1978.

Bhardwaj, R.K. : *Indian Police Administration*, National Publishing House, New Delhi, 1978.

Bloom. B.S. : *Stability and Change in Human Characteristics*, Wiley New York, 1964.

Bopp, William J. : *Police Administration Selected Readings*, Helbrook Press Inc Boston, 1975.

B.P.R&D., *Crime in India*, 1976, New Delhi, 1980.

Boolsen, Frank : Directory of Colleges and Universities offering Programmes in Law Enforcement Criminalistics Corrections, 1961.

Chaturvedi, T.N. : *Public Service and Modern Challenges ; Need for Continuing Education*, Training Division, New Delhi.

C.P.T.C., Mt. Abu, Seminar on Police Training, Oct. 1961.

Coatman, John : *Police*, Oxford University Press, London, 1959.

Curry, J.C. : *Indian Police*, London, Faber and Faber, 1934.

C.P.T.C., Mt. Abu, *Training of Constables in Modern Set-up*, IX Advanced Course, 1964.

C.P.T.C., Mt. Abu. Training I Advanced Course, 1960.

Craig, Robert L. and Bittel, Laster R. : *Training and Development Handbook*, McGraw Hill Book Co., New York, 1967.

Dayal, Ishwar : *Management Training in Organisations*, Printice Hall of India, New Delhi, 1970.

Diaz, S.M. : *New Dimensions to Police Role and Functions in India*, SV NPA Magazine Sec., Hyderabad.

Earayil, L. Alphouse and Vadackumcherry, James : *Public Relations at the Cutting Edge Level*, Police Training College, Trivandrum, Kerala, 1982.

Gammage, Allen Z. : *Police Training in the United States*, Charles C. Thomas, Springfield, Illinois.

Ghosh, S.K. : *Indian Police at the Cross-Roads*, Eastern Law House, Allahabad.

Gupta, Anand Swarup : *The Police in British India 1861-1947*, Concepts Publishing Co., New Delhi, 1979.

German, A.C. : *Police Personnel Management*, Charles C. Thomas, Illinois, USA, 1958.

Griffiths, P. : To Guard my people : The History of Indian Police, Allied Publishers P. Ltd., Bombay, 1971.

Hale, D. Charles : *Fundamentals of Police Administration*, Holbrook Press, Boston, 1977.

Harris, Richard H. : *The Police Academy : An Inside view*, John Wiley and Sons, New York, 1973.

Hansen, David A. and Culley, Thomas R. : *The Police Training Officer*, Charles C. Thomas (Publisher), Springfield, Illinois, USA, 1973.

Herbert, A. Thelan : *Dynamics of Group at Work*, Chicago University Press, 1954.

Iyer, V.R. Krishna : *Police in a Welfare State*, Asia Book Centre, New Delhi, 1959.

Institute of Criminology and Forensic Science, New Delhi,

"*Training Courses in Criminology*", United Nations Handbook.

Katz and Kohn : *The Social Psychology of Organisations* Wiley, New York, 1966.

Kenney, John P. : *Police Administration*, Charles C. Thomas, Springfield, Illinois, 1972.

Kuykendell, Jack L. and Unsinger, Peter C. : *Community Police Administration*, Nelson Hall, Law Enforcement series, Chicago, 1975.

Lahiri, B.N. : *Before and After* : Chugh Publications, Allahabad, 1974.

Lynton, Rolf P. and Pareek, Udai, : *Training for Development*, Sons and Co. Pvt. Ltd., Bombay, 1967.

Mahajan, Amritjit : *Indian Police Women*, (A Sociological study of a new role), Deep & Deep Pub , New Delhi.

Mager, Robert P. : *Preparing Instructional Objectives*, Fearn Publishers, California, 1962.

Maaner, Johnvan (Ed) : *Policing: A View from the Street*, Goodyear Publishing Co., in California, 1978.

Mathew, B. Miles (Ed) *Innovation in Education*, New York : Teachers College, Columbia University, 1964.

Maheswari, S.R. : *Indian Administration*, Orient Longman, New Delhi, 1974.

Monappa, Arun and Sanyadam, Mirza S. : *Personnel Management*, Tata Mc Graw Hill Pub. Co. Ltd., New Delhi, 1979.

Misra, S.C. : *Police Administration in India*, National Police Academy, Abu, 1970.

Misra, S.C. : *State Police Organisation in India*, C.R.P.F. Press, New Delhi, 1975.

Mc Gehee, N. and Thayer, P.W. : *Training in Business and Industry*, Wiley, New York, 1961.

National Police Academy, Hyderabad, cases on training XXVIII S, 1974.

N.P.A. Hyderabad, Transactions, Vol. XXII, April, 1976.

Nath. T. : *Forty Years of Indian Police*, Concepts Pub. Co., New Delhi, 1981.

Niederhoffer, Arthur, : *Behind the Shield: The Police in Urban Society*, Double-day and Co., Garden City, New York.

Nigam. S.R. : *Scotland Yard and the Indian Police*, Kitab Mahal Pvt. Ltd., Allahabad, 1963.

Otto, Calvin P. and Glaser R.O. : *The Management of Training — A Handbock of Training and Development Personnel*, Addison Wesley Pub. Co., Massachusetts, 1970.

Panakal, J.J. : *Special Training of Police for Prevention of Juvenile Delequency (Paper II)*, All India Police Science Congress, Bombay, Sept., 1961.

Pareek, Udai and Rao, T.V. : *Designing and Managing Human Resources*, Oxford and I.B.H. Pub. Co. Ltd., New Delhi, 1981.

Pandey, D.C. : *Police Coercion in India*, Service Pub. House, New Delhi.

Publications Division, G. of I, M.H.A. The Civil List of the Indian Police Service 1976, New Delhi.

Publication Division, Govt. of India, The Constitution of India, 1981.

Report of the Assam Police Commission, 1971.

Report of the Bihar Police Commission, 1961.

Report of the Madhya Pradesh Police Commission, 1965-66.

Report of the Maharashtra Police Commission, 1964.

Report of the Punjab Police Commission, 1962.

Report of the U.P. Police Commission, 1962.

Report of the Indian Police Commission, 1902-03.

Reddy, G. Ram and Seshadri, K. (Edited) : *Developing Society and Police*, Osmania University, Hyderabad, 1972.

Rao, S. Venugopal, *Facets of Crime in India*, Allied Publishers, New Delhi, 1962.

Rose, H.C. : *The Development and Supervision of Training Programmes*, N.P.P., American Technical Society, 1966.

Sharma, P.D. : *Police, Polity and People in India*, Uppal Pub. House, New Delhi, 1981.

Sharma, P.D., : *Indian Police, A Development Approach Research*, Delhi, 1977.

Saxena, A.P. : *Training and Development in Government*, The I.I.P.A., New Delhi, 1974.

Sarason, S.B. : *The Culture of the School and the Problem of a Change*, Allyn and Bacon, Boston 1971.

SVP NPA Hyderabad—Transactions, Vol. XXIV, April, 1977.

Skolnick, Jerome : *Justice Without Trial* (*Law Enforcement in Democratic Society*) Willey, N.Y. 1966.

Smith, Bruce : *Police Systems in the United States*, Harpur and Bog., New York, 1949.

Sethi, R.B. : *The Police Acts* (*Central & States*), Law Book Co., Allahabad, 1959.

Sinha, A.K. : *Thirty Two years in Police and After*, Published by the author, 1952.

Saxena, A.P. : *The Training Function—Identification and Implementation*, Training Monograph No. 6, Training Division, New Delhi, 1970.

Training Division, D.P.&A.R., Cabinet Secretariat, New Delhi : *Development of Administrators in Selected Countries*, Training Monograph No. 18, 1972.

Training Division, M.H A., Govt. of India, New Delhi : *Administrative Reforms Commission on Training*—Training, Monograph No. 2, New Delhi, 1969.

Training Division M.H.A., Govt. of India : *State Administrative Reforms—Committee on Training*—Training Monograph No. 7, New Delhi, 1970.

Training in the Public Services (Handbook), United Nations, New York, 1966.

Wadhwani, M. : *Methodology of Training*, Training Monograph No. 16, Training Division, Dept. of Personnel, Cabinet Secretariat, New Delhi, 1972.

Wadhwani, M. : *Training of Civil Servants in the U.K.*, Training Division, D.P.&A.R., Cabinet Secretariat, New Delhi, 1972. Training Monograph No. 12.

Warren, M.W. : *Training for Results : Reading Mass,* Addison Wesley, New York, 1969.

Whisenand, Paul M. : *Police Supervision : Theory and Practice,* Prentice Hall Inc, New Jersey, 1976.

Wilson, Orlando : *Police Administration,* Mc Graw Hill Book Company, New York, 1963.

ARTICLES

Aleem, M.A. : *Recruitment and Promotion Policy for Police Personnel in Andhra Pradesh,* In G. Reddy and K. Seshadri (eds) : *Developing Society and Police,* Hyderabad, Osmania University.

Ali, A.A. : *The role and range of training,* National Police Academy Magazine, November, 1973 p. 85.

Arul, P.V. : *Police training,* Indian Police Journal, July 1958, p. 39.

Bawa, P.S. : *Rationale of training for integrity,* XIII. All India Police Science Congress Papers, Bhopal, December, 1975, p. 48.

Dhillon, K.S. : *Attitudinal Changes in Police* ; M.P. Police Journal, No. 1 Jan. 1976, p. 17.

Doig, James W. : *Police Problems, Proposals and Strategies for change,* Public Administrative Review Symposium on Police in a Democratic Society, Sep. Oct., 1968.

Dube, B.F. : *Training Methodology and their distinctive feature,* M.P. Police Journal, Vol. XVI, No. 3-4, July-Oct. 1974, p. 7.

Gokhale, S.G. : *Police : Attitudes, training institute, organisational climate,* N.P.A. Magazine, Nov. 1973, p. 43.

Jamadar, S.M. : *Police Training,* Times of India, Jan. 31, 1976.

Kalia, V.K. : *Need for ethical training in Police* : SVP NPA Magazine, Nov. 1977, p. 125.

Luthra, B.R. : *The Committee on Police Training,* Police Research and Development Journal, Jan-June, 1974, p. 2

Mathur, K.M. : *Training the Trainers,* The Crapler, April 30, 1977, p. 20.

Muhammad, Mahmood Bin : *Planning and Research for Crime Prevention*, SVP NPA Magazine, Nov. 1975, p. 20.

Muhammad, Mahmood Bin : *Areas for research and further study in Police Administration.* In G. Ram Reddy and K. Seshadri (eds) : Developing Society and Police, Hyderabad Osmania University, 1972, p. 173.

Naik, V.V. : *The meaning of training* : NPA Magazine, Nov. 1969, p. 7.

Naik, V.V. : *Police training : A world symposium*, Integrated Management, August 1973, p. 24.

Parker, Glenn M. : *Human relations training : improving police-community relations* ; training and development journal, Oct. 1974, p. 7

Police Research and Development Journal Quarterly IV 1971, Oct. Dec. 1971.

Prasad, K.N. : In Retrospect, N.P.A. Magazine Vol. XXIII, Nov. 1971.

Saksena, N.S. : *What is wrong with Police Training*, SVP NPA Magazine, Vol. XXVII, No. 1 June, 1977, p. 7.

Singhvi, G.C. : *What ails Police training*, Indian Journal of Public Administration, Jan-Mar. 1972, p. 51.

Singhvi, G.C. : *Police Training Perspective*, C.B.I. Bulletin Vol. VI, No. 9.

Stracey, E.L. : *A Century of Police training*, N.P.A. Magazine Oct. 1961, p. 1

Tandon, Shrawan : *Importance of Research and Development in Modernising Police Force*, Police Research and Development Journal Quarterly, Oct-Dec. 1977.

Trikha, M.C. : *Aspects of Police Training in the U.K.*, Police Research and Development Journal, July-Dec. 1974. p. 37

Tyagi, A.R. : *Recruitment and Training of the Police*, Journal of the L.B.S. Academy of Administration, Vol. XVIII, No 1, Spring 1973, p. 122.

Venugopal, Rao S. : *Police Research : An Overview*, The Crapler, April 30, 1976, p. 21.

N.P.A. : *Specialised training in law and order duties for police officers and magistrates*, Abu N.P.C., 1977.

The Recruitment and training of police officers ; Seminar organised by the Society for Study of State Govts.

Training : I Advanced Course-1960, Central Police Training College, Mt. Abu.

Training of Constables in Modern set-up : IX Advanced course-1964, Central Police Training College, Mt. Abu.

INDEX